Journalism Ethics and Mass Management

Journalism Ethics and Mass Management

Dr. Neha Arora

RANDOM PUBLICATIONS
NEW DELHI (INDIA)

Journalism Ethics and Mass Management

ISBN 978-93-5111-214-3

Published in 2014 in India by

RANDOM PUBLICATIONS

4376-A/4B, Gali Murari Lal, Ansari Road
New Delhi-110 002
Phone : +91-11-43580356, +91-11-23289044
e-mail: randomexports@gmail.com, sales@randompublications.com, info@randompublications.com

Reprinted 2019

Type Setting by : Keystoneprintads, Delhi-110051
Digitally Printed at : Replika Press Pvt. Ltd.

Preface

Journalism ethics comprise principles of ethics and of good practice as applicable to the specific challenges faced by journalists. Historically and currently, this subset of media ethics is widely known to journalists as their professional "code of ethics" or the "canons of journalism". The basic codes and canons commonly appear in statements drafted by both professional journalism associations and individual print, broadcast, and online news organizations. While various existing codes have some differences, most share common elements including the principles of-truthfulness, accuracy, objectivity, impartiality, fairness and public accountability-as these apply to the acquisition of newsworthy information and its subsequent dissemination to the public. Like many broader ethical systems, journalism ethics include the principle of "limitation of harm." This often involves the withholding of certain details from reports such as the names of minor children, crime victims' names, or information not materially related to particular news reports release of which might, for example, harm someone's reputation. Some journalistic Codes of Ethics, notably the European ones, also include a concern with discriminatory references in news based on race, religion, sexual orientation, and physical or mental disabilities. The Parliamentary Assembly of the Council of Europe approved in 1993 Resolution 1003 on the Ethics of Journalism which recommends journalists to respect the presumption of innocence, in particular in cases that are still sub judice.

The title of this book is intended to reflect an approach which is prepared to see beyond simple black and white, and acknowledge shades of grey. Good ethical decision making requires thought, time, and discussion. That may seem an unattainable luxury in Indian newsrooms, too many of which are under constant pressure to produce more with less. But journalists have a responsibility to find the time for this work. It's possible to be a successful journalist without taking time to confront ethical issues, but you can't be a good one. In the long run, trustworthy journalism is in the interests of the bottom line, too. In India, the debate about journalism ethics has taken particular turns in recent years. Issues of transformation and race have sparked heated debates in the profession, and there have been calls for the codes themselves to be revisited, to bring them into line with the new Indian reality. This book grew out of these discussions. Among other things, it attempts to measure the traditional standards of journalism against the demands of a changing society. Besides the discussion of various areas of ethics, the chapters contain a set of case studies drawn from real events. They also include talking points - short contributions by some of the most prominent people in Indian journalism. They provide additional voices on the various areas, offering a different perspective or sometimes discussing the way an issue plays itself out in particular circumstances. The text is intended to be as practical as possible. There is also a set of discussions and exercises that could be used in a classroom situation. Finally, a selection of codes have also been included - chiefly the industry codes used in print and broadcasting. Editors and owners have responsibilities, too: they need to create the right conditions for careful, thoughtful, and ethical journalism. I hope that this book will encourage journalists to take the time and trouble to explore ethical decision making as a professional skill that is as important as any other.

I thank all members of my team who have helped in the preparation of the book. My special thanks go to "Random Publications" who have published the book.

– Dr. Neha Arora

Contents

1

Issues in Journalism Ethics

Journalism ethics and standards comprise principles of ethics and of good practice as applicable to the specific challenges faced by professional journalists. Historically and currently, this subset of media ethics is widely known to journalists as their professional "code of ethics" or the "canons of journalism." The basic codes and canons commonly appear in statements drafted by both professional journalism associations and individual print, broadcast, and online news organizations.

"Every news organization has only its credibility and reputation to rely on." - Tony Burman, editor-in-chief of CBC News While various existing codes have some differences, most share common elements including the principles of — truthfulness, accuracy, objectivity, impartiality, fairness and public accountability — as these apply to the acquisition of newsworthy information and its subsequent dissemination to the public.

Like many broader ethical systems, journalism ethics include the principle of "limitation of harm." This often involves the withholding of certain details from reports such as the names of minor children, crime victims' names or information not materially related to particular news reports release of which might, for example, harm someone's reputation.

EVOLUTION AND PURPOSE OF CODES OF JOURNALISM

The principles of Journalistic codes of ethics are designed as guides through numerous difficulties, such as conflicts of interest, to assist journalists in dealing with ethical dilemmas.

CODES OF PRACTICE

While journalists in the United States and European countries have led in formulation and adoption of these standards, such codes can be found in news reporting organizations in most countries with freedom of the press. The written codes and practical standards vary somewhat from country to country and organization to organization, but there is a substantial overlap among mainstream publications and societies. The International Federation of Journalists launched a global Ethical Journalism Inititiative in 2008 aimed at strengthening awareness of these issues within professional bodies.

One of the leading voices in the U.S. on the subject of Journalistic Standards and Ethics is the Society of Professional Journalists. The Preamble to its Code of Ethics states:

Public enlightenment is the forerunner of justice and the foundation of democracy. The duty of the journalist is to further those ends by seeking truth and providing a fair and comprehensive account of events and issues. Conscientious journalists from all media and specialties strive to serve the public with thoroughness and honesty. Professional integrity is the cornerstone of a journalist's credibility.

The Radio-Television News Directors Association, an organization exclusively centered on electronic journalism, maintains a code of ethics centering on — public trust, truthfulness, fairness, integrity, independence and accountability. RTDNA publishes a pocket guide to these standards. Examples of journalistic codes of ethics held by international news gathering organizations may be found as follows:

- British Broadcasting Corporation: Editorial Guidelines.
- Canadian Broadcasting Corporation: *Journalistic Standards and Practices*
- Al Jazeera: Code of Ethics.
- Code of Journalists of the Republic of Slovenia

COMMON ELEMENTS

The primary themes common to most codes of journalistic standards and ethics are the following.

Objectivity:

- Unequivocal separation between news and opinion. Editorials and op-eds are clearly separated from news pieces. News reporters and editorial staff are distinct.
- Unequivocal separation between advertisements and news. All advertisements must be clearly identifiable as such.
- Reporter must avoid conflicts of interests—incentives to report a story with a given slant. This includes not taking bribes and not reporting on stories that affect the reporter's personal, economic or political interests.
- Competing points of view are balanced and fairly characterized.
- Persons who are the subject of adverse news stories are allowed a reasonable opportunity to respond to the adverse information before the story is published or broadcast.
- Interference with reporting by any entity, including censorship, must be disclosed.

Sources:

- Confidentiality of anonymous sources.

- Avoidance of anonymous sources if possible.
- Accurate attribution of statements made by individuals or other news media.
- Pictures, sound, and quotations must not be presented in a misleading context (or lack thereof). Simulations, reenactments, alterations, and artistic imaginings must be clearly labelled as such, if not avoided entirely.
- Plagiarism is strongly stigmatized and in many cases illegal.

Accuracy and standards for factual reporting:

- Reporters are expected to be as accurate as possible given the time allotted to story preparation and the space available, and to seek reliable sources.
- Events with a single eyewitness are reported with attribution. Events with two or more independent eyewitnesses may be reported as fact. Controversial facts are reported with attribution.
- Independent fact-checking by another employee of the publisher is desirable
- Corrections are published when errors are discovered
- Defendants at trial are treated only as having "allegedly" committed crimes, until conviction, when their crimes are generally reported as fact (unless, that is, there is serious controversy about wrongful conviction).
- Opinion surveys and statistical information deserve special treatment to communicate in precise terms any conclusions, to contextualize the results, and to specify accuracy, including estimated error and methodological criticism or flaws.

Slander and libel considerations:

- Reporting the truth is never libel, which makes accuracy very important.
- Private persons have privacy rights that must be balanced against the public interest in reporting information about them. Public figures have fewer privacy rights in U.S. law, where reporters are immune from a civil case if they have reported without malice. In Canada, there is no such immunity; reports on public figures must be backed by facts.
- Publishers vigorously defend libel lawsuits filed against their reporters, usually covered by libel insurance.

HARM LIMITATION PRINCIPLE

During the normal course of an assignment a reporter might go about — gathering facts and details, conducting interviews, doing research, background checks, taking photos, video taping, recording sound — harm limitation deals with the questions of whether everything learned should be reported and, if so, how. This principle of limitation means that some weight needs to be given to the negative consequences of full disclosure, creating a practical and ethical dilemma. The Society of Professional Journalists' code of ethics offers the following advice, which is representative of the practical ideals of most professional journalists.

Quoting directly:

- Show compassion for those who may be affected adversely by news coverage. Use special sensitivity when dealing with children and inexperienced sources or subjects.
- Be sensitive when seeking or using interviews or photographs of those affected by tragedy or grief.
- Recognize that gathering and reporting information may cause harm or discomfort. Pursuit of the news is not a license for arrogance.
- Recognize that private people have a greater right to control information about themselves than do public officials and others who seek power, influence or attention. Only an overriding public need can justify intrusion into anyone's privacy.
- Show good taste. Avoid pandering to lurid curiosity.
- Be cautious about identifying juvenile suspects or victims of sex crimes.
- Be judicious about naming criminal suspects before the formal filing of charges.
- Balance a criminal suspect's fair trial rights with the public's right to be informed.

Presentation

Ethical standards should not be confused with common standards of quality of presentation, including:

- Correctly spoken or written language (often in a widely spoken and formal dialect, such as Standard English)
- Clarity
- Brevity (or depth, depending on the niche of the publisher)

SELF-REGULATION

In addition to codes of ethics, many news organizations maintain an in-house Ombudsman whose role is, in part, to keep news organizations honest and accountable to the public. The ombudsman is intended to mediate in conflicts stemming from internal and or external pressures, to maintain accountability to the public for news reported, and to foster self-criticism and to encourage adherence to both codified and uncodified ethics and standards. This position may be the same or similar to the public editor, though public editors also act as a liaison with readers and do not generally become members of the Organisation of News Ombudsmen.

An alternative is a news council, an industry-wide self-regulation body, such as the Press Complaints Commission, set up by UK newspapers and magazines. Such a body is capable perhaps of applying fairly consistent standards, and of dealing with a higher volume of complaints, but may not escape criticisms of being toothless.

ETHICS AND STANDARDS IN PRACTICE

As with other ethical codes, there is a perennial concern that the standards of journalism are being ignored. One of the most controversial issues in modern reporting is media bias, especially on political issues, but also with regard to cultural and other issues. Sensationalism is also a common complaint. Minor factual errors are also extremely common, as almost anyone who is familiar with the subject of a particular report will quickly realize. There are also some wider concerns, as the media continue to change, for example that the brevity of news reports and use of soundbites has reduced fidelity to the truth, and may contribute to a lack of needed context for public understanding.

From outside the profession, the rise of news management contributes to the real possibility that news media may be deliberately manipulated. Selective reporting (spiking, double standards) are very commonly alleged against newspapers, and by their nature are forms of bias not easy to establish, or guard against. This section does not address specifics of such matters, but issues of practical compliance, as well as differences between professional journalists on principles. Journalism scandals are high-profile incidents or acts, whether intentional or accidental, that run contrary to the generally accepted ethics and standards of journalism, or otherwise violate the 'ideal' mission of journalism: to report news events and issues accurately and fairly.

As the investigative and reporting face of the media, journalists are usually required to follow various journalistic standards. These may be written and codified, or customary expectations. Typical standards include references to honesty, avoiding journalistic bias, demonstrating responsibility, striking an appropriate balance between privacy and public interest, shunning financial conflict of interest, and choosing ethical means to obtain information. Journalistic scandals are public scandals arising from incidents where in the eyes of some party, these standards were significantly breached. In most journalistic scandals, deliberate or accidental acts take place that run contrary to the generally accepted ethics and standards of journalism, or otherwise violate the 'ideal' mission of journalism: to report news events and issues accurately and fairly.

Journalistic scandals include: plagiarism, fabrication, and omission of information; activities that violate the law, or violate ethical rules; the altering or staging of an event being documented; or making substantial reporting or researching errors with the results leading to libelous or defamatory statements.

All journalistic scandals have the common factor that they call into question the integrity and truthfulness of journalism. These scandals shift public focus and scrutiny onto the media itself. Because credibility is journalism's main currency, many news agencies and mass media outlets have strict codes of conduct and enforce them, and use several layers of editorial oversight to catch problems before stories are distributed.

However, in many of the cases listed below, investigations later found that long-established journalistic checks and balances in the newsrooms failed. In some cases, senior editors fail to catch bias, libel, or fabrication inserted into a story by a reporter. In other cases, the checks and balances were omitted in the rush to get an important, 'breaking' news story to press (or on air). Furthermore, in many libel and defamation cases, the publication would have had full support of editorial oversight in case of yellow journalism.

Media bias is a term used to describe the real and perceived bias of journalists and news producers within the mass media, in the selection of which events will be reported and how they are covered. The term "media bias" usually refers to a pervasive or widespread bias contravening the standards of journalism, rather than the perspective of an individual journalist or article. The direction and degree of media bias in various countries is widely disputed, although its causes are both practical and theoretical. Practical limitations to media neutrality include the inability of journalists to report all available stories and facts, and the requirement that selected facts be linked into a coherent narrative.

Since it is impossible to report everything, some selectivity is inevitable. Government influence, including overt and covert censorship, biases the media in some countries. Market forces that can result in a biased presentation include the ownership of the news source, the selection of staff, the preferences of an intended audience, pressure from advertisers, or reduced funding due to lower ratings or governmental funding cuts. Political affiliations arise from ideological positions of media owners and journalists. The space or air time available for reports, as well as deadlines needing to be met, can lead to incomplete and apparently biased stories.

Types of bias:

- Advertising bias, corporate media depends on advertising revenue for funding. This relationship promotes a bias to please the advertisers.
- Ethnic or racial bias, including racism, nationalism.
- Corporate bias, coverage' of political campaigns in such a way as to favour or oppose corporate interests, and the reporting of issues to favour the interests of the owners of the news media or its advertisers. Some critics view the financing of news outlets through advertisers as an inherent bias.
- Class bias, including bias favoring one social class and bias ignoring (or exaggerating) social or class divisions.
- Political bias, including bias in favour of or against a particular political party, candidate, or policy. Other complaints are: the American media has an "either or" view by only focusing on Republicans or Democrats, and ignoring other lines of thought such as socialism and libertarianism.

- Mainstream bias, a tendency to report what everyone else is reporting, and to gather news from a relatively small number of easily available sources.
- Religious and cultural bias, including bias in which one religious or nonreligious viewpoint is given preference over others.
- Bias based on sex, age, background, education, language, among others. (For instance woman's issues are rarely featured in mainstream news, and a poorly written letter won't make it into the Letters to the Editor section.)
- Sensationalism, bias in favour of the exceptional over the ordinary. This includes the practice whereby exceptional news may be overemphasized, distorted or fabricated to boost commercial ratings; entertainment news is often subjected to sensationalism.
- Exaggerated influence of minority views: Like sensationalism, this is a tendency to emphasize the new and the different over the *status quo* or existing consensus. This may be done in an attempt to be "fair", or to find something worth reporting.
- Bias toward ease or expediency: This can be a tendency to present information which is already widely reported in other news media, i.e. "jumping on the bandwagon" or "following the leader", presentation of "fluff pieces" which are of questionable journalistic merit (such as coverage in news media of the personal lives of celebrities, or "news you can use"-style reporting which offers consumer advice which is widely viewed as common sense), and over representation of crime reporting, particularly street crime. This type of bias is largely attributed to the relatively low cost of presenting these stories (compared to investigative journalism which tends to require more time and research, and thus more money, to produce), competition between commercial news media for consumers, ratings and ad revenue, and a 24-hour news cycle which demands constant output.
- "Accidental bias" which could include errors and misinformation (re: expediency) or editors accidentally reinterpreting a reporter's work.

SOURCES OF MEDIA BIAS

Whether or not media bias exists is a seemingly endless debate. Yet valid questions remain about media performance and the role of public communications practitioners in shaping perception. There are some researchers who use a "social construction of reality" framework to analyse media and the ways in which information is filtered. According to scholar Richard Alan Nelson's (2003) study *Tracking Propaganda to the Source: Tools for Analyzing Media Bias,* media effects findings suggest that when bias occurs it stems from a combination of 10 factors:

- The media are neither objective nor completely honest in their portrayal of important issues.
- Framing devices are employed in stories by featuring some angles and downplaying others.
- The news is a product not only of deliberate manipulation, but of the ideological and economic conditions under which the media operate.
- While appearing independent, the news media are institutions that are controlled or heavily influenced by government and business interests experienced with manufacturing of consent/consensus.
- Reporters' sources frequently dominate the flow of information as a way of furthering their own overt and hidden agendas. In particular, the heavy reliance on political officials and other-government related experts occurs through a preferential sourcing selection process which excludes dissident voices.
- Journalists widely accept the faulty premise that the government's collective intentions are benevolent, despite occasional mistakes.
- The regular use of the word "we" by journalists in referring to their government's actions implies nationalistic complicity with those policies.
- There is an absence of historical context and contemporary comparisons in reportage which would make news more meaningful.
- The failure to provide follow up assessment is further evidence of a pack journalism mentality that at the conclusion of a "feeding frenzy" wants to move on to other stories.
- Citizens must avoid self-censorship by reading divergent sources and maintaining a critical perspective on the media in order to make informed choices and participate effectively in the public policy process.

SCHOLARLY TREATMENT OF MEDIA BIAS

Media bias is studied at schools of journalism, university departments (including Media studies, Cultural studies and Peace studies) and by many independent watchdog groups from various parts of the political spectrum. In the United States, many of these studies focus on issues of a conservative/liberal balance in the media. Other focuses include international differences in reporting, as well as bias in reporting of particular issues such as economic class or environmental interests. A widely-cited public opinion study documents a correlation between news source and certain misconceptions about the Iraq war. Conducted by the Programme on International Policy Attitudes in October 2003, the poll asked Americans whether they believed statements about the Iraq war that were known to be false.

Respondents were also asked which was their primary news source: Fox News, CBS, NBC, ABC, CNN, "Print sources," or NPR. By cross referencing the responses according to primary news source, the study showed that higher numbers of Fox News watchers held certain misconceptions about the Iraq war. The director of Programme on International Policy (PIPA), Stephen Kull said, "While we cannot assert that these misconceptions created the support for going to war with Iraq, it does appear likely that support for the war would be substantially lower if fewer members of the public had these misperceptions."

The Glasgow Media Group carried out the Bad News Studies, a series of detailed analyses of television broadcasts (and later newspaper coverage) in the United Kingdom. Published between 1976 and 1985, the Bad News Studies used content analysis, interviews and covert participant observation to conclude that news was biased against trade unions, blaming them for breaking wage negotiating guidelines and causing high inflation. Martin Harrison's *TV News: Whose Bias?* (1985) criticized the methodology of the Glasgow Media Group, arguing that the GMG identified bias selectively, via their own preconceptions about what phrases qualify as biased descriptions. For example, the GMG sees the word "idle" to describe striking workers as pejorative, despite the word being used by strikers themselves.

Herman and Chomsky (1988) proposed a propaganda model hypothesizing systematic biases of U.S. media from structural economic causes. They hypothesize media ownership by corporations, funding from advertising, the use of official sources, efforts to discredit independent media ("flak"), and "anti-communist" ideology as the filters that bias news in favour of U.S. corporate interests. Their propaganda model first and foremost disuses self censorship through the corporate system; that reporters and especially editors share and/or acquire values with corporate elites in order to further their careers. Those that don't are usually weeded out or marginalized. Such examples have been dramatized in fact based movie dramas as "Good Night, and Good Luck" and "The Insider" or demonstrated in the documentary "The Corporation". George Orwell originally wrote a preface for his book "Animal Farm", which focuses on British self censorship.

"The sinister fact about literary censorship in England is that it is largely voluntary.... [Things are] kept right out of the British press, not because the Government intervened but because of a general tacit agreement that 'it wouldn't do' to mention that particular fact." As if to prove the point, the preface itself was censored and is not published with most copies of the book.

The propaganda model posits that advertising dollars are essential for funding most media sources and clearly have an effect on the content of the media. For example, according to Fair, 'When Al Gore proposed launching a progressive TV network, a Fox News executive told Advertising Age (10/13/03): "The problem with being associated as liberal is that they wouldn't be going in a direction that advertisers are really interested in.... If you go out and say that you are a liberal network, you are cutting your potential audience, and certainly your potential advertising pool, right off the bat."

Furthermore "an internal memo from ABC Radio Networks to its affiliates reveals scores of powerful sponsors have a standing order that their commercials never be placed on syndicated Air America programming that airs on ABC affiliates.... The list, totaling 90 advertisers, includes some of largest and most well-known corporations advertising in the U.S.: Wal-Mart, GE, Exxon Mobil, Microsoft, Bank of America, Fed-Ex, Visa, Allstate, McDonald's, Sony and Johnson & Johnson. The U.S. Postal Service and the U.S. Navy are also listed as advertisers who don't want their commercials to air on Air America."

The academic study cited most frequently by critics of a "liberal media bias" in American journalism is *The Media Elite,* a 1986 book co-authored by political scientists Robert Lichter, Stanley Rothman, and Linda Lichter. They surveyed journalists at national media outlets such as the New York Times, Washington Post, and the broadcast networks. The survey found that most of these journalists were Democratic voters whose attitudes were well to the left of the general public on a variety of topics, including such hot-button social issues such as abortion, affirmative action, and gay rights. Then they compared journalists' attitudes to their coverage of controversial issues such as the safety of nuclear power, school busing to promote racial integration, and the energy crisis of the 1970s.

The book's most thorough case study involved nuclear energy. The survey of journalists showed that most were highly skeptical about nuclear safety. However, the authors conducted a separate survey of scientists in energy related fields, who were much more sanguine about nuclear safety issues. They then conducted a content analysis of nuclear energy coverage in the media outlets they had surveyed. They found that the opinions of sources who were cited as scientific experts reflected the antinuclear sentiments of journalists, rather than the more pro-nuclear perspectives held by most energy scientists. The authors concluded that journalists' coverage of controversial issues reflected their own attitudes, and the predominance of political liberals in newsrooms therefore pushed news coverage in a liberal direction. They presented this tilt as a mostly unconscious process of like-minded individuals projecting their shared assumptions onto their interpretations of reality.

At the time the study was embraced mainly by conservative columnists and politicians, who adopted the findings as scientific proof of liberal media bias. Many of the positions in the preceding study are supported by a 2002 study by Jim A. Kuypers: Press Bias and Politics: How the Media Frame Controversial Issues. In this study of 116 mainstream US papers (including The New York Times, the Washington Post, Los Angeles Times, and the San Francisco Chronicle), Kuypers found that the mainstream print press in America operate within a narrow range of liberal beliefs. Those who expressed points of view further to the left were generally ignored, whereas those who expressed moderate or conservative points of view were often actively denigrated or labeled as holding a minority point of view.

In short, if a political leader, regardless of party, spoke within the press-supported range of acceptable discourse, he or she would receive positive press coverage. If a politician, again regardless of party, were to speak outside of this range, he or she would receive negative press or be ignored. Kuypers also found that the liberal points of view expressed in editorial and opinion pages were found in hard news coverage of the same issues. Although focusing primarily on the issues of race and homosexuality, Kuypers found that the press injected opinion into its news coverage of other issues such as welfare reform, environmental protection, and gun control; in all cases favoring a liberal point of view.

Studies reporting perceptions of liberal bias in the media are not limited to studies of print media. A joint study by the Joan Shorenstein Centre on Press, Politics and Public Policy at Harvard University and the Project for Excellence in Journalism found that people see liberal media bias in television news media such as CNN.. Although both CNN and Fox were perceived in the study as being left of centre, CNN was perceived as being more liberal than Fox. Moreover, the study's findings concerning CNN's perceived liberal bias are echoed in other studies. There is also a growing economics literature on mass media bias, both on the theoretical and the empirical side. On the theoretical side the focus is on understanding to what extent the political positioning of mass media outlets is mainly driven by demand or supply factors. According to Dan Sutter of the University of Oklahoma, a systematic liberal bias in the U.S. media could depend on the fact that owners and/or journalists typically lean to the left.

Along the same lines, David Baron of Stanford GSB presents a game-theoretic model of mass media behaviour in which, given that the pool of journalists systematically leans towards the left or the right, mass media outlets maximise their profits by providing content that is biased in the same direction. They can do so, because it is cheaper to hire journalists that write stories which are consistent with their political position. A concurrent theory would be that supply and demand would cause media to attain a neutral balance because consumers would of course gravitate towards the media they agreed with. This argument fails in considering the imbalance in self-reported political allegiances by journalists themselves, that distort any market analogy as regards offer: (...) *Indeed, in 1982, 85 per cent of Columbia Graduate School of Journalism students identified themselves as liberal, versus 11 per cent conservative"*, quoted in Sutter, 2001.

This same argument would have news outlets in equal numbers increasing profits of a more balanced media far more than the slight increase in costs to hire unbiased journalists, notwithstanding the extreme rarity of self-reported conservative journalists. As mentioned above, Tim Groseclose of UCLA and Jeff Milyo of the University of Missouri at Columbia use think tank quotes, in order to estimate the relative position of mass media outlets in the political spectrum. The idea is to trace out which think tanks are quoted by various mass media outlets within news stories, and to match these think tanks with the political position of members of the U.S. Congress who quote them in a non-negative way. Using this procedure, Groseclose and Milyo obtain the stark result that all sampled news providers -except Fox News' Special Report and the Washington Times- are located to the left of the average Congress member, i.e. there are signs of a liberal bias in the US news media.

However, the news media also show a remarkable degree of centrism, just because all outlets but one are located –from an ideological point of view- between the average Democrat and average Republican in Congress. The methods Groseclose and Milyo used to calculate this bias have been criticized by Mark Liberman, a professor of Computer Science at the University of Pennsylvania. Liberman concludes by saying he thinks "that many if not most of the complaints directed against G&M are motivated in part by ideological disagreement — just as much of the praise for their work is motivated by ideological agreement. It would be nice if there were a less politically fraught body of data on which such modeling exercises could be explored."

Sendhil Mullainathan and Andrei Shleifer of Harvard University construct a behavioural model, which is built around the assumption that readers and viewers hold beliefs that they would like to see confirmed by news providers. When news customers share common beliefs, profit-maximizing media outlets find it optimal to select and/or frame stories in order to pander to those beliefs. On the other hand, when beliefs are heterogeneous, news providers differentiate their offer and segment the market, by providing news stories that are slanted towards the two extreme positions in the spectrum of beliefs.

Matthew Gentzkow and Jesse Shapiro of Chicago GSB present another demand-driven theory of mass media bias. If readers and viewers have a priori views on the current state of affairs and are uncertain about the quality of the information about it being provided by media outlets, then the latter have an incentive to slant stories towards their customers' prior beliefs, in order to build and keep a reputation for high-quality journalism. The reason for this is that rational agents would tend to believe that pieces of information that go against their prior beliefs in fact originate from low-quality news providers.

The economics empirical literature on mass media bias mainly focuses on the United States. Steve Ansolabehere, Rebecca Lessem and Jim Snyder of the Massachusetts Institute of Technology analyse the political orientation of endorsements by U.S. newspapers. They find an upward trend in the average propensity to endorse a candidate, and in particular an incumbent one. There are also some changes in the average ideological slant of endorsements: while in the 40s and in the 50s there was a clear advantage to Republican candidates, this advantage continuously eroded in subsequent decades, to the extent that in the 90s the authors find a slight Democratic lead in the average endorsement choice.

John Lott and Kevin Hassett of the American Enterprise Institute study the coverage of economic news by looking at a panel of 389 U.S. newspapers from 1991 to 2004, and from 1985 to 2004 for a subsample comprising the top 10 newspapers and the Associated Press. For each release of official data about a set of economic indicators, the authors analyse how newspapers decide to report on them, as reflected by the tone of the related headlines. The idea is to check whether newspapers display some kind of partisan bias, by giving more positive or negative coverage to the same economic figure, as a function of the political affiliation of the incumbent President. Controlling for the economic data being released, the authors find that there are between 9.6 and 14.7 per cent fewer positive stories when the incumbent President is a Republican.

Riccardo Puglisi of the Massachusetts Institute of Technology looks at the editorial choices of the *New York Times* from 1946 to 1997. He finds that the *Times* displays Democratic partisanship, with some watchdog aspects. This is the case, because during presidential campaigns the Times systematically gives more coverage to Democratic topics of civil rights, health care, labour and social welfare, but only when the incumbent president is a Republican. These topics are classified as Democratic ones, because Gallup polls show that on average U.S. citizens think that Democratic candidates would be better at handling problems related to them. According to Puglisi, in the post-1960 period the Times displays a more symmetric type of watchdog behaviour, just because during presidential campaigns it also gives more coverage to the typically Republican issue of Defence when the incumbent President is a Democrat, and less so when the incumbent is a Republican.

Alan Gerber and Dean Karlan of Yale University use an experimental approach to examine not whether the media are biased, but whether the media influence political decisions and attitudes. They conduct a randomized control trial just prior to the November 2005 gubernatorial election in Virginia and randomly assign individuals in Northern Virginia to (a) a treatment group that receives a free subscription to the Washington Post, (b) a treatment group that receives a free subscription to the Washington Times, or (c) a control group. They find that those who are assigned to the Washington Post treatment group are eight percentage points more likely to vote for the Democrat in the elections. The report also found that "exposure to either newspaper was weakly linked to a movement away from the Bush administration and Republicans."

Another unaffiliated group, Media Study Group, established seven categories of poor journalistic practice: for example, the journalist stating personal opinion in a report, asserting incorrect facts, applying unequal space or treatment to two sides of a controversial issue; then analyzed The Age Newspaper (Melbourne Australia) for the frequency of infraction of this code of practice. The resultant instances were then analyzed statistically with respect to the frequency they supported one or other side of the two-sided controversial issue under consideration. The goal of this group was to establish a quantitative methodology for the study of bias.

A self-described progressive media watchdog group, Fairness and Accuracy in Reporting, in consultation with the Survey and Evaluation Research Laboratory at Virginia Commonwealth University, sponsored a rigorous academic study in which journalists were asked a range of questions about how they did their work and about how they viewed the quality of media coverage in the broad area of politics and economic policy. "They were asked for their opinions and views about a range of recent policy issues and debates. Finally, they were asked for demographic and identifying information, including their political orientation". They then compared to the say or similar questions posed with "the public" based on Gallup, and Pew Trust polls. Their study concluded that a majority of journalists, although relatively liberal on social policies, were significantly to the right of the public on economic, labour, health care and foreign policy issues.

This study continues: "we learn much more about the political orientation of news content by looking at sourcing patterns rather than journalists' personal views. As this survey shows, it is government officials and business representatives to whom journalists "nearly always" turn when covering economic policy. Labour representatives and consumer advocates were at the bottom of the list. This is consistent with earlier research on sources. For example, analysts from the centrist Brookings Institution and conservative think tanks such as the Heritage Foundation and the American Enterprise Institute are those most quoted in mainstream news accounts; liberal think tanks are often invisible. When it comes to sources, 'liberal bias' is nowhere to be found."

EXPERIMENTER BIAS

A major problem in studies is experimenter bias. Research into studies of media bias in the United States shows that Liberal experimenters tend to get results that say the media has a conservative bias, while conservatives experimenters tend to get results that say the media has a liberal bias, and those who do not identify themselves as either liberal or conservative get results indicating little bias, or mixed bias. This same problem with experimenter bias extends to the studies of experimenter bias, of course. Whether bias is toward the left or the right depends on where you stand. The study "A Measure of Media Bias" (pdf) by political scientist Timothy J. Groseclose of UCLA and economist Jeffrey D. Milyo of the University of Missouri-Columbia, purports to rank news organisations in terms of identifying with liberal or conservative values relative to each other. They used the Americans for Democratic Action

(ADA) scores as a quantitative proxy for political leanings of the referential organizations. Thus their definition of "liberal" includes the RAND Corporation, a nonprofit research organization with strong ties to the Defence Department. According to Media Matters for America (a non-profit progressive research and information centre), "the study employed a measure of "bias" so problematic that its findings are next to useless". What is "liberal" in the United States may not be "liberal" by world standards. FAIR suggests that a benchmark for each country be set by scientific polling of a cross-section of the citizens. Another source of bias is the fact that some studies are reported by the media, and other stories are not. The case study "A Measure of Media Bias" discussed above was widely reported in the United States. George Orwell pointed out that in the UK during the last century businesses did not undermine their own interests by reporting leftist (anti business or pro-labour) information. In the United States Ben Bagdikian documents a long history of advertisers pulling out support when media content becomes too controversial.

TOOLS FOR MEASURING AND EVALUATING MEDIA BIAS

Richard Alan Nelson's (2003) study cited above on *Tracking Propaganda to the Source: Tools for Analyzing Media Bias* reports there are at least 12 methods used to analyse the existence of and quantify bias:

- Surveys of the political/cultural attitudes of journalists, particularly members of the media elite, and of journalism students.
- Studies of journalists' previous professional connections.
- Collections of quotations in which prominent journalists reveal their beliefs about politics and/or the proper role of their profession.
- Computer word-use and topic analysis searches to determine content and labeling.
- Studies of policies recommended in news stories.
- Comparisons of the agenda of the news and entertainment media with agendas of political candidates or other activists.
- Positive/negative coverage analysis.
- Reviews of the personal demographics of media decision makers.
- Comparisons of advertising sources/content which influence information/entertainment content.
- Analyses of the extent of government propaganda and public relations (PR) industry impact on media.
- Studies of the use of experts and spokespersons etc. by media vs. those not selected to determine the interest groups and ideologies represented vs. those excluded.
- Research into payments of journalists by corporations and trade associations to speak before their groups and the impact that may have on coverage.

EFFORTS TO CORRECT BIAS

One technique used to avoid bias is the "point/counterpoint" or "round table," an adversarial format in which representatives of opposing views comment on an issue. This approach theoretically allows diverse views to appear in the media. However, the person organizing the report still has the responsibility to choose people who really represent the breadth of opinion, to ask them non-prejudicial questions, and to edit or arbitrate their comments fairly. When done carelessly, a point/counterpoint can be as unfair as a simple biased report, by suggesting that the "losing" side lost on its merits.

The Skeptics Society has accused reporters of misusing the point/counterpoint format by giving more time to superstitions than to their scientific rebuttals. Using this format can also lead to accusations that the reporter has created a misleading appearance that viewpoints have equal validity (sometimes called "false balance"). This may happen when a taboo exists around one of the viewpoints, or when one of the representatives habitually makes claims that are easily shown to be inaccurate. One such allegation of misleading balance came from Mark Halperin, political director of ABC News. He stated in an internal e-mail message that reporters should not "artificially hold [George W. Bush and John Kerry] 'equally' accountable" to the public interest, and that complaints from Bush supporters were an attempt to "get away with... renewed efforts to win the election by destroying Senator Kerry."

When the Drudge Report published this message, many Bush supporters viewed it as "smoking gun" evidence that Halperin was using ABC to propagandize against Bush to Kerry's benefit, by interfering with reporters' attempts to avoid bias. An academic content analysis of election news later found that coverage at ABC, CBS, and NBC was more favorable toward Kerry than Bush, while coverage at Fox News Channel was more favorable toward Bush. Scott Norvell, the London bureau chief for Fox News, stated in a May 20, 2005 interview with the Wall Street Journal that "Even we at Fox News manage to get some lefties on the air occasionally, and often let them finish their sentences before we club them to death and feed the scraps to Karl Rove and Bill O'Reilly. And those who hate us can take solace in the fact that they aren't subsidizing Bill's bombast; we payers of the BBC license fee don't enjoy that peace of mind. Fox News is, after all, a private channel and our presenters are quite open about where they stand on particular stories. That's our appeal. People watch us because they know what they are getting. The Beeb's (British Broadcasting Corporation) (BBC) institutionalized leftism would be easier to tolerate if the corporation was a little more honest about it".

With the release of the 2008 book *What Happened: Inside the Bush White House and Washington's Culture of Deception* by George W. Bush's press secretary Scott McClellan, there are some who contend that this is evidence of Mark Halperin being correct instead of biased. In his book, McClellan admits to lying to the media, and describes the contempt he felt for reporters who so easily believed his lies, and were cowed by the fear that if they exposed the lies, they would be accused of "liberal bias".

Another technique used to avoid bias is disclosure of affiliations that may be considered a possible conflict of interest. This is especially apparent when a news organization is reporting a story with some relevancy to the news organization itself or to its ownership individuals or conglomerate. Often this disclosure is mandated by the laws or regulations pertaining to stocks and securities. Commentators on news stories involving stocks are often required to disclose any ownership interest in those corporations or in its competitors.

In rare cases, a news organization may dismiss or reassign staff members who appear biased. This approach was used in the Killian documents affair and after Peter Arnett's interview with the Iraqi press. This approach is presumed to have been employed in the case of Dan Rather over a heavily biased story that he ran on 60 Minutes in the month prior to the 2004 election that attempted to impugn the military record of George W. Bush by relying on obviously fake documents that were provided by a Democrat Party operative. Finally, some countries have laws enforcing balance in state owned media. Since 1991, the CBC and Radio Canada, its Francophone counterpart, are governed by the Broadcasting Act. This act states, amongst other things:

The programming provided by the Canadian broadcasting system should (i) be varied and comprehensive, providing a balance of information, enlightenment and entertainment for men, women and children of all ages, interests and tastes, (...) (iv) provide a reasonable opportunity for the public to be exposed to the expression of differing views on matters of public concern.

BIAS IN THE MASS MEDIA

Political bias has been a feature of the mass media since its birth with the invention of the printing press. The expense of early printing equipment restricted media production to a limited number of people. Historians have found that publishers often served the interests of powerful social groups. John Milton's pamphlet *Areopagitica, a Speech for the Liberty of Unlicensed Printing*, published in 1644, was one of the first publications advocating freedom of the press. In the nineteenth century, journalists began to recognize the concept of unbiased reporting as an integral part of journalistic ethics. This coincided with the rise of journalism as a powerful social force. Even today, though, the most conscientiously objective journalists cannot avoid accusations of bias.

Like newspapers, the broadcast media (radio and television) have been used as a mechanism for propaganda from their earliest days, a tendency made more pronounced by the initial ownership of broadcast spectrum by national governments. Although a process of media deregulation has placed the majority of the western broadcast media in private hands, there still exists a strong government presence, or even monopoly, in the broadcast media of many countries across the globe. At the same time, the concentration of media in private hands, and frequently amongst a comparatively small number of individuals, has also lead to accusations of media bias. There are many examples of accusations of bias being used as a political tool, sometimes resulting in government censorship.

In the United States, in 1798, Congress passed the Alien and Sedition Acts, which prohibited newspapers from publishing "false, scandalous, or malicious writing" against the government, including any public opposition to any law or presidential act. This act was in effect until 1801.

During the American Civil War, President Abraham Lincoln accused newspapers in the border states of bias in favour of the Southern cause, and ordered many newspapers closed. Chancellor Adolf Hitler of Germany, in the years leading up to World War II, accused newspapers of Marxist bias, an accusation echoed by pro-German media in England and the United States. Politicians who favored the United States entering World War II on the German side asserted that the international media were controlled by Jews, and that reports of German mistreatment of Jews were biased and without foundation. Hollywood was said to be a hotbed of Jewish bias, and films such as Charlie Chaplin's The Great Dictator were offered as proof.

In the 1980s, the government of South Africa accused newspapers of liberal bias and instituted government censorship. In 1989, the newspaper *New Nation* was closed by the government for three months for publishing anti-apartheid propaganda. Other newspapers were not closed, but were extensively censored. Some published the censored sections blacked out, to demonstrate the extent of government censorship. In the USA during the labour union movement and the civil rights movement, newspapers supporting liberal social reform were accused by conservative newspapers of communist bias. Film and television media were accused of bias in favour of mixing of the races, and many television programs with racially mixed casts, such as *I Spy* and *Star Trek*, were not aired on Southern stations.

During the war between the United States and North Vietnam, Vice President Spiro Agnew accused newspapers of anti-American bias, and in a famous speech delivered in San Diego in 1970, called anti-war protesters "The nattering nabobs of negativism."

Not all accusations of bias are political. Science writer Martin Gardner has accused the entertainment media of anti-science bias. He claims that television programs such as *The X-Files* promote superstition. In contrast, the Competitive Enterprise Institute accuses the media of being biased in favour of science and against business interests, and of credulously reporting science that purports to show that greenhouse gasses cause global warming.

ROLE OF LANGUAGE

Mass media, despite its ability to project worldwide, is limited in its cross-ethnic compatibility by one simple attribute - language. Ethnicity, being largely developed by a divergence in geography, language, culture, genes and similarly, point of view, has the potential to be countered by a common source of information. Therefore, language, in the absence of translation, comprises a barrier to a worldwide community of debate and opinion, although it is also true that media within any given society may be split along class, political or regional lines. Furthermore, if the language is translated, the translator has room to shift a bias by choosing weighed words for translation.

Language may also be seen as a political factor in mass media, particularly in instances where a society is characterized by a large number of languages spoken by its populace. The choice of language of mass media may represent a bias towards the group most likely to speak that language, and can limit the public participation by those who do not speak the language. On the other hand, there have also been attempts to use a common-language mass media to reach out to a large, geographically dispersed population, such as in the use of Arabic language by news channel Al Jazeera.

Many media theorists concerned with language and media bias point towards the media of the United States, a large country where English is spoken by the vast majority of the population.

Some theorists argue that the common language is not homogenizing; and that there still remain strong differences expressed within the mass media. This viewpoint asserts that moderate views are bolstered by drawing influences from the extremes of the political spectrum. In the United States, the national news therefore contributes to a sense of cohesion within the society, proceeding from a similarly informed population. According to this model, most views within society are freely expressed, and the mass media are accountable to the people and tends to reflect the spectrum of opinion. Language may also be a more subtle form of bias. Use of a word with positive or negative connotations rather than a more neutral synonym can form a biased picture in the audience's mind. It makes a difference whether the media calls a group "terrorist" or "freedom fighters" or "insurgents". For example, a 2005 memo to the staff of the CBC states:

Rather than calling assailants "terrorists," we can refer to them as bombers, hijackers, gunmen (if we're sure no women were in the group), militants, extremists, attackers or some other appropriate noun. In a widely criticized episode, initial online BBC reports of the 7 July 2005 London bombings identified the perpetrators as terrorists, in contradiction to the BBC's internal policy. But by the next day, Tom Gross and many others noted that the online articles had been edited, replacing "terrorists" by "bombers".

In another case, March 28, 2007, the broadcaster paid almost $400,000 in legal fees in a London court to keep an internal memo dealing with alleged anti-Israeli bias from becoming public. BBC was accused of pro-Palestinian bias over a documentary about Israel developing a nuclear weapon during the second Palestinian intifada in 2000.

NATIONAL AND ETHNIC VIEWPOINT

Many news organizations reflect or are perceived to reflect in some way the viewpoint of the geographic, ethnic, and national population that they primarily serve. Media within countries is sometimes seen as being sycophantic or unquestioning about the country's government. Western media are often criticized in the rest of the world (including eastern Europe, Asia, Africa, and the Middle East) as being pro-Western with regard to a variety of political, cultural and economic issues.

Al Jazeera has been frequently criticized in the West about its coverage of Arab world issues. The Israeli-Palestinian conflict and wider Arab-Israeli issues are a particularly controversial area, and nearly all coverage of any kind generates accusation of bias from one or both sides. This topic is covered in a separate article.

ANGLOPHONE BIAS IN THE WORLD MEDIA

It has been observed that the world's principal suppliers of news, the news agencies, and the main buyers of news are Anglophone corporations and this gives an Anglophone bias to the selection and depiction of events. Anglophone definitions of what constitutes news are paramount; the news provided originates in Anglophone capitals and responds first to their own rich domestic markets. Despite the plethora of news services, most news printed and broadcast throughout the world each day comes from only a few major agencies, the three largest of which are the Associated Press, Reuters and Agence France-Presse.

Although these agencies are 'global' in the sense of their activities, they each retain significant associations with particular nations, namely France (AFP), the United States (AP) and the United Kingdom (Reuters). Chambers and Tinckell suggest that the so-called global media are agents of Anglophone values which privilege norms of 'competitive individualism, laissez faire capitalism, parliamentary democracy and consumerism.' They see the presentation of the English language as international as a further feature of Anglophone dominance.

VIS-A-VIS RELIGIOUS ISSUES

Media bias towards religion is most obvious in countries where the media are controlled by the state, which is in turn dominated by a particular religion. In these instances, bias against other faiths can be explicit and virulent. But even in countries with freedom of religion and a free press, the dominant religion exerts some amount of influence on the media. In nations where Christianity is the majority faith, reporters tend to focus on the activities of the Christian community, to the exclusion of other faiths. But the opposite may also occur, with media self-consciously avoiding reporting on any religious matters at all in order to avoid the appearance of favoring one faith over another, or presenting religious faith and phenomenon in a negative light.This type of bias is often seen with reporting on new religious movements. It is often the case that the only view the public gets of a new religious movement, controversial group or purported cult is a negative and sensationalized report by the media. For example, most new or minority religious movements only receive media coverage when something sensational occurs, e.g. the mass suicide of a cult or illegal activities of a leader in the religious movement. According to the Encyclopedia of Social Work (19th edition), the news media play an influential role in the general public's perception of cults.

As reported in several studies, the media have depicted cults as problematic, controversial, and threatening from the beginning, tending to favour sensationalistic stories over balanced public debates. It furthers the analysis that media reports on cults rely heavily on police officials and cult "experts" who portray cult activity as dangerous and destructive, and when divergent views are presented, they are often overshadowed by horrific stories of ritualistic torture, sexual abuse, mind control, etc. Furthermore, unfounded allegations, when proved untrue, receive little or no media attention.

OTHER INFLUENCES

The apparent bias of media is not always specifically political in nature. The news media tend to appeal to a specific audience, which means that stories that affect a large number of people on a global scale often receive less coverage in some markets than local stories, such as a public school shooting, a celebrity wedding, a plane crash, or similarly glamorous or shocking stories. For example, the deaths of millions of people in an ethnic conflict in Africa might be afforded scant mention in American media, while the shooting of five people in a high school is analyzed in depth. The reason for this type of bias is a function of what the public wants to watch and/or what producers and publishers believe the public wants to watch.

Bias has also been claimed in instances referred to as conflict of interest, whereby the owners of media outlets have vested interests in other commercial enterprises or political parties. In such cases in the United States, the media outlet is required to disclose the conflict of interest. However, the decisions of the editorial department of a newspaper and the corporate parent frequently are not connected, as the editorial staff retains freedom to decide what is covered as well as what isn't. Biases, real or implied, frequently arise when it comes to deciding what stories will be covered and who will be called for those stories.

Accusations that a source is biased, if accepted, may cause media consumers to distrust certain kinds of statements, and place added confidence on others. For example, if readers believe that a particular newspaper is conservatively biased, they may feel that a pro-liberal article in that paper *must* be true. Conversely, they may assume that a pro-conservative article in that paper is suspect. Because of the possibility of influencing the public in this way, accusations about which media outlets are biased, and how, have become a very common occurrence.

Media ethics is the subdivision of applied ethics dealing with the specific ethical principles and standards of media, including broadcast media, film, theatre, the arts, print media and the internet. The field covers many varied and highly controversial topics, ranging from war journalism to Benetton advertising.

AREAS OF MEDIA ETHICS

ETHICS OF JOURNALISM

The ethics of journalism is one of the most well-defined branches of media ethics, primarily because it is frequently taught in schools of journalism. Journalistic ethics tends to dominate media ethics, sometimes almost to the exclusion of other areas.

Topics covered by journalism ethics include:

- News manipulation. News can manipulate and be manipulated. Governments and corporations may attempt to manipulate news media; governments, for example, by censorship, and corporations by share ownership. The methods of manipulation are subtle and many. Manipulation may be voluntary or involuntary. Those being manipulated may not be aware of this.
- Truth. Truth may conflict with many other values.
  - Public interest. Revelation of military secrets and other sensitive government information may be contrary to the public interest, even if it is true. The definition of public interest is hard.
  - Privacy. Salacious details of the lives of public figures are a central content element in many media. Publication is not necessarily justified simply because the information is true. Privacy is also a right, and one which conflicts with free speech.
  - Fantasy. Fantasy is an element of entertainment, which is a legitimate goal of media content. Journalism may mix fantasy and truth, with resulting ethical dilemmas.
  - Taste. Photo journalists who cover war and disasters confront situations which may shock the sensitivities of their audiences. For example, human remains are rarely screened. The ethical issue is how far one risk shocking an audience's sensitivities in order to correctly should and fully report the truth.
- Conflict with the law. Journalistic ethics may conflict with the law over issues such as the protection of confidential news sources. There is also the question of the extent to which it is ethically acceptable

to break the law in order to obtain news. For example, undercover reporters may be engaging in deception, trespass and similar torts and crimes.

ETHICS OF ENTERTAINMENT MEDIA

Issues in the ethics of entertainment media include:

- The depiction of violence and sex, and the presence of strong language. Ethical guidelines and legislation in this area are common and many media (e.g. film, computer games) are subject to ratings systems and supervision by agencies. An extensive guide to international systems of enforcement can be found under motion picture rating system.
- Product placement. An increasingly common marketing tactic is the placement of products in entertainment media. The producers of such media may be paid high sums to display branded products. The practice is controversial and largely unregulated. Detailed article: product placement.
- Stereotypes. Both advertising and entertainment media make heavy use of stereotypes. Stereotypes may negatively affect people's perceptions of themselves or promote socially undesirable behaviour. The stereotypical portrayals of men, affluence and ethnic groups are examples of major areas of debate.
- Taste and taboos. Art is about the questioning of our values. Normative ethics is often about the enforcement and protection of our values. In media ethics, these two sides come into conflict. In the name of art, media may deliberately attempt to break with existing norms and shock the audience. The extent to which this is acceptable is always a hotbed of ethical controversy.

MEDIA AND DEMOCRACY

In democratic countries, a special relationship exists between media and government. Although the freedom of the media may be constitutionally enshrined and have precise legal definition and enforcement, the exercise of that freedom by individual journalists is a matter of personal choice and ethics. Modern democratic government subsists in representation of millions by hundreds.

For the representatives to be accountable, and for the process of government to be transparent, effective communication paths must exist to their constituents. Today these paths consist primarily of the mass media, to the extent that if press freedom disappeared, so would most political accountability. In this area, media ethics merges with issues of civil rights and politics.

Issues include:

- Subversion of media independence by financial interests.
- Government monitoring of media for intelligence gathering against its own people.

CONTEXTS OF MEDIA ETHICS

MEDIA ETHICS AND THE LAW

Like ethics the law seeks to balance competing aims. In most countries there are laws preventing the media from doing or saying certain things when this would unduly breach another person's rights. For instance, slander and libel are forms of defamation, a tort. Slander occurs when a person's good name is unfairly slurred. Libel is concerned with attacks on reputation through writing.

A major area of conflict is between the public's "right to know", or freedom of the press, and individual's right to privacy. This clash often occurs regarding reporting into the private lives of public figures. There are restrictions in most countries on the publication of obscence material, particularly where it depicts nudity, desecration of religious objects or symbols (blasphemy), human remains or violent or sexual crime.

MEDIA ETHICS AND MEDIA ECONOMICS

Media ethics also deals with the relationship of media and media economics where things such as — deregulation of media, concentration of media ownership, FCC regulations in the U.S, media trade unions and labour issues, and other such worldwide regulating bodies, citizen media (low power FM, community radio) — have ethical implications.

INTERCULTURAL DIMENSIONS OF MEDIA ETHICS

If values differ interculturally, the issue arises of the extent to which behaviour should be modified in the light of the values of specific cultures. Two examples of controversy from the field of media ethics:

- Google's self-censorhip in China.
- The Jyllands-Posten Muhammad cartoons controversy in Denmark, and subsequently worldwide.

META-ISSUES IN MEDIA ETHICS

One theoretical question for media ethics is the extent to which media ethics is just another topical subdivision of applied ethics, differing only in terms of case applications and raising no theoretical issues peculiar to itself. The oldest subdivisions of applied ethics are medical ethics and business ethics. Does media ethics have anything new to add other than interesting cases?

SIMILARITIES BETWEEN MEDIA ETHICS AND OTHER FIELDS OF APPLIED ETHICS

Privacy and honesty are issues extensively covered in medical ethical literature, as is the principle of harm-avoidance. The trade-offs between economic goals and social values has been covered extensively in business ethics.

DIFFERENCES BETWEEN MEDIA ETHICS AND OTHER FIELDS OF APPLIED ETHICS

The issues of freedom of speech and aesthetic values (taste) are primarily at home in media ethics. However a number of further issues distinguish media ethics as a field in its own right. A theoretical issue peculiar to media ethics is the identity of *observer* and *observed*. The press is one of the primary guardians in a democratic society of many of the freedoms, rights and duties discussed by other fields of applied ethics. In media ethics the ethical obligations of the guardians themselves comes more strongly into the foreground. Who guards the guardians? This question also arises in the field of legal ethics.

A further self-referentiality or circular characteristic in media ethics is the questioning of its own values. Meta-issues can become identical with the subject matter of media ethics. This is most strongly seen when artistic elements are considered. Benetton advertisements and Turner prize candidates are both examples of ethically questionable media uses which question their own questioner. Another characteristic of media ethics is the disparate nature of its goals. Ethical dilemmas emerge when goals conflict. The goals of media usage diverge sharply. Expressed in a consequentialist manner, media usage may be subject to pressures to maximize: economic profits, entertainment value, information provision, the upholding of democratic freedoms, the development of art and culture, fame and vanity.

Yellow journalism is a type of journalism that downplays legitimate news in favour of eye-catching headlines that sell more newspapers. It may feature exaggerations of news events, scandal-mongering, sensationalism, or unprofessional practices by news media organizations or journalists. Campbell (2001) defines Yellow Press newspapers as having daily multi-column front-page headlines covering a variety of topics, such as sports and scandal, using bold layouts (with large illustrations and perhaps colour), heavy reliance on unnamed sources, and unabashed self-promotion. The term was extensively used to describe certain major New York City newspapers about 1900 as they battled for circulation. By extension the term is used today as a pejorative to decry any journalism that treats news in an unprofessional or unethical fashion, such as systematic political bias. Yellow Journalism can also be the practice of over-dramatizing events. Frank Luther Mott (1941) defines Yellow Journalism in terms of five characteristics:

- Scare headlines in huge print, often of minor news
- Lavish use of pictures, or imaginary drawings
- Use of faked interviews, misleading headlines, pseudo-science, and a parade of false learning from so-called experts
- Emphasis on full-colour Sunday supplements, usually with comic strips (which is now normal in the U.S.)
- Dramatic sympathy with the "underdog" against the system.

Present day (successful) exponents of the yellow journalistic style would include the British red top tabloids, notably The Sun and its German equivalent Bild, and in Australia the Daily Telegraph. The term originated during the Gilded Age with the circulation battles between Joseph Pulitzer's New York World and William Randolph Hearst's New York Journal. The battle peaked from 1895 to about 1898, and historical usage often refers specifically to this period. Both papers were accused by critics of sensationalizing the news in order to drive up circulation, although the newspapers did serious reporting as well. The New York Press coined the term *yellow kid journalism* in early 1897 after a then-popular comic strip to describe the down market papers of Pulitzer and Hearst, which both published versions of it during a circulation war. This was soon shortened to *yellow journalism* with the New York Press insisting, "We called them Yellow because they are Yellow."

Joseph Pulitzer purchased the World in 1883 after making the *St. Louis Post-Dispatch* the dominant daily in that city. The publisher had gotten his start editing a German-language publication in St. Louis, and saw a great untapped market in the nation's immigrant classes. Pulitzer strove to make *The World* an entertaining read, and filled his paper with pictures, games and contests that drew in readers, particularly those who used English as a second language. Crime stories filled many of the pages, with headlines like "Was He a Suicide?" and "Screaming for Mercy." In addition, Pulitzer only charged readers two cents per issue but gave readers eight and sometimes 12 pages of information (the only other two cent paper in the city never exceeded four pages).

While there were many sensational stories in the *World*, they were by no means the only pieces, or even the dominant ones. Pulitzer believed that newspapers were public institutions with a duty to improve society, and he put the *World* in the service of social reform. During a heat wave in 1883, *World* reporters went into the Manhattan's tenements, writing stories about the appalling living conditions of immigrants and the toll the heat took on the children. Stories headlined "How Babies Are Baked", "Burning Babies Fall From The Roof" and "Lines of Little Hearses" spurred reform and drove up the *World's* circulation.

Just two years after Pulitzer took it over, the *World* became the highest circulation newspaper in New York, aided in part by its strong ties to the Democratic Party. Older publishers, envious of Pulitzer's success, began criticizing the *World*, harping on its crime stories and stunts while ignoring its more serious reporting — trends which influenced the popular perception of yellow journalism, both then and now. Charles Dana, editor of the New York Sun, attacked *The World* and said Pulitzer was "deficient in judgment and in staying power." Pulitzer's approach made an impression on William Randolph Hearst, a mining heir who acquired the *San Francisco Examiner* from his father in 1887. Hearst read the *World* while studying at Harvard University and resolved to make the Examiner as bright as Pulitzer's paper..

Under his leadership, the *Examiner* devoted 24 per cent of its space to crime, presenting the stories as morality plays, and sprinkled adultery and "nudity" (by 19th century standards) on the front page. A month after taking over the paper, the *Examiner* ran this headline about a hotel fire:

HUNGRY, FRANTIC FLAMES. They Leap Madly Upon the Splendid Pleasure Palace by the Bay of Monterey, Encircling Del Monte in Their Ravenous Embrace From Pinnacle to Foundation. Leaping Higher, Higher, Higher, With Desperate Desire. Running Madly Riotous Through Cornice, Archway and Facade.

Rushing in Upon the Trembling Guests with Savage Fury. Appalled and Panic-Striken the Breathless Fugitives Gaze Upon the Scene of Terror. The Magnificent Hotel and Its Rich Adornments Now a Smoldering heap of Ashes. The "Examiner" Sends a Special Train to Monterey to Gather Full Details of the Terrible Disaster. Arrival of the Unfortunate Victims on the Morning's Train — A History of Hotel del Monte — The Plans for Rebuilding the Celebrated Hostelry — Particulars and Supposed Origin of the Fire.

Hearst could go overboard in his crime coverage; one of his early pieces, regarding a "band of murderers," attacked the police for forcing *Examiner* reporters to do their work for them. But while indulging in these stunts, the *Examiner* also increased its space for international news, and sent reporters out to uncover municipal corruption and inefficiency. In one celebrated story, *Examiner* reporter Winifred Black was admitted into a San Francisco hospital and discovered that indigent women were treated with "gross cruelty." The entire hospital staff was fired the morning the piece appeared.

NEW YORK

With the *Examiner's* success established by the early 1890s, Hearst began shopping for a New York newspaper. Hearst purchased the New York Journal in 1895, a penny paper which Pulitzer's brother Albert had sold to a Cincinnati publisher the year before. Metropolitan newspapers started going after department store advertising in the 1890s, and discovered the larger the circulation base, the better. This drove Hearst; following Pulitzer's earlier strategy, he kept the *Journal's* price at one cent (compared to *The World's* two cent price) while providing as much information as rival newspapers. The approach worked, and as the *Journal's* circulation jumped to 150,000, Pulitzer cut his price to a penny, hoping to drive his young competitor (who was subsidized by his family's fortune) into bankruptcy. In a counterattack, Hearst raided the staff of the *World* in 1896. While most sources say that Hearst simply offered more money, Pulitzer — who had grown increasingly abusive to his employees — had become an extremely difficult man to work for, and many *World* employees were willing to jump for the sake of getting away from him. Although the competition between the *World* and the *Journal* was fierce, the papers were temperamentally alike. Both were Democratic, both were sympathetic to labour and immigrants (a sharp contrast to publishers like the *New York Tribune's* Whitelaw Reid, who blamed their poverty on moral defects), and both invested enormous resources in their Sunday publications, which functioned like weekly magazines, going beyond the normal scope of daily journalism.

Their Sunday entertainment features included the first colour comic strip pages, and some theorize that the term yellow journalism originated there, while as noted above the New York Press left the term it invented undefined. *Hogan's Alley,* a comic strip revolving around a bald child in a yellow nightshirt (nicknamed The Yellow Kid), became exceptionally popular when cartoonist Richard Outcault began drawing it in the *World* in early 1896. When Hearst predictably hired Outcault away, Pulitzer asked artist George Luks to continue the strip with his characters, giving the city two Yellow Kids.

The use of "yellow journalism" as a synonym for over-the-top sensationalism in the U.S. apparently started with more serious newspapers commenting on the excesses of "the Yellow Kid papers."

In 1890, Samuel Warren and Louis Brandeis published "The Right to Privacy," considered the most influential law review article of all time, as a critical response to sensational forms of journalism, which they saw as an unprecedented threat to individual privacy. The article is widely considered to have led to the recognition of new common law privacy rights of action.

SPANISH-AMERICAN WAR

Pulitzer and Hearst are often credited (or blamed) for drawing the nation into the Spanish-American War with sensationalist stories or outright lying. However, the vast majority of Americans did not live in New York City, and the decision makers who did live there probably relied more on staid newspapers like the *Times, The Sun* or the *Post.* The most famous example of the exaggeration is the apocryphal story that artist Frederic Remington telegrammed Hearst to tell him all was quiet in Cuba and "There will be no war." Hearst responded "Please remain. You furnish the pictures and I'll furnish the war." The story (a version of which appears in the Hearst-inspired Orson Welles film *Citizen Kane*) first appeared in the memoirs of reporter James Creelman in 1901, and there is no other source for it. But Hearst became a war hawk after a rebellion broke out in Cuba in 1895. Stories of Cuban virtue and Spanish brutality soon dominated his front page. While the accounts were of dubious accuracy, the newspaper readers of the 19th century did not expect, or necessarily want, his stories to be pure nonfiction. Historian Michael Robertson has said that "Newspaper reporters and readers of the 1890s were much less concerned with distinguishing among fact-based reporting, opinion and literature."

Pulitzer, though lacking Hearst's resources, kept the story on his front page. The yellow press covered the revolution extensively and often inaccurately, but conditions on Cuba were horrific enough. The island was in a terrible economic depression, and Spanish general Valeriano Weyler, sent to crush the rebellion, herded Cuban peasants into concentration camps and caused hundreds of thousands of deaths. Having clamored for a fight for two years, Hearst took credit for the conflict when it came: A week after the United States declared war on Spain, he ran "How do you like the *Journal's* war?" on his front page.

In fact, President William McKinley never read the *Journal*, and newspapers like the *Tribune* and the *New York Evening Post*. Moreover, journalism historians have noted that yellow journalism was largely confined to New York City, and that newspapers in the rest of the country did not follow their lead. The *Journal* and the *World* were not among the top ten sources of news in regional papers, and the stories simply did not make a splash outside New York City. War came because public opinion was sickened by the bloodshed, and because leaders like McKinley realized that Spain had lost control of Cuba. These factors weighed more on the president's mind than the melodramas in the *New York Journal.*

Hearst sailed directly to Cuba, when the invasion began, as a war correspondent, providing sobre and accurate accounts of the fighting. Creelman later praised the work of the reporters for exposing the horrors of Spanish misrule, arguing, "no true history of the war... can be written without an acknowledgment that whatever of justice and freedom and progress was accomplished by the Spanish-American war was due to the enterprise and tenacity of *yellow journalists,* many of whom lie in unremembered graves."

AFTER THE WAR

Hearst was a leading Democrat who promoted William Jennings Bryan for president in 1896 and 1900. He later ran for mayor and governor and even sought the presidential nomination, but lost much of his personal prestige when outrage exploded in 1901 after columnist Ambrose Bierce and published separate columns months apart that suggested the assassination of McKinley. When McKinley was shot on September 6, 1901, critics accused Hearst's Yellow Journalism of driving Leon Czolgosz to the deed. Hearst did not know of Bierce's column and claimed to have pulled Brisbane's after it ran in a first edition, but the incident would haunt him for the rest of his life and all but destroyed his presidential ambitions. Pulitzer, haunted by his "yellow sins," returned the *World* to its crusading roots as the new century dawned. By the time of his death in 1911, the *World* was a widely-respected publication, and would remain a leading progressive paper until its demise in 1931. Other newspapers, especially the new tabloids in the big cities, adopted the flashy techniques of Yellow Journalism, most notably the New York *Daily News*, founded in 1919.

STANDARDS AND REPUTATION

Among the leading news organizations that voluntarily adopt and attempt to uphold the common standards of journalism ethics described herein, adherence and general quality varies considerably. The professionalism, reliability and public accountability of a news organization are three of its most valuable assets. An organization earns and maintains a strong reputation, in part, through a consistent implementation of ethical standards, which influence its position with the public and within the industry.

GENRES AND ETHICS

Advocacy journalists — a term of some debate even within the field of journalism — by definition tend to reject "objectivity", while at the same time maintaining many other common standards and ethics. Creative nonfiction and Literary journalism use the power of language and literary devices more akin to fiction to bring insight and depth into often book-length treatment of the subjects about which they write. Such devices as dialogue, metaphor, digression and other such techniques offer the reader insights not usually found in standard news reportage. However, authors in this branch of journalism still maintain ethical criteria such as factual and historical accuracy as found in standard news reporting. Yet, with brilliant prose, they venture outside the boundaries of standard news reporting in offering richly detailed accounts. One widely regarded author in the genre is Joyce Carol Oates, as with her book on boxer Mike Tyson.

New Journalism and Gonzo journalism also reject some of the fundamental ethical traditions and will set aside the technical standards of journalistic prose in order to express themselves and reach a particular audience or market segment. Tabloid journalists are often accused of sacrificing accuracy and the personal privacy of their subjects in order to boost sales. Supermarket tabloids are often focused on entertainment rather than news.

A few have "news" stories that are so outrageous that they are widely read for entertainment purposes, not for information. Some tabloids do purport to maintain common journalistic standards, but may fall far short in practice. Others make no such claims. Some publications deliberately engage in satire, but give the publication the design elements of a newspaper, for example, The Onion, and it is not unheard of for other publications to offer the occasional, humorous articles appearing on April Fool's Day.

RELATIONSHIP WITH FREEDOM OF THE PRESS

In countries without freedom of the press, the majority of people who report the news may not follow the above-described standards of journalism. Non-free media are often prohibited from criticizing the national government, and in many cases are required to distribute propaganda as if it were news. Various other forms of censorship may restrict reporting on issues the government deems sensitive.

VARIATIONS, VIOLATIONS, AND CONTROVERSIES

There are a number of finer points of journalistic procedure that foster disagreements in principle and variation in practice among "mainstream" journalists in the free press. Laws concerning libel and slander vary from country to country, and local journalistic standards may be tailored to fit. For example, the United Kingdom has a broader definition of libel than does the United States. Accuracy is important as a core value and to maintain credibility, but especially in broadcast media, audience share often gravitates toward outlets that are reporting new information first. Different organizations may balance speed and accuracy in different ways.

The New York Times, for instance, tends to print longer, more detailed, less speculative, and more thoroughly verified pieces a day or two later than many other newspapers. 24-hour television news networks tend to place much more emphasis on getting the "scoop." Here, viewers may switch channels at a moment's notice; with fierce competition for ratings and a large amount of airtime to fill, fresh material is very valuable. Because of the fast turn-around, reporters for these networks may be under considerable time pressure, which reduces their ability to verify information. Laws with regard to personal privacy, official secrets, and media disclosure of names and facts from criminal cases and civil lawsuits differ widely, and journalistic standards may vary accordingly. Different organizations may have different answers to questions about when it is journalistically acceptable to skirt, circumvent, or even break these regulations.

Another example of differences surrounding harm reduction is the reporting of preliminary election results. In the United States, some news organizations feel that it is harmful to the democratic process to report exit poll results or preliminary returns while voting is still open. Such reports may influence people who vote later in the day, or who are in western time zones, in their decisions about how and whether or not to vote. There is also some concern that such preliminary results are often inaccurate and may be misleading to the public. Other outlets feel that this information is a vital part of the transparency of the election process, and see no harm (if not considerable benefit) in reporting it.

TASTE, DECENCY AND ACCEPTABILITY

Audiences have different reactions to depictions of violence, nudity, coarse language, or to people in any other situation that is unacceptable to or stigmatized by the local culture or laws (such as the consumption of alcohol, homosexuality, illegal drug use, scatological images, etc.). Even with similar audiences, different organizations and even individual reporters have different standards and practices.

These decisions often revolve around what facts are necessary for the audience to know. When certain distasteful or shocking material is considered important to the story, there are a variety of common methods for mitigating negative audience reaction. Advance warning of explicit or disturbing material may allow listeners or readers to avoid content they would rather not be exposed to. Offensive words may be partially obscured or bleeped. Potentially offensive images may be blurred or narrowly cropped. Descriptions may be substituted for pictures; graphic detail might be omitted. Disturbing content might be moved from a cover to an inside page, or from daytime to late evening, when children are less likely to be watching. There is often considerable controversy over these techniques, especially concern that obscuring or not reporting certain facts or details is self-censorship that compromises objectivity and fidelity to the truth, and which does not serve the public interest.

For example, images and graphic descriptions of war are often violent, bloody, shocking and profoundly tragic. This makes certain content disturbing to some audience members, but it is precisely these aspects of war that some consider to be the most important to convey. Some argue that "sanitizing" the depiction of war influences public opinion about the merits of continuing to fight, and about the policies or circumstances that precipitated the conflict. The amount of explicit violence and mutilation depicted in war coverage varies considerable from time to time, from organization to organization, and from country to country. Reporters have also been accused of indecency in the process of collecting news, namely that they are overly intrusive in the name of journalistic insensitivity. War correspondent Edward Behr recounts the story of a reporter during the Congo Crisis who walked into a crowd of Belgian evacuees and shouted, "Anyone here been raped and speaks English?"

CAMPAIGNING IN THE MEDIA

Many print publications take advantage of their wide readership and print persuasive pieces in the form of unsigned editorials that represent the official position of the organization. Despite the ostensible separation between editorial writing and news gathering, this practice may cause some people to doubt the political objectivity of the publication's news reporting. (Though usually unsigned editorials are accompanied by a diversity of signed opinions from other perspectives.) Other publications and many broadcast media only publish opinion pieces that are attributed to a particular individual (who may be an in-house analyst) or to an outside entity. One particularly controversial question is whether media organizations should endorse political candidates for office. Political endorsements create more opportunities to construe favoritism in reporting, and can create a perceived conflict of interest.

INVESTIGATIVE METHODS

Investigative journalism is largely an information-gathering exercise, looking for facts that are not easy to obtain by simple requests and searches, or are actively being concealed, suppressed or distorted. Where investigative work involves undercover journalism or use of whistleblowers, and even more if it resorts to covert methods more typical of private detectives or even spying, it brings a large extra burden on ethical standards. Anonymous sources are double-edged - they often provide especially newsworthy information, such as classified or confidential information about current events, information about a previously unreported scandal, or the perspective of a particular group that may fear retribution for expressing certain opinions in the press.

The downside is that the condition of anonymity may make it difficult or impossible for the reporter to verify the source's statements. Sometimes sources hide their identities from the public because their statements would otherwise quickly be discredited. Thus, statements attributed to anonymous sources may carry more weight with the public than they might if they were attributed. The Washington press has been criticized in recent years for excessive use of anonymous sources, in particular to report information that is later revealed to be unreliable. The use of anonymous sources increased markedly in the period before the 2003 invasion of Iraq.

SCIENCE ISSUES

The mainstream press is often criticized for poor accuracy in reporting science news. Many reporters are not scientists, and are thus not familiar with the material they are summarizing. Technical information is also difficult to contextualize for lay audiences, and short-form reporting makes providing background, context, and clarification even harder. Food scares are an example of the need for responsible science journalism, as are stories connected with the safety of medical procedures.

EXAMPLES OF ETHICAL DILEMMAS

One of the primary functions of journalism ethics is to aid journalists in dealing with many ethical dilemmas they may encounter. From highly sensitive issues of national security to everyday questions such as accepting a dinner from a source, putting a bumper sticker on one's car, publishing a personal opinion blog, a journalist must make decisions taking into account things such as the public's right to know, potential threats, reprisals and intimidations of all kinds, personal integrity, conflicts between editors, reporters and publishers or management, and many other such conundra. The following are illustrations of some of those.

- The Pentagon Papers dealt with extremely difficult ethical dilemmas faced by journalists. Despite government intervention, The Washington Post, joined by The New York Times, felt the public interest was more compelling and both published reports. (The cases went to the Supreme Court where they were merged and are known as New York Times Co. v. United States, 403 U.S. 713.
- The Washington Post also once published a story about a listening device that the United States had installed over an undersea Soviet cable during the height of the cold war. The device allowed the United States to learn where Soviet submarines were positioned. In that case, Post Executive Editor Ben Bradlee chose not to run the story on national security grounds. However, the Soviets subsequently discovered the device and, according to Bradlee, "It was no longer a matter of national security. It was a matter of national embarrassment." However, the U.S. government still wanted The Washington Post not to run the story on the basis of national security, yet, according to Bradlee, "We ran the story. And you know what, the sun rose the next day."
- The Ethics Advice Line, a joint venture, public service project of Chicago Headline Club Chapter of the Society of Professional Journalists and Loyola University Chicago Centre for Ethics and Social Justice, provides some examples of typical ethical dilemmas reported to their ethical dilemma hotline and are typical of the kinds of questions faced by many professional journalists.

A partial listing of questions received by The Ethics Advice Line:

- Is it ethical to make an appointment to interview an arsonist sought by police, without informing police in advance of the interview?
- Is lack of proper attribution plagiarism?
- Should a reporter write a story about a local priest who confessed to a sex crime if it will cost the newspaper readers and advertisers who are sympathetic to the priest?
- Is it ethical for a reporter to write a news piece on the same topic on which he or she has written an opinion piece in the same paper?
- Under what circumstances do you identify a person who was arrested as a relative of a public figure, such as a local sports star?
- Freelance journalists and photographers accept cash to write about, or take photos of, events with the promise of attempting to get their work on the AP or other news outlets, from which they also will be paid. Is that ethical?
- Can a journalist reveal a source of information after guaranteeing confidentiality if the source proves to be unreliable?

2

The Free Press and Democracy

Press in a democracy is known as the Fourth Estate meaning thereby that it is as important as other three known organs of the State i.e. Legislature, Executive and the Judiciary. Its main objective is to create a healthy public opinion that may preserve and strengthen the rule of law. The Press in India is however not able to discharge this function properly. There is therefore the need for full and detailed discussion of the role of Press in India. With this in view, the Central India Law institute organised a seminar on-Freedom of Press at Jabalpur on 26th January 1996. The Seminar was presided over by Hon. Justice S.M.N. Raina, Retired Judge of the High Court of M.P. Justice Gulab Gupta.

Executive Chairman of the Institute initiated the discussion on the subject, which was followed by comments, questions and explanation by the audience. Smt. Shobha Menon, Advocate Jabalpur presented here paper on "Need for Limitation on Freedom of Press" which also provoked good deal of discussion by -the audience. Shri K.P. Mishra, Advocate Jabalpur then presented his paper on "Obscenity and the Press" which was very much appreciated. It also provoked good deal of discussion. The Seminar ended with a vote of thanks by Justice S.Awasthy, Director of the Institute. The following is the summary of the main presentations in the Seminar. Justice Gulab Gupta- Obligations of the Fourth Estate Though the Press in the context of Freedom of speech and Expression may also include Radio.

Television and other similar media, the law and public morality imposes similar obligations on them and hence the word 'Press' is us in a comprehensive sense. As regards newspapers they are either national or local and all are not only controlled by business houses but also motivated by economic gains.

Referring to Hindi newspapers of M.P., it was stated that many of them publish their editions from several cities giving some national news and mostly local news. As a result these newspapers do not publish even the regional news. A newspaper in Bilaspur neither publishes news from other centres nor is read in other centres. This localization has reduced their value in our context of democratic social order. Such newspapers are termed as 'regional' only to charge higher advertisement rates. There is therefore need to have a fresh look in the matter. Referring to Yellow Journalism, Justice Gupta said that local newspapers in particular show this tendency and the same is increasing day by day. Since sensational, morbid or offensive matter easily attract attention of readers, they are considered the basis of good earning and resorted to knowingly. If such reporting relates to law courts, they become subject to the law of contempt. Decisions of the Supreme Court in Vishwa Dev Sharma v. State of Rajasthan,' and In Re. Vinayak Chandra Sharma were cited in support of the view. Yellow Journalism according to Justice was wide enough to include not only contemptuous publication but also obscene publications and since it was against our cultural heritage and values; that deserved to be avoided.

Mrs. Shobha Menon-Need for Limitations 'Freedom' means absence of control, interference or restriction. Hence, the expression 'freedom of the Press' means the right to print and publish without any intereference from the State or any public authority. But, as will be seen presently, this freedom, like other freedoms, cannot be absolute but is subject to well-known exceptions acknowledged in the public interest, which in India are enumerated in Art. of the Constitution. Since in India, freedom of expression is guaranteed by Art. 19(1) (a) of the Constitution, and it has been held by Supreme Court that freedom of the 'press' is included in that wider guarantee, it is unnecessary to plead for the freedom of the Press in this country.

Nevertheless, the principles which lie at the background of the Press and the limitation thereto-are relevant to every legislation relating to the Press. Since its constitutionality can be challenged in India, it would be not only useful but also essential to keep before one's mind's eye the basis and historic principles on which the demand for freedom of the Press is founded. This has become particularly important in India, when the zeal for establishing a welfare and socialist State is apt to relegate all individual rights to the background, for the time being. Need for Limitations If the Press is such a useful or rather an indispensable instrument for information and exchange of views and opinions in a modern democracy, the question at once arises, why should there by any need for regulating or controlling this freedom by law.

The reason is obvious: If no guarantee of individual right can be absolute, so is the freedom of the Press-it must be reconciled with the collective interests of the society, otherwise known as the 'public interest. The need for balancing these with competing interests has been pithily expressed by the eminent English Judge, Lord Denning. "The freedom of the press is extolled as one of the great bulwarks of liberty. It is entrenched in the constitutions of the world. But it is often misunderstood. It does not mean that the press is free to ruin a reputation or to break a confidence or to pollute the course of justice or to do any thing that it is unlawful. It means that there is to be censorship. Not by lacewing system. Not by executive direction, Nor by court injunction. "It means that the press is to be free from what Blackstone calls 'previous restrain'. In short, the press is not entitled to any absolute immunity from unlawful conduct any more than any other individual.

Rights are dependent upon the existence of the State and the maintenance of order so that the rights may be ensured and enforced. Hence, no right or freedom can be allowed to be exercised in such manner as would jeopardize the very existence of the State or the maintenance of public order, or under public normality, or a fair and impartial administration of justice, which are essential for a civilized existence. Again since a pre-condition of the enforcement of individual rights is guarded, the freedom of expression cannot be so exercised as to undermine the reputation of any member of the public. When the danger to such countervailing public interest assumes a serious dimension, the State would be justified in curtailing or controlling even the freedom of the Press.

Freedom of the Press cannot, therefore, mean an uncontrolled license for or immunity to every possible use of language. Every human institution is liable to be abused and every liberty, is left unbridled, has the tendency to become a licence. It should be pointed out that when there is a conflict between the public interest behind a free press and some other competing interest arises, it is for the Courts to strike the balance between the two interests. In India, the Court's role in balancing the two competing public interests is reserved in the Constitution itself by the expression 'reasonable restriction' in C1.(2)-(6)of Art. 19.

In every civilized society whew individual rights are declared and enforced, whether by ordinary law or 13y the Constitution, the right implies a duty not to abuse that right, for, the right being guaranteed to all citizens alike, it would be hollow to others unless one individual respects the similar rights of others or transgresses the bounds of his own right, and affects the other rights of other individuals. As early as 1789, the French Declaration of the Rights of Man, which declared that "free communication of thoughts and ideas is one of the most precious rights of man", in the same breath stated that this freedom of every citizen was "subject to responsibility for abuse of this liberty in cases contemplated by law".

AVENUES OF ABUSE OF FREEDOM OF THE PRESS

The avenues of abuse of the Press in modern times, should be noticed in. brief: The foremost danger is that since the Press is a most potent instrument of mass communication, newspapers are sought to be used by powerful parties and financial groups or even individuals having vested interests, for purposes of 'propaganda', i.e., to further their private interests to the detriment of the public, as a result of which the Press, instead of creating a free market of ideas, tend to become an instrument for suppression of view, and an agency of monopolistic contrail or eve news and reports. The basic assumption that freedom of the Press is indispensable to offer to the public all points of view involved in public issues and to give a truthful account of events so that the reader may freely form his considered view on each issue is defeated if every newspaper gives a biased or coloured report of news and advocates only one of the solutions, namely, that advocated by the party or group which conducts that newspaper.

SAFEGUARDS AGAINST ABUSE OF FREEDOM OF THE PRESS

Though the likelihood of freedom of the Press to be abused is now evident in all modern countries, the remedy of this serious problem is not so easy. The reason is that it is a necessary evil since freedom of the Press is the ' Ark of the Covenant of Democracy' it cannot be dispensed with. Though it "has some disagreeable results, the wholesome ones are greater and more numerous." If that be so, the Press' cannot be suppressed nor does the remedy lie in State monopoly or nationalization of newspaper, because that would be the assumption by the State of the guardianship of the public mind a very antithesis of democracy.

The result would be the same of the State acquires complete control by a system of censorship of day-to-day regulation. That is why Pundit Jawaharlal once said-" I would rather have a completely free press with all the dangers involved in the wrong use of that freedom than a suppressed or a regulated press". The remedy against abuse of.freedom of the Press has, in fact, been provided, in India, by Art of the Constitution itself. In c1.(2) it empowered the State to impose ' reasonable restriction' in the countervailing social interests such as security of the State, public order and the like, which are enumerated in that clause.

"The exercise of these freedoms, since it carries with it duties and responsibilities, may be subject to such formalities condition, restrictions or penalties as are prescribed by law and are necessary in a democratic society, in the interests of national security, territorial integrity or public safety, for the prevention of disorder or crime, for the protection of health or morals for the protection of the reputation or rights of others, for preventing the disclosure of information received in confidence or for maintaining the authority and impartiality of the judiciary". Thus, apart from the interest of security of the State, freedom of the Press may have to be controlled to protect an individual from any damage to his reputation, privacy property and the like, by irresponsible publications through the Press.

"The Press is the servant, not the master, of the citizenry and its freedom does not carry with it an unrestricted hunting license to prey on the ordinary citizen". In short, "Without a lively sense of responsibility a free press may readily become a powerful inst5ument of injustice". Classification of the limitation In India, a journalist, a printer, publisher or proprietor of newspaper or an author has to take care that he does not violate any of the restrictions which have been imposed on the freedom of the Press by a number of Statute founded on different aspects of the need for social or public control. Some of these statutes, again, have a constitutional foundation, e.g. those which have been passed to enforce the grounds of restriction envisaged by cl. (2) or (6) of Art while others are general laws applicable to the public, including the Press.' Besides statutory limitations, there are certain limitations which are founded on English common law, and are still uncodified, e.g., those founded on the common law of torts, such as the civil wrongs of defamation breach of confidence, invasion of privacy and the like. Some of the limitations, again founded on reasons of State or public policy, such as 'official secrets', while others are founded on private rights, such as copyright.

EXTRA LEGAL RESTRAINTS

The need for an institution to ensure a high standard of responsibilities on the part of the Press arises from the fact that the freedom of the Press is likely to be abused by what is called 'yellow journalism', i.e.. the publication of matters which debase public taste or indulge in intrusion into public lives even though such publication may not be punishable under the provisions of the existing law. Almost every modern country has therefore set up a body which could serve as a watchdog over the standards of journalism and at the same time maintain the freedom of the Press against unwarranted government intrusion. In England, the Press Council (1953) is non-statutory body, having no legal powers.

It is composed of representatives of journalists as well as eminent men and academicians who constitute about one-third of the Council, and is headed by a non-political Chairman. In India, the Press Council is a statutory body. It was first established by the Press Council Act, 1965, on the lines recommended by the first Press Commission (1954). In the main, its functions followed the British precedent, to include:

- The preservation of the freedom of the Press.
- To maintain and improve the standards of newspaper in India
- To form a code of conduct to prevent writings which were not legally punishable but where yet 'objectionable'?

The Press Council Act, 1965 was, however repealed during Mrs. Gandhi's regime, by enacting the Press Council (Repeal) Act, 1976. The Press Council was, therefore abolished with effect from January, 1976, on the following grounds offered by the Government while bringing the Ordinance which later become the Act: The Press Council has failed to set out and enforce any code of conduct, as envisaged by the Act of 1965. It also failed to build up any respectable body of case-law because only complaints of comparatively minor importance were dealt with by the Council. After coming into power, the

Janata Government enacted a fresh Press Council Act, 1978, to re-establish the Press Council, with a different composition and powers. Censorship which, when imposed by law, operates as a restriction upon the freedom of the Press, ceases to be so when it is self-imposed. In many countries, therefore, newspaper and journals have put their heads together to formulate a code of conduct or guidelines they would observe to prevent abuses of the freedom of these. In U.S.A., for instance, such guidelines have been formulated in many States, by the news media in consultation with the Bar, as to matters which should not be published to the prejudice of an accused in pending or impending trial, e.g. confessions, opinions on the guilt or innocence of the accused, statements as might influence the outcome of trial.

In U.K. the Press Council itself is an institution of self-censorship. Its 'adjudication' on complaints received from members of the public against the Press are thus regarded as having moral authority and have thus been developing a code of conduct of journalists. Self-censorship imposed by voluntary restraints must be distinguished from guidelines issued by a Censor, an instance of which was when in India during the 1975-76 Emergency.

Newspaper editors hardly have to be told about the importance of press freedom. Nor do they need to be lectured on the virtues of peace. But surprisingly, few editors seem to be aware of or articulate the strong connection between the two. Quite simply, a free press promotes peace; creating a universally free press would promote universal peace. The bridge between the two is democracy. Only to academics is democracy a complex term requiring elaborate definition. To most people, correctly I argue, democracy is easily defined by certain rights: that of voting and the secret ballot, of being able to run for any political office, including the highest, and of freedom of speech.

And the latter, of course, means not only the freedom to publish criticism of the government, but even to advocate revolution. Except in a time of war, censorship and democracy are not only seen as incompatible—they *are* incompatible. This is clear from a survey of governments around the world. For all countries, without exception, as shown by the latest Freedom House survey of freedom, the most democratic have the freest media; the least democratic have the least free media. Indeed, it is inconceivable that it could be otherwise. Plainly, a free press is essential to democracy, but I would put this even in stronger terms: promoting freedom of the press also promotes democracy—a way to democracy is by working to create a free press. I think that most newsmen would agree with this.

Now, on the other side of the coin, research on war and peace has shown the following results. First, democracies do not make war on each other. There has been no war and virtually no threat of violence between two countries that are democratic. The most war occurs between the least free countries. Note that there are 167 sovereign nations in the world today, 60 of them democracies. Not only has there been or is there no war between them, but there is not even the threat of war; none of these democracies arm against each other. Not one. In its long, bloody history, for example, Western Europe is finally at peace. There is not even the expectation of war among these countries. And, it is no accident that Western Europe is also totally democratic.

Second, democracies tend to have the least internal violence (riots, revolutions, guerrilla warfare, civil war); those countries with the least freedom tend to have the most. Finally, democratic governments just do not kill their own citizens for any but the most reprehensible civil crimes, such as executions for murder; the least free tend to kill their citizens by the millions for political, religious, or racial reasons. In many parts of the world, genocide and totalitarianism are almost synonymous. Consider that in this century alone, aside from foreign or domestic wars, totalitarian governments have killed in cold blood more than 115,000,000 people, over three times the number killed in battle in all wars in this century, including the two world wars.

The major perpetuators are well known; disagreement now only exists about the numbers: Hitler may have slaughtered as many as 14,000,000 people, including near 5,000,000 Jews; Stalin surely outdid him by murdering well over 20,000,000; Mao Tse-tung possibly liquidated even more; Pol Pot in Cambodia exterminated around 2,000,000 Cambodians; the Young Turks killed over 1,000,000 Armenians during World War I. And then there were the assorted butcheries in Ethiopia, Vietnam, Syria, Uganda, Rwanda, Burundi, Indonesia, East Pakistan, and elsewhere. A twentieth century, global blood bath of over 100,000,000; over 140,000,000 people when battle-deaths in foreign and domestic wars are included. But not one of these millions were killed in a war or violence between democracies; few, if any, citizen of a democracy have been killed by their own government for other than civil crimes like murder (the number of criminals executed in the whole history of the United State by federal and local authorities up to 1982 is 13,630).

It should be clear that democracies are a way to nonviolence. In fact, promoting democracy is promoting world peace. For were democracy universalized, the lesson of history and contemporary events is that international war would be eliminated, domestic violence minimized, and genocide and governmental mass murder of its citizens ended. The conclusion is now manifest. Since advancing freedom of the press furthers democracy, spreading freedom of the press promotes world peace. And the reverse logic is also true. Without democracies, there will be war; without freedom of the press, democracies cannot exist. Newsmen everywhere should realize this simple equation, then. *To foster peace, foster freedom of the press.*

The recent happenings in Tamil Nadu where six journalists were sentenced to 15 days simple imprisonment for alleged breach of privilege and contempt by the state Legislative Assembly brings back the not so pleasant memories of the Emergency. There is a saying that those who forget history are wont to repeat it. The action is condemnable as the intent of those who passed the judgment is, itself, questionable. The threat to freedom of the press in this country or for that matter in all of Asia hangs like the proverbial sword of Damocles. In India, no political party can boast of respecting the freedom of the press. There have been numerous instances of newspaper offices being vandalised and editors and journalists being roughed up by political flunkeys for publishing articles that were critical of their leaders whose credentials were suspect, to say the least. This sorry state of affairs has increased in recent years.

Not long ago, an article published by Alex Perry, a foreign journalist, on Prime Minister Vajpayee's fitness, thereby questioning his ability to lead the nation, considerably angered the ruling party. The press is considered the watchdog of democracy. Sadly, there is scant regard for this truism in a country which is, ironically, the world's largest democracy. Self-discipline, which is so crucial for the survival of any democracy, is fast disappearing from the Indian polity. Tolerance levels are declining and arrogance is all-pervasive. More often than not political power is used to further the cause of the power-hungry rather than to serve the masses. When obedience to the enforceable is itself neglected, obedience to the unenforceable is out of the question. Even after more than five decades of Independence, democracy in India has still not matured and the quality of public life is declining alarmingly.

Today, political leaders are voted to power because of their oratory and manipulative skills and not for their wisdom and virtue. We cannot expect better governance if we continue to elect people with criminal track records and malafide intentions. Fortunately, the Indian citizen can depend on a strong judiciary, which has so often come to the rescue. The press, on its part, should bear in mind that freedom of the press does not mean a license to write anything. This freedom is precious and it has to be used judiciously. When this freedom is misused, public respect for this profession will diminish. The press has to guard against this.

There is a common understanding that democracy and press freedom are strongly connected and mutually reinforcing. Mass media fulfill an essential function in democracy as a link between the citizens and their political representatives. The information and representation function of the media is thought to be best performed if the media are free, that is to say autonomous. In all dissident movements in Eastern-Europe the demand for democracy was accompanied by the demand for a free press. In Russia, Gorbachev stressed the importance of glasnost' (not the equivalent of press freedom but a step in that direction) as a sine qua non for democratic reform.

Yeltsin affirmed that he could not conceive of a democratic society 'without the freedom of expression and the press'. And also Putin stressed the relationship: 'without a truly free media, Russian democracy will not survive'. In this paper we discuss the relationship between press freedom and democracy in post- communist Russia. Post-communist Russia represents a unique historical and socio- political setting, which does not readily allow for generalization. Nevertheless, the observations on Russia can contribute to a deeper understanding of the connection between press freedom and democracy in other contexts as well. Although widely used words, the concepts of democracy and press freedom are not uniformly defined.

Different perceptions of democracy cause different perceptions of the role of the media in democracy. In order to avoid confusion of ideas, we start by having a closer look at both concepts. The concept of democracy Press freedom and democracy are words with a highly positive emotional value. Amartya Sen (1999) has pointed out that while democracy is not yet universally practiced, nor indeed uniformly accepted, in the general climate of world opinion, democratic governance has now achieved the status of being taken to be generally right. Because of its positive emotional value the word is highly vulnerable for abuse and 'cooptation' which leads to a shift, and in the end an emptiness, of meaning.

In the Soviet Union a distinction was made between the real 'socialist democracy' and the fake 'bourgeois democracy'. The meaning of the word democracy became even more obscured by the use of the prefixes pseudo-, new-, or 'not consolidated' in combination with democracy. Post- communist Russia has been labelled all of this, due to the gap between its democratic quality and its democratization rhetoric. Other labels have been used that question the genuineness of Russian democracy even more: Russia as 'delegative democracy', 'totalitarian democracy' or 'authoritarian democracy'.

With the same half-heartedness, Olcott and Ottaway (1999) speak of 'semi-authoritarianism', Zhelev (1999) of 'a multiparty authoritarian system', Sergej Kovalev of an 'authoritarian-police regime that will preserve the formal characteristics of democracy and market economy' and the Russian commentator Mikhail Delyagin of a 'liberal dictatorship' and 'manipulative democracy'. Koshkareva and Narzhikulov (1998: 164) speak of a 'nomenklatura democracy'. Diamond (1996) calls this a characteristic of the 'third wave' of democratization: the gap between the so called electoral (formal, political) and liberal (substantial, social) democracies.

At a minimum, democracy is a political system based on free, competitive and regular elections. This 'electoral' democracy presumes space for political opposition movements and political parties that represent a significant range of voter choice and whose leaders can openly compete for and be elected to positions of power in government. The concept of 'liberal' or 'substantial' democracy extends the key element of free competition with a bunch of political and civil rights (freedom of speech, freedom of association, freedom of religion, etc.) and the notions of the rule of law, inclusive citizenship and civil society. The concept of substantial democracy cannot easily be reduced to a set of procedures and institutions but is described as 'a way of regulating power relations in such a way as to maximize the opportunities for individuals to influence the conditions in which they live, to participate in and influence debates about the key decisions that affect society'. Democracy in this sense is not a dichotomic but continuous variable. The choice is not between democracy or no democracy but between more or less democracy, which comes down very often to 'old' and 'new' democracies. Linz and Stepan (1996) distinguish 'consolidated' and 'transitional' democracies. Consolidation is attained to when democracy became 'the only game in town', constitutionally as well as behaviourally and attitudinally. At this stage, institutions and laws alone are not sufficient anymore, and the element of political culture joins in. The concept of political culture builds largely on the book of Almond and Verba, The Civic Culture, and experiences some renaissance in the last decennia.

The idea however, that one 'culture' - one constellation of values, norms, belief systems, and attitudes - fits democracy closer than the other, is not new. Plato already pointed out that forms of government (oligarchy, democracy, tyranny, aristocracy) differ according to dispositions of men. More recently, Miller, White and Heywood (1998: 66) have expressed this as 'democracies require democrats'. The concept of political culture provides a link between the macro level of the society and the micro level of the individual. The concept of culture also suggests some continuity over time: 'neither an individual's values nor those of a society as a whole are likely to change overnight. Instead, fundamental value change takes place gradually'.

The value that has singled out as most contributive to a 'civic' or 'democratic' culture is trust, and more specifically impersonal trust, in contrast with personal trust. In the 'democratic' culture, the individual is considered an end in itself and a rational being, capable of making independent judgments and choices (eg. voting) and able to construct his own 'truth' out of widely divergent messages. 'Authoritarian culture', in contrast, places truth in the hands of a few 'wise men' whereas the common man is distrusted and considered a dependent, irrational being, a 'cog in the wheel', not capable of making independent judgments and choices.

Merrill and Lowenstein (1990: 159-160) speak of a 'democratic orientation' (with examples such as John Locke and John Milton) versus an 'elitarian orientation'. The former can be linked to individualism, pluralism and trust; the latter to collectivism, dominance (unitary truth) and distrust. Russia has traditionally been an elitist country. Tsarist Russia was characterized by a wide gap between the ruling elite and the common men. Communist Russia was, despite its claims to be egalitarian, very elitist oriented. Lenin stressed the role of the Communist Party as a vanguard party.

Hence, the mass lacked class consciousness and organization and had need of the guidance of the Party. According to Kropotkin, Lenin's attitude was dictated by a fundamental distrust in mankind (cited in Krug, 1990: 106). The American journalist Robert Kaiser (1976: 22) has stated it very crude when he wrote: 'The Soviet system is built on the assumption that the citizenry cannot be trusted'. The sharp dichotomy between the Party and the people outlived Lenin. Pavao Novosel speaks of a division of the Soviet society in 'first and second class citizens', formalized through the nomenklatura system. Postcommunist Russia is characterized by a more diversified social stratification but the contrast between the 'elite' (oligarchs and rulers) and 'the people' remains.

The distinction is expressed more frequently than before in terms of money and standard of living, but remains present in the mentality of the Russians as well. Also Zhelev (1996: 7) sees this as a constant between the past and the present: 'the sense that 'we, the people' are of no consequence' and the tension between 'us' and 'them'. Truth has traditionally been unitary in Russia and so was the community, as words like sobornost' (a kind of mystic unity) testify to.

In the Marxist interpretation too there was only one right position. Opposition and diversity were considered falsehood and therefore deserved no hearing. William Zimmerman (1995: 631) has called this 'synoptic thinking': 'the view that there is only one correct philosophy'. This view is diametrically opposed to the pluralistic view of truth and the parliamentarian model that 'by contrast is based on the assumption that the existence of groups or factions that express and defend particular interests in a representative institution is not only natural but its sole justification'.

THE CONCEPT OF PRESS FREEDOM

A free press is a cornerstone of (liberal) democracy. It is essential for holding government accountable, and for citizens to get informed, to communicate their wishes, to participate in the political decisionmaking. In principle, and on the analogy of democracy, press freedom has been accepted worldwide as the norm. The Soviet mass media enjoyed, in contrast with 'bourgeois' mass media and on the analogy of 'real democracy', 'real freedom'. Hence, media were freed from the obligation to be profitable: 'Freedom of the press was equated with freedom from private ownership: being freed from the profit motive, the media were free to do their duties as instruments of the state and the Party'. The communist model embraced the notion of the so called 'positive freedom', namely the freedom to, whereas in the liberal view, common in the West, the concept of 'negative freedom' or freedom from, prevailed: freedom from external goals (eg. building of a communist society, class homogenization) and external control and pressures (eg. government, parties, industry).

A free press, in other words, is an autonomous press: free to determine its own tasks and policies. In line with this view of freedom, 'traditional free press theory lacks a prescriptive character. It does not in its simple and most basic form say anything of what the press ought to do'. Media autonomy, or independence, implies that the media are clearly separated from state and political institutions and free from/of inhibiting forms of economic, political or other dependency. Karol Jakubowicz (2000) distinguishes three levels of media independence:

- External independence of media organizations, that is freedom to establish and operate media outlets without legal, political, or administrative interference or restraint.
- Internal independence of editorial staff, that is editorial autonomy, respected by owners, publishers and managers.
- Personal/professional independence of media practitioners, both management and journalists, which implies their impartiality and detachment from social, political and economic interests in their performance of journalistic duties and a sense of high professionalism and dedication to journalistic ethics.

Whereas laws, codes and institutions can contribute a lot to the first two levels of independence (media institutions and editorial staff) – one could speak of a 'formal press freedom' in accordance with the notion of 'formal democracy' – the third level, that is the individual level, is situated more on the field of (political) culture (i.e. attitudes, norms, values). And whereas the first two levels can be possibly realized without the third, absence of the third level on the other hand makes external and internal independence to a large degree meaningless. In other words: as democracy, press freedom is not considered a dichotomic but a continuous variable.

The choice is not between press freedom or no press freedom but between more or less press freedom. In every country and every system one can distinguish factors that spur press freedom on the one hand and factors that curtail press freedom on the other hand. The American organization Freedom House (2002) concentrates on the external factors that endanger press autonomy as the most measurable criteria: laws, regulations and administrative decisions that influence media content, political pressures and controls on media content, economic influences over media content and repressive actions (censorship, physical violence, arrests, killing of journalists). On the basis of these criteria Russia enjoys a 'partial press freedom'. Very often the issue of 'press freedom' is linked to the issue of 'press responsibility' or 'social responsibility'.

Together with Freedom House (2002) we want to stress the demand for 'freedom' above the demand for responsibility. Hence, the issue of 'press responsibility' often is voiced to defend governmental control of the press. It is linked more with the concept of 'positive freedom' than with the concept of freedom as such ('negative freedom'). Another frequently made association is that of press freedom with 'freedom of information' and the 'right to know'. This aspect is crucial indeed and complementary to press freedom as it relates to the perspective of the citizen. We'll come back to it later.

THE PARADOX OF DEMOCRACY AND PRESS FREEDOM: THE POLITICIAN'S SIDE

The process of democratization in Russia paradoxically became a justification to curtail press freedom and to keep the media instrumentalized. The instrumental use of the mass media in postcommunist Russia is a continuation of the communist past. Although the external (societal) goal has changed from the building of the communist society into support for the democratic society, the mobilization of the mass media as a means to a goal remained unchanged. Gorbachev considered the mass media main instruments in promoting his politics of glasnost and gaining support for his reforms. As before, mass media mobilized people for the ideology of socialism but now in a more dynamic way. Yassen Zassoursky, dean of the Faculty of Journalism of the Moscow State University, has labelled the media model in the glasnost era (1985-1991) successively the 'glasnost-model' and the 'instrumental model'.

The first label (glasnost- model) points out an element of change, namely the break with the previous 'administrative-bureaucratic model'. Also in this model, however, Zassoursky points at the instrumental use of the mass media. In the name he later used (instrumental model), this aspect of continuity is brought to the forefront. The first Yeltsin-years received from Zassoursky the label of 'fourth power model'. The expectations, however, were pitched too high, and from 1995-'96 onward this label was changed in for that of 'authoritarian-corporate model'. It seems that the press could not meet the requirements for being called an independent 'Fourth Power'.

'Whatever good or bad happened to the Russian media in the 90s was directly tied to Yeltsin's views and acts in the information sphere', states media law specialist Andrei Richter. Yeltsin presented himself as the self-constituted personal guarantor of democracy and press freedom. While it is obvious that Yeltsin 'allowed' more freedom than any of his predecessors, he never questioned his presumed right to allow such freedom. And in exchange he expected loyal support from the mass media for his policy.

Yeltsin embodied the belief that in order to improve the democratic procedures one has to step 'beyond' these procedures. In the name of democracy he fired upon Parliament in October 1993 and banned opposition newspapers. In the name of democracy he ruled largely by decree thus ignoring a whole series of 'horizontal checks'. In times of elections - 'the lifeblood' of democracy– the mobilization of mass media reaches a peak. In the name of democracy Yeltsin blatantly expected the mass media to support and arrange his re-election as President in 1996.

The mass media were committed to an anti-communist crusade. The whole election campaign was reduced to a duel between President Yeltsin and oppositional candidate Zhuganov, between the future and the past, between democracy and communism, between press freedom and press control. The tone of the campaign was set by the sacking on 15 February 1996 of Oleg Poptsov, head of the state-owned television station RTR. The right to appoint and dismiss media functionaries are one of the most powerful means of direct influence in the media for the executive. The President appoints the chairman of the 'public' television channel ORT and the government channels RTR and Kul'tura.

The government appoints the chairmen of the central radio channels. Another way of direct control are the state organizations directly subordinated to the executive, especially the Media Ministry but also an ad hoc institution such as Boris Yeltsin's 'Federal Information Centre of Russia' or an institution with no direct authority over the media such as the Security Council. The possibilities for indirect control are even greater. There is the reliance of many media outlets on economic sponsorship, either through state subsidies or by businesses, either open or secret. There is the use of courts as weapons deployed against journalists (esp. libel and slander). There is the dependency on the Kremlin – instead of an independent agency – for the issuance and revoking of broadcast and publishing licenses.

There is the dependency on state facilities such as printing houses, transmission facilities, and distribution systems. There is the accreditation of journalists and the unequal access to information. There is the use of violence against journalists. To this we can add the legal insecurity caused by the rapid succession of decrees, government orders and procedures, and the unpredictable changes in policy and practice of, for example, tax collection (eg. massively tolerated tax-evasion, followed by repressive controls on a large scale).

The paradox of democracy and press freedom: the media's side It does not appear fair to exclusively blame the authorities for the described system. The label 'authoritarian-corporate model' implies next to the 'authoritarian' aspect (that is, the media subordinated to the authorities) also the 'corporate' aspect (that is, the cooperation and alliances). The distinction comes down to the question whether the media are 'forced' rather than 'free' partners of the authorities. The question of quilt is inappropriate. We can only observe and conclude. In the early years of the Russian Federation, marked by the conflict between President and Parliament, 'most of the Russian media appeared to adopt a strongly pro-government stance'.

A content analysis of central television programs in the run-up to the referendum of 25 April 1993, showed 'the obtrusive partisanship of state television'. The majority of media voluntarily opted for the new, hence democratic partiality. Their leaders approached Yeltsin on their own initiative for protection and promised loyalty (read: partiality) instead. In the presidential elections of 1996, the majority of journalists and media professionals rallied behind Yeltsin again and voluntarily agreed with the mobilization function of the media. As Shevelov, vice president of television channel ORT, stated: 'you can only refer to pressure if there is resistance. There is none.' The journalists adhered to partisanship not only for material reasons but also out of normative considerations. Igor Malashenko, president of the private television station NTV, who joined the Yeltsin re-election campaign in April 1996 as chief media advisor, explained this logic as following: if the private media provided "unbiased, professional, and objective" campaign coverage, Zyuganov would win the election, and journalists would lose their freedom permanently. Better to become a temporary "instrument of propaganda" in the hands of the Kremlin, Malashenko argued. Partijnost' was justified for the protection of democracy and consequently for press freedom. In the name of democracy the journalists voluntarily gave up their autonomy and their freedom.

Elections in general, and the 1996 elections in particular, can be considered critical but not atypical periods. Hence, it is not possible to treat the electoral period as being distinct from the context in which media normally operate. Quite the reverse, if we may believe Brzezinski: 'A perceptive formula is easier to articulate in a moment of special stress. (..) The situation of crisis permits sharper value judgments'. In general, and apart from election context, research has shown that many Russian journalists do not reject the paternalistic character of power and therefore accept its tutelage in mass communication. The journalist considers himself, in line with the tradition, a missionary of ideas, not a neutral observer or autonomous information disseminator.

The concept adhered to is that of the active or participant journalist as described by the Hungarian writer Janos Horvat: someone who wants to influence politics and audiences according to his political beliefs. The restriction to the presentation of mere facts is even commonly regarded as a devaluation of the profession of journalist. The attitude of the individual journalists suits the media-owners who like to use the argument of press freedom to protect their own freedom and their particular interests. As the majority of media-holdings form part of larger financial-industrial groups and as money is still made through political connections, political, economic and media-interests go closely together.

Political and economic elites try to secure via the media their own positions. Oligarchs and media magnates like Boris Berezovsky and Vladimir Gusinsky are the classic examples. When the media outlets of Vladimir Gusinsky became the target of prosecution, Gusinsky immediately alarmed that press freedom and in extension even democracy was endangered. His alarm was taken over by other journalists in Russia as well as in foreign countries (the USA in the first place).

There were, however, also skeptical voices. Robert Coalson (2000) wrote in a column in The Moscow Times: 'Gusinsky has shown very little genuine concern for press freedom. Like the other oligarchs, he only appears when his own interests are directly at risk'. In the same way Sergej Markov noticed with reference to a rally on freedom of speech, organized in connection with the NTV-case: '.. all speeches by NTV stars were about NTV's freedom. Such egoism could not inspire champions of freedom of expression'. Also in line is the following reflection: 'Where were the voices of protest from this 'independent' press when Yeltsin attacked the legitimate Russian parliament with military force, when the Soviet Union became dissolved by the signatures of a few officials, when the country's resources passed into the hands of a few oligarchs, and when corruption allowed Yeltsin's chosen family and friends to suddenly acquire wealth and transfer this wealth out of the country? That 'independent' press manipulated a government that served its interests.'

'The concept of freedom of speech has become hackneyed after Gusinsky and somewhat awkward to use' concludes the however not neutral General Director of Gazprom-Media, Alfred Kokh (2001: 20) and the public? As Price and Krug (2000: 4) state: 'for free and independent media to 'work', the community in question must value the role that the media play'. The public however seems to accept the 'Russian interpretation' of press freedom. Or, in any case, is adapted to it. The people react to mass media information by asking themselves not 'is this true' but 'komu eto vygodno?' (to who's advantage ?). News is interpreted in function of the news source, whether 'Berezovsky's channel', 'Gusinsky's channel' or 'the government's channel', or whether Potanin's newspaper, LUKoil's newspaper or the Communist Party's newspaper.

It is telling that 'independent' media in Russia are identified with 'opposition' media. Media independence is considered illusory, and partisanship the norm. Many Russians endorse the proposition that the mass media have the obligation to support 'the system'. A poll at the end of 2000, for example, shows that 34% of the Russians agree that the mass media have to give 'full support' to the President and that opposition is not desirable. 'In today's Russia, media freedom is not the most fashionable and popularly supported notion' declared television presentator and journalist Evgeny Kiselev in an interview with Jeremy Drukker. And Elena Androunas (1993: 35) points to the absence of 'freedom as a state of mind'.

FREEDOM OF OPINION, NOT OF INFORMATION

The result is a pluralist but not an independent (autonomous) press. Pluralist, in the sense of representation in the media system of a broad range of political expression, opinions and interests. In this sense, postcommunist Russia is hardly less pluralistic than older democracies and probably even more, as it is not hindered to the same degree by 'political correctness' or 'la pensée unique'. Peter Humphreys (1996: 312) points in his book on media policy in Western Europe at a systematic decline of pluralism in the 20st century, caused by a de-ideologization of the traditional politics and commercialization, standardization and concentration of the media.

While the Russian media system is characterized by a high degree of concentration as well, this concentration is not at all linked with depolitization: 'money in the CIS is still made through connections in the government, and in this game it helps to own newspapers and stations as instruments of political influence'. Ivan Sigal (1997) has named Russian news coverage 'a part of politics'. 'In such circumstances', says Izvestiya-journalist Sergej Agafonov, 'a free independent press is doomed, but an unfree and dependent press can flourish'. Alexei Pankin speaks of a unique result: 'a genuinely pluralistic unfree media'.

However, a pluralism that derives the right to exist from the presence of different power groups in society is an uncertain pluralism. Hence, when the different power groups join forces because they feel threatened in their positions, as was the case in the 1996 presidential elections, this pluralism dies. The greatest victim of this kind of pluralism is the (factual) information. Every newspaper and every television channel brings its own versiya of the facts. In order to get an accurate picture of what happened, one has to read daily about six newspapers and watch several television stations, claims Andrei Fadin (1997). But who does? 'What we have is not freedom of information, and this 'freedom' is not exhaustive stimulating readers to buy half a dozen newspapers, but rather discouraging them from reading anything other than gossip columns and cheap sensations, and even more importantly, from organising their own actions on the basis of information received' reacts Alexei Pankin (1997).

The skepticism of the public is illustrated by its small confidence in the media: down from 70% in 1990 to only 13% in 2000. To fulfil their information function, the media need not only to break with the view of journalism as 'politics conducted with other means'. They also are in need, more concretely, for guaranteed access to information and transparency of governance. Press freedom presumes that, though independent, the press is not shielded away from government and industry. Worldwide, a correlation is determined between press freedom and transparency, and consequently between transparency and democracy: 'Information gathering is a vital component of freedom of information.

Without access to information, journalists are engaged primarily in the presentation of opinions. And while openness in the statement of opinions is an important element of democratic society, it is not sufficient for its development and maintenance. The possibility for an informed citizenry depends on the ability of journalists to have access to sources. Without this kind of journalistic effectiveness, a society can have free and independent media, but their utility toward advancement of democratic institution-building might be severely limited.' A climate of open access clings to the principle of information as a universal right, adjudged to everyone on an equal basis according to laws and procedures (universalism) whereas a culture of secrecy considers information a privilege, dependent on position or connections (particularism). Laws concerning transparency include those that recognize and guarantee public access to government-controlled information and institutions, with limited exceptions for national security, protection of personal privacy, crime prevention, and other goals. Laws concerning the licensing and accredititation of journalists also relate to his question. Russia has always been characterized by a culture of secrecy rather than transparency.

Always in Russian history, information was considered a privilege not a universal right - a property of the 'elite' who could dispose of it arbitrarily. In the Soviet Union, access to news sources depended on one's hierarchical (Party) position. The privileges of the nomenklatura 'first class' citizens not only included material goods, such as high salaries, access to 'diplomatic' shops, country houses, and the like, but also enhanced access to information: from the right to see foreign movies, or to read books, declared unsuited for general distribution to the receipt of special foreign news bulletins, on a daily basis compiled by TASS and distributed on paper of different colors according to the degree of detail and the intended public.

Though the high-placed functionaries received significantly more information, they too received their information on a 'need-to-know' basis. The result of this information policy was an information deficit: information became one of the most sought after commodities in the Soviet Union. Informal networks and rumours filled the vacuum. Parallel to the official information circuit, and on the analogy of the 'black market', an unofficial information circuit (e.g. samizdat) was functioning. The use of personal networks and informal contacts for obtaining scarce information, services or goods is indicated in Russian by the word blat or the term ZIS (znakomstva i svyazi). In the Soviet Union, the use of informal information networks primarily had an economic function, namely the survival in an economy of scarcity.

In the transition to a free market economy, privileged access to information played a key role in the process of privatizations, which became indicated as 'insider privatizations'. Personal (particularistic) relations (e.g. corruption, loyalties, privileges) continue to dominate the post-communist Russian economy and politics alike. Postcommunist leaders continue to see secrecy as a method to control the information flow. The panelists that IREX brought together to discuss the media situation in Russia agreed unanimously that 'access to some publicly relevant information is not free: authorities continue to view information as their property, and want to control access.' Defence-related security topics that are not state secrets have the status of classified information.

As a result 'obtaining publicly relevant information has become an increasingly challenging and dangerous job for Russian journalists, especially in cases of investigating authorities' abuses, corruption, fraud during election campaigns, and the war in Chechnya'. Banai sums up the three most efficient processes of information gathering in Russia as 'trust, relationship and integration'. Authorities still offer privileges to some periodicals and journalists. Mikhail Gulyaev names as 'privileged media' under President Yeltsin the news agencies ITAR-TASS and Interfaks, the newspapers Kommersant' and Izvestiya, and the weekly Argumenty i Fakty.

More recent examples support the enduring culture of secrecy. The way in which the Kremlin handled the disaster with the sunken submarine Kursk in the summer of 2000 fuelled speculations that the government was trying to withhold information from the public. Media coverage of the disaster was restricted, only state-controlled television channel RTR was granted full access to the disaster scene. The dissemination of false and misleading information led to confusion and government officials provided obscure answers to justified questions. The adoption by the Security Council of the 'Doctrine of the Information Security of the Russian Federation' on September 9th, 2000 roused fear that the government intended to limit the free flow of information and conceal information from the public.

Among others, the doctrine promotes a feeling of distrust towards the foreign press whereas the unrestricted access to foreign media nowadays is guaranteed by the Russian mass media law of 27 December 1991. The Russian mass media law gives the citizens only an indirect right to information that is they have the right to efficient reception through the mass media of correct information on the activities of state organs, societal organizations and their functionaries. Mass media however have guaranteed access to government and administration information. Unlawful refusals from government or administration functionaries to communicate information requested upon are punishable by law.

In reality however, refusal of information remain a problem. Since 1993, the Glasnost Defence Foundation draws up an inventory of all infringements of the rights of journalists and mass media. The majority of violations are tied up with precisely the refusal and restriction of access to information. What's more, the number of infringements increases throughout the 90s. Very few journalists however, claim their rights before court. Again, we have to conclude that the existence of laws alone is not a sufficient condition for their implementation. Kathryn Hendley (1999) points out that the 'demand for law' lags behind the 'supply of law'.

The demand for law implies respect for the law and trust in law, or, in other words a 'juridical culture'. We started from the common understanding that presses freedom and democracy are closely associated concepts. Both concepts, however, are not unequivocally defined. Democracy implies participation of the citizens in the decision making process, at the least in the election of the government. But gradations are legion. Press freedom implies media autonomy, freedom from external goals and controls. Again, gradations are numerous. Having said that, the correlation seems to exist: in the sense that there was 'no democracy' and 'no press freedom' in the Soviet Union and only 'partial democracy' and 'partial press freedom' in post-communist Russia. A third concept should be added, crucial to both press freedom and democracy, namely the right to know or the right to information coupled up to transparency of governance and administration. Information has to be considered a key concept in democracy and, at times, an antidote to opinion. The close integration of democracy with press freedom and in extension of politics with mass media has to be considered not only in terms of manipulation and force but also in terms of sharing a common political and information culture. Hence, the same values underly both 'cultures'.

All observations come down to the same conclusion: laws and institutions alone are not sufficient. Attitudes and values do play a role - whether named juridical culture, political culture, information culture, or culture tout court. The concept of culture suggests some communality of values: politicians, media workers and public alike share the same political culture and in extension the same information and communication culture. The concept of culture also suggests some continuity over time: not only over the communist and postcommunist period but also dating back to the time of the czars.

Culture is not unchangeable, but too high expectations concerning the role of media as triggers of democracy are doomed to fail. Media and society's development go together in coherent patterns. Howie Severino raises an interesting question in his latest blog post: how can a country that supposedly enjoys so much press freedom, such as the Philippines, be so corrupt? Isn't sunshine the best disinfectant? If we are a nation of tattletales, how come many are still stealing and cheating? Howie cites data that suggest that countries with high press-freedom rankings are less corrupt.

The conventional wisdom is that a free and courageous press exposes, thus helps to eliminate, corruption. One of the exception, Howie points out, seems to be the Philippines. We all have our own theories on why this is so. I'm not about to offer mine, except to point out my disagreement with the premise of this whole democracy-equals-press-freedom thing in the context of the Philippines. Press freedom, as we all know, does not exist in a vacuum. In a truly functioning democracy, press freedom should flourish. It is a gauge of democracy's efficacy. Without genuine democracy, it would be impossible for press freedom to exist.

The key word in that last sentence is "genuine." If we define democracy by its classic meaning — that people are free to choose their leaders and chart their own political course - then it would seem that what the Philippines have is indeed a democracy. But Philippine democracy has gone through a lot of permutations ever since the Americans introduced the concept to us more than a century ago. (It was, to be sure, an alien idea, which is probably why for much of the period since then, we were merely experimenting with democracy, not quite sure what to do with it, not quite fully grasping its potential.) We have been told, since 1986 at least, that a military coup d'etat that is subsequently backed by a throng of people rushing to Edsa is democracy in action. We were told about this again in 2001. Today, we tend to equate democracy in action with the upheavals of a mob - a well-meaning mob, sure, but a mob just the same. The bastardization of democracy continues to this day. Every election time, we are told that a few select families ruling over us for years and years is democracy in action.

An elite political family is good for us, we are told. Political dynasties in the Philippines are the antithesis of democracy and yet we are relentlessly made to accept them as part of our democratic way of life. Never mind that the evidence that elections in the Philippines are far from democratic has always been plain for all to see: the fraud, the vote buying, the violence, the manipulations, to name a few. The consequence of this bastardization, of course, is the poisoning and emasculation of our democratic institutions. This allows politicians to easily steal elections and make us all believe - through the media — that that is the work of God.

We have a Commission on Elections that has shown its capacity to be the chief agent not in upholding democracy but in subverting it. We have a judicial system that tends to favour the rich and those in power. We have an executive branch that is populated by a few select families who harbor a sense of entitlement to the positions that they had either stole or bought. Not surprisingly, we have had a media that, through all these years, has served the cause of the elite, the rich and the powerful more than they do the common man.

The Philippine press, with a few exceptions, has not changed since the end of World War II, which is to say that it remains either a weapon or a plaything by those rich or influential enough to literally buy a newspaper or a broadcast network or pay off reporters, editors and news managers. Filipino journalists work on pittance wages, if at all, making them the most abused of professionals. As such, they are easily corrupted not just by the owners of their newspapers or stations but by those who have the money to buy them and influence how they write or present the news. Again, there are exceptions but these exceptions are not significant enough to empower the press to function properly and professionally.

Perhaps with the exception of the mosquito press during the martial-law years, the Philippine press has never quite shown us why it deserves to be called the "fourth estate," supposedly a vanguard for the people that would come to democracy's rescue if the other three estates — the executive branch, the legislative branch and the judiciary — failed. So what we have now is a democracy that is not quite the democracy that many of us may have wished for. And what we have is a media that is an outgrowth of this anomaly of democracy, a corrupted and incompetent press so weak it cannot function as the sunshine to disinfect the rot in our system.

3

Journalistic Ethics and Ordinary Morality

Over the years, thousands of reporters' morals and ethics have been called into question through the duration of high-profile stories. Journalists are trained, and often forced, to abandon their personal beliefs in order to capitalize on a major event, ruthlessly capturing the private lives of citizens through print, video, and radio. One such instance was during the Columbine Shootings, when reporters snagged teenagers on their way to safety to ask them how they felt and what their reactions were. Where does it end? Is there a limit to the voracity of journalists who are paid to get the scoop no matter what the costs? And to whom do they answer when they go to far, as so many of them have over the course of history?

Freedom of speech protects the careers of reporters who are paid to 'tell the truth,' but sometimes it seems that they abuse their right to share the 'truth' with the public. Their gruesome accounts of murders; their invasive stories about affairs; and their constant pursuit of the rich and the famous has labeled them the 'black sheep' of society. The fact of the matter is that people are outraged. When citizens suffer tragedies, the last thing that they want is a barrage of microphones slung in their faces as they attempt to cope with their loss.

Most people are private about their lives, and though there are occassional exceptions to this rule, most people don't want their most secret affairs splashed across the front paper of USA Today. They don't want vivid images of their pain-contorted faces captured on film for the evening news. And they don't want everyone in the world talking about their experiences as though it were a fictional story recorded in a novel. Journalists are supposed to abide by the Society of Professional Journalists' (SPJ) Code of Ethics. The four main points in this code are:

- Seek Truth and Report It
- Minimize Harm
- Act Independently
- Be Accountable

It states that, "Journalists believe that public enlightenment is the forerunner of justice and the foundation of democracy. The duty of the journalist is to further those ends by seeking truth and providing a fair and comprehensive account of events and issues." Supposedly, journalists are supposed to abide by this code, though it rarely seems that they do. Rather than treating their subjects as human beings, they do their best to find the worst possible information, and that is the angle from which they choose to work. There are also laws governing the uses of sources in journalism. For example, if a reporter hears the words, "Off the record," they are supposed to keep whatever they have just heard confidential.

This isn't always followed, however, and several law suits have ensued regarding the breach of this rule. Unfortunately, judges rule in the favour of the journalist 86% of the time, just because it is so difficult to prove. According to the Project for Excellence in Journalism, which issued its first annual report in 2004, the authors stated that "Journalists believe they are working in the public interest, and are trying to be fair and independent in that cause. The public thinks these journalists are either lying or deluding themselves."

It also concluded that of seven major media sources (newspapers, web sites, network TV, cable TV, local TV, radio and alternative) all of them are losing their public following except for online sources and the radio. This shows that the public is disgusted with journalistic endeavors, and that they would rather not subject themselves to the degrading and ruthless probing into the lives of innocent citizens. There is also a relatively new controversy existing between "bloggers," who essentially publish daily journals on the Internet in order to attract attention to a particular product or service. Rober McLaws, a renowned developer who has his own blog, brought up the issue of journalistic integrity in blogs, which should really follow the same guidelines as other print media.

Journalistic integrity should be placed under the microscope and reevaluated by both reporters and their superiors. Newspapers, television shows, radio networks, and magazines should take responsibility for what they report, and show at least some measure of concern for the average citizen. How will this story effect the public? Who will this anger? Is my viewpoint objective? The SPJ is responding to the attacks of the public, and plans to begin efforts to put a stop to some of the less tasteful reporting in the United States.

The construction of a formal discourse on ethics is a direct contribution to the formation of identity within and outside a would-be professional group. Three successive approaches struggled and finally mixed to form the ethics that has, since the 1950s expressed the idealized moral independence of journalists from the commercial interests of the media. In Quebec, that dominant conception is currently being challenged by the rise of a "good employee's model" which in turn challenges the quasi-professional status of journalists. Claude-Jean Bertrand, a well known French commentator of the media scene in America recently wrote: "One impression a European observer gets of the American media in the mid-1980s is that they are running scared.

They seem timely concerned about their credibility, about the hostility which the public is claimed to feel towards them." And he goes to expose the growing interest in ethics, at the highest levels of media management, as a response to growing criticism. The move is not new. Ever since its birth, the media have cloaked their activities with a rhetoric of public service and ethical standards to improve public relations.

One can even claim that, in a sense, private media industries proclaim respectability and civic responsibility, in order to justify a private production apparatus for satisfying the public need for information. The province of Quebec has not recently (or ever?) experienced the equivalent of a Janet Cooke affair, or a propaganda situation like the Grenada invasion, let alone a libel suit by a person of national stature like General Westmoreland. But, in spite of the barrier of the (French) language, Quebec is part of the North American continental economy and is culturally at the pace with the United States. So, it is easy to interpret recent events on the media scene in French Canada as expressions of the same defensive civic responsibility trend as those found outside of the province.

Among these is June 1987 decision of the editor of LAPRESSE, Montreal's second French language daily, to enforce a set of ethical conflict of interest guidelines which were publicized in the proper circles. These forbid gifts from potential sources, trips paid by somebody other than the newspaper and sidelines for editorial employees. But more important than these events are long term trends which seem to indicate that the French-Canadian media and their journalists are not as beleaguered as their American counterparts. Primary among these, are the profound economic and cultural changes that are transforming the Quebec media industry as they are the rest of the western world.

These forces seem to push in two apparently contradictory directions: toward an ever growing concentration of ownership at the multinational level and, at the same time, toward a proliferation of (the same) products at the consumer level. The multiplication of titles resulting from technological developments and the narrowing of each individual market have decreased the growth of general news media and increased opportunities for specialised media that market a very specific style or sound. Increased refinements in marketing techniques enable these media to pinpoint their customers more and more effectively.

The result is a new burst of competition which makes use of recent technological advances in the fields of telecommunications and computerization. What may be considered particular to Quebec is that these trends became full-blown realities in the first half of the 1980s amid the political depression that followed the failure of the nationalist fervor that dominated the intellectual scene during the preceding two decades. Undoubtedly, the resulting change in the socio- cultural and technological environment has also affected the ways in which French-Canadian journalists view their social role. These changes are best chronicled in the changing discourse on ethics. This article examines these changes based on the following three propositions:

- It makes sense to talk of ethics for journalists only if we consider that they as a group engage in a particular activity which is in need of moral guidance. In that light, the ethics of journalism will be different from those of ordinary citizen, or other wage earners. This does not mean that journalists do not have to follow accepted personal ethical practices. It simply emphasizes that his or her professional ethics address specific areas of social responsibility.
- There will also be a radical difference between the ethics espoused by the professional group called journalists, even though they are salaried and not liberal entrepreneurs, and the ethics promoted by media corporations, even if a large part of the contents of these ethics are acceptable to journalists and even if the managers of the media are journalists. This proposition is important to the argument in that it points up the situation of the "dependent professional" which journalists find themselves by virtue of their status as employees. There is "dependency" in at least two senses: financial and moral because the media industries, their employers, have the legal obligation to provide information within the framework of a free press. As a consequence journalists either succeed in justifying their activity in terms of their own professional values or they fall within the moral definitions of their duties and ideals, drawn up by the media. In short, to be considered a professional group, journalists must be able to formulate their own standards in terms of their own social mission, rather than simply adhere to the standards, explicit or implicit, of the corporations that hire them.
- In North America, three historically situated sets of values competed in the past, and produced the dominant ethical model which has undergirded journalistic activity and legitimated the social existence of the trade. In Quebec this model developed in opposition to media industries, taking on an "adversarial stance" which strengthened the journalists' own discourses and organisations. But that dominant model is rapidly losing ground to a modem version of the "good employee's" ethic which seems to leave no room for moral independence from the employing corporations and consequently no place for an autonomous professional status.

A WOULD BE PROFESSION

During the past two centuries it was believed that journalistic activity required distinctive technical knowledge and skills as well as an intellectual formation beyond that of general culture. Gradually, practitioners in the field created professional associations, clubs and specialized publications. At the turn of the century, journalism became a separate field in teaching institutions. Scholars began to identify the intellectual and technical requirements of the field, scrutinized journalistic practice and converted it into an organized system of knowledge which could be taught as opposed to being acquired "on the job".

As a result, journalists began to be classed as a distinctive professional group and their sense of self-identity grew in proportion. It must be noted here that the word "professional" is ambiguous. It refers to a variety of general as well as specific components. On the general level a professional is someone who earns a living from a particular occupation. Here the meaning refers to an opposition with the amateur. Another definition states that a professional is someone who acts professionally, that is with technical mastery and a concern for well done work. For a journalist, that would mean mastery of such routine skills as factual accuracy, speed at meeting deadlines, style in presentation, a shared set of news values, and so on.

These two meanings of the term can be equally well applied to the subordinate status of the hired technician. The professionalism discussed here includes the first two meanings of the term, but it also refers to types of social behaviour associated with journalism, the social cohesion of the group itself, and its status relative to other groups. "We define the professional", writes Esther Dhm, "as a person preoccupied, among other things, by liberty and professional autonomy in his activities, and by final control of his activities by his peers (and by the public) rather than by his hierarchical superiors, without denying their importance on other aspects." (1987: 21-22, my translation). At this level, professionalism is much more a process, a struggle for something rather than something already achieved.

For this reason the struggle journalistic toward "professionalism" creates unease among media employers who fear the potential independence of their employees if they adopted a spiritual attitude similar to that of doctors or lawyers. Stating that journalists have a professional responsibility as a specific group of employees means that they are allowed not only a certain technical freedom of action in their everyday work, but also a certain power in designing the way in which every publishing or broadcasting operation intervenes socially. For those who claim journalists are mere executants, or even worse, who deny them any autonomy whatsoever, the matter of professional ethics has but one meaning: are they or are they not doing their job in terms of the technical standards of the craft and the ethical standards of their media employer.

For those who, on the contrary, state that journalists have small spaces of liberty even in rigidly supervised press enterprises and that they should demand even more on behalf of the public's right to information, ethics symbolizes an ideal of professional practice and a tool with which to create an autonomous profession. The persistent demand for liberty and autonomy, a formal discourse on ethics, may already be a valid criterion for considering journalism as a profession, even though this "trade" as yet lacks other professional qualities. Medicine, law and engineering have already attained the legal status of professions. Journalists, for their part, at least in Canada, are still considered common citizens in the eye of the law. Traditional professions rest on the privileged relationship between a professional and his client, while journalists are defined in terms of their relationship with a collectivity, even though they have individual clients such as employers and sources.

Doctors, lawyers and engineers have their conduct supervised through peer committees which evaluate their activities in accordance with the corporation's rules and an official code of ethics. They may also inflict sanctions. Professional associations furthermore control the quality of the professional acts of their members, access to the professional title and thereby to practice. In addition a system of values to which professionals are requested to adhere, have been codified into a formal code of ethics.

All together these features of accepted professions create a corporative sys- tem which is publicly justified on the grounds that it protects consumers from a power used in secrecy and from a practice that only fellow-members can really understand and value. In the case of journalism and its practices, in contrast, there are no such protective rules and anyone seems to be allowed to judge the quality of their work. Journalists, for their part, are sometimes judged by public opinion, ombudsmen or press councils, but the sanctions these bodies impose are only moral ones.

If they are punished, it is by their employers or by the courts. Journalists not only do not constitute a corporation, but the majority of them are salaried workers. Invoking their own professional ethics and their own social mission puts them in conflict with their employers. This does not negate the fact that journalists are bound by a kind of moral loyalty to the enterprise that hires them and that good-quality work must be exchanged for the salary obtained. Journalists must also not intentionally hinder the operation of the enterprise, a duty which is not unique to media employees but applies to all workers in any field. So the evolution of a coherent set of rules to form an ethic is one of the means through which journalists have tried to strengthen their collective social position. And this was done mostly by making their moral rules explicit.

It is probably because of the importance of the informal side of ethical training that many critics of journalism teaching believe that apprenticeship while working is superior to any academic formula as the best way for journalism students be socialized into their chosen profession. Formal teaching, they will argue, obtains little success in regard to internal compliance, even when the teacher is a personality able to build a fan club, even when the Journalism School attempts to faithfully reproduce the reality of the newsroom, and even when a collection of heroes, portraits of celebrity journalists, can be presented to students through films and documentaries. Ethics are in large part acquired informally through socialisation in the newsroom. During this training, the beginner day after day absorbs the values of the environment.

The newcomer will identify emotionally with other journalists who act as role models. In the working situation penalties, explicit or not, and rewards distinguish unacceptable from valued behaviors. In short, the journalistic neophyte will learn ethics by breathing it, the same way a junior gets journalistic flair imitating senior members of the team, modeling his sensibility on theirs, training himself to look at the world the way they do. Sound judgment together with the feeling for news become a reflex, a kind of sixth sense intermingled with the consciousness of being part of the group. This description indicates that the moral formation acquired "on the job" is of a very local nature. The ways of a specific newsroom and the microculture it creates usually differ much from those of other media and frequently transmit values which serve the commercial purposes of the individual media outlets. Differences are particularly evident in the values accepted by the general press and the specialised press and between the popular press and the "quality press".

These differences persist even though the standardised procedures of industrial news production and the growing uniformity of news material sources are beginning to undermine these differences. More important for our argument however is the formal dimension of ethical training, which focuses on the normative bases of a given ethic. This investigates the collective and cultural choices which have led to the promotion of certain behaviors and condemnation of others. The dictionary corroborates the action orientation of ethics by defining it as the "science of morals, art of behaviour". Such a definition indicates that ethics is on the one hand an instrument to guide action and on the other hand a set of choices made according to normative distinctions between good and evil.

The "science of morals", component furthermore elaborates that ethics is more than a list of duties and moral commandments. It incorporates the foundations of morals, the hazy realm of values and ideals -not to mention "essential myths" from which codes of honour and morality are deduced. It is from this source that beliefs about what life and journalism should be originate. That is the main reason why the domain of ethics has become such a battlefield where, in spite of his or her neutral, professional role, the journalist must takes sides for an ideal society. In these circumstances learning rhetoric of ethics, both offensive and defensive, is a professional necessity for the contemporary journalist.

Being at the centre of the message producing process, the journalist is continually submitted to contradictory pressures from employers, sources, friends, etc. An enunciated set of ethic values are indispensable in mediating these contradictions. Also, ethics are frequently used by others (employers, sources or the public) in a self-interested attempt to tame journalists for their own purposes. The genuine memory of professional ethics is the one governed by "opinion" in the sense used by John Stuart Mill. It refers to the realm of opinions which should proceed from personal convictions rather than from fear of punishment And if there have to be penalties, let them be reduced to moral culpability and collective reprobation by (public) "opinion", or to personal guilty conscience, tarnished reputation, social boycott and reproof by a tribunal of peers like a Press Council, etc.

ESSENTIAL MYTHS

What are the main features of the various normative models of journalistic ethics that are so intimately linked to the idea of the journalist as an autonomous professional which are challenged today? The most central features derive from the opinion press of the XVIII and XIX centuries, which enunciated freedom of speech as the quintessential mark of the activity of the publisher, a freedom that had to prevail against censorship, by king or church. From the journalistic point of view this implies support for the principle that all opinions expression is socially legitimate. It also implies rejection of legal barriers on freedom of speech such as forbidding hate literature, protecting individuals against slander and libel, defending individual rights by so-called Charters of Rights, etc. Journalists subscribing to the first version of a normative model take literally the liberal assumption according to which every citizen is an adult provided with a grown-up's judgment and understanding.

They will, in general, support freedom of the press, that is the institutional form of freedom of speech. Because of these principles however such journalists may also turn against the owners of the media, who are the de facto implementors of freedom of the press, in order to have their own freedom of speech acknowledged. For them then proclaiming professional status means that freedom of the press pertains (principally?) to media workers and only secondarily the entrepreneurs. Because of its insistence first and foremost on the freedom of the commentator, this school of thought is close to that supporting artistic freedom, which justifies the total absence of rules as necessary preconditions for the creative process. It will logically emphasize the authenticity of proclaimed opinions.

The truth to be conveyed, in journalistic work is not a precise reflection of "reality" existing independently from the media and the journalists, but rather a faithful rendition of the real opinions of columnists, critics or editorialists. The ethics of freedom of speech in this version boils down to an ethics of honesty. Journalists fight openly for their point of view and, in doing so behave in a socially responsible manner. In the marketplace of ideas displayed by the media, hypotheses and invective, along with blunders, bias and partisanship are essential ingredients for the constitutional democratic life. A more recent tradition, is directly related to the reporting activity rather than to editorializing. It adapts freedom of speech the commercial press, the so-called information press. This tradition requires of the media only that they circulate the information that the consumer will buy. It did not emerge until the economic possibility existed for newspapers to survive financially by selling their product to advertisers and consumers. In the process news became viewed as a commodity.

The journalistic mission in this context became redefined as "excavating" society in order to find therein anything of interest to the consumer. In the process the reporter practices the ascetics of neutrality and commits himself to the search for truth in the accurate account of events. In this tradition the reporter's ethic is one of objectivity, and information production a process which is free from the opinions of both journalists and their employers. In this setting opinions are formally eliminated from reports by locking up them in the editorial space.

THE DOMINANT MODEL

A third model of the journalistic ethic had its origin in the Hutchins Commission convoked in the United States after World War II. It developed what has become known as the social responsibility theory of the media. This conception derives from the growth of monopolies, oligopolies and the concentration of ownership in the press which put an end to the free market of ideas. This model extends the idea of news as "objective data" which reporters are enmeshed to circulate without distortion in order to fulfill their public service function. The social responsibility theory also contributed to the development of the idea of the public's right to that service. Many intellectuals tried to use this doctrine as an argument against sensationalism and stressed the obligation of the media to search for and publish only socially important news.

Accordingly, they claimed most of the energies of the media should be devoted to investigative reporting of political institutions. Gradually, these three different models of the journalistic ethic which were built on very different assumptions were blended into a mix that idealised journalism into a kind of public service activity. From the era of censorship, it retained the notion of independence, mainly from governments. From the objectivity era, and its cultural environment of scientific positivism, it kept the ideal of personal neutrality and individual thought which incidentally steered journalists away from organising for collective action.

The Quebec Press Council (1987: 3) summarizes this tenet as follows: "When media and information professionals evaluate what is and what is not in the public interest, they have to set aside their personal interests and prejudices. Editorial choices are their responsibility. They must be made independently from any considerations other than those which follow from the exercise of the activity of journalism and from the laws of the land." The social responsibility era finally made journalists into the guardians of the right to information. It gave reporters as independent individuals the right to fight against their employers' mercantilism, the propaganda distributed by institutional sources of information and the public's morbid curiosity.

This interpretation of the freedom of speech ethic will urge journalists to demand their own speech freedom at the risk of "displeasing" their employer. It also supports them in a monopoly or quasi-monopoly situation like a one-paper town to demand that newspapers publish a wide variety of opinions even though this might infringe on the publisher's right of management. Reporters, following this individualistic ethics will demand the greatest freedom of action possible, not in order to express their own opinions but to investigate any issue including the workings of the enterprise that employs them.

Some Quebec reporters even went so far as to demand, if not for themselves as individuals, at least for the collectivity of the editorial staff, the right to decide what to investigate and what topics were to be tackled. Reporters justify this broad definition of choice of subject matter on the grounds that it helps to reveal aspects of outside reality that would otherwise remain inaccessible to public scrutiny. The ethics of social responsibility diminishes the commercial freedom of the enterprise to choose financially viable entertaining content.

It defines the publishing task primarily in political terms which emphasises issues relevant to an understanding of democratic life. It invites journalists and the media to educate the public rather than to flatter it in summary, each one of the three conceptions of the journalistic ethic argues that journalists should not submit entirely to the commercial interests of the media. They offer three different rationales for the professional autonomy of journalists from the media enterprises that hire them.

STRUGGLE FOR INFLUENCE

The present retreat from the ethic of journalistic autonomy among the Quebec's journalistic community is in large part explainable by the intellectual depression following the defeat of the nationalist referendum of 1980 and the economic crisis of 1981. This defeat engendered a widespread sense of malaise clearly evident in the anguished testimony of leading journalists published in a special edition of "Le 30 (December 1988) which celebrated the twentieth anniversary of the FPJQ.

It also paved the way for Quebec's post referendum philosophy: the ideal of financial success. This mood is evident in a new respect for businessmen, a surge of popularity in economic and business programming in both television and the press and an editorial campaign for the entrepreneurial spirit. The renewed faith in free enterprise as the way to social development is also evident in stock holding plans which draw employees into the corporation both financially and spiritually. In the journalistic milieu, these changed socio-political circumstances provided the context for a new model of behaviour which might be called the "good employee's model". The rise of this model, two or three years ago, coincided with a wave of media interest in Japanese industrial relations a phenomenon which some commentators branded the "Japanese syndrome".

Media reports described the employer-employee relations in the Japanese corporation as enlightened paternalism in which the employees total devotion is rewarded with life-long financial security. Supposedly, that devotion also contributed to the international success of Japanese corporations. We argue here that the "good employee's model" represents a threat for journalistic autonomy and professionalism because it undermines the group's will to counterbalance the commercial incentives of the media corporations. This is accomplished through a fundamental change in the ethics of the trade.

Firstly, it subordinates the individual's ethical framework to the interests of the company itself. In a conflict, the individual's moral obligation, including professional values are outweighed for the true employee by the employer's interests. Secondly, it strengthens the social position of media enterprises in claiming that they are the sole guardians of the information transmission function in modem society. Particularly in Quebec, the "good employee's model" undermines the hard won gains in professional autonomy which journalists had acquired by challenging their employers on the issues of information as a public service.

The different interpretations of "public service" offered by French and English Canadians are well documented by Lysiane Gagnon (1981). She points to such factors as the Cartesian mentality inherited from French culture; the clerical attitude of the intellectual elites; and an intellectual tradition which aims to "form" rather than to "inform". She also mentions the importance granted to politics in French culture, to a fondness for collective rights and to support for State intervention. Added to this there was the rapid concentration of the press in Quebec at the end of the 1960s which Gagnon fails to mention as a triggering point for the confrontation between media owners and intellectuals. She merely remarks that "The phenomenon of concentration began to become apparent at the very height of political and labour dissatisfaction, which may be said to have been much stronger in Quebec than everywhere in Canada."

What she does not note is that, in the political confrontation, the media and their owners were clearly identified with the conservative forces, the federalists, the opponents of a strong Quebec State, the authoritarians, etc. The main demarcation line in all of these confrontations was nationalism in all its forms. In the media industry, the confrontation was strong enough to fuel the creation of not one but two federations of journalists, the FPJQ and the F6dCration Nationale des Communications affiliated to the CNTU. The latter groups together most of the unions of journalists and other unionized media employees in Qu6bec.

The FPJQ, founded in 1969, has a membership of about 1 000 and the FNC, created in 1972, has more than 5 000 members. Both of these organisations promoted a much more radical interpretation of information as a public service than the social responsibility theory. They still consider themselves the main (if not the real) advocates of the public's right to know. In certain occasions in the 1970s, their advocacy even confronted the liberty of the press invoked by the media. The new 1980's socio-political environment as we have seen has undermined that spirit. With financial success as the main value the notion of the "public interest" has become reduced to "what interests the public".

Translated into media content, this means that media marketing departments and business managers now control the type of information which will be published. It is generally known that "entertainment" packaging has reduced the hard news focus in most papers. The new environment has also elevated the "good employee" model to prominence which defines journalism as nothing more than a job without any moral responsibility beyond producing technically competent work. In such a situation, there is no way of distinguishing between the professional ethics of information workers and the social responsibility of corporate media institutions.

The role of professional ethic is precisely to establish the boundaries of the media's social responsibility and consequently the limits of their power. Turning ethical questions over to the media furthermore entitles press employers to lay down "their" ethical code to "their" journalists making them part of the public relations cadre of these enterprises. In such a situation, journalists can no longer be viewed as potential allies of the public, nor should they count on their support against the media. Because without a separate ethic, the public can no longer judge how journalists intend to use their professional liberty, however small it may be. Thus, for example, partisans of objectivity are supported by common sense and the average reader.

Those who subscribe to the social responsibility ethic are helped by well-meaning intellectuals. And journalists who favour an opinion ethic and subjectivity are sustained by readers who believe in the values of democracy and public service. In the public discussion about the media today the options seem to be narrowing. Those who believe in the social responsibility of the press include many politicians, well-meaning pressure groups and some prestigious journalists from the quality press, who wish to "educate" the public. But this position is losing ground. On the other side, are the partisans of information that seduces the consumer. They comprise most managers and a loose grouping of all those who oppose any hindrance to liberty, as a matter of principle.

Together, they support a commercial version of the public's right to information which is anchored in nothing more than what the public is willing to buy in a very competitive market. We have already noted that the journalist's responsibility in this setting is to look for the story that will please the largest number of consumers because this will improve the position in the market of the business that hired him. Whether the "good employee's" model as the dominant journalistic ethic will be as useful to the public is highly doubtful. I would argue that it is not and that it may in fact constitute a threat to democracy. Society will be better off if journalists remain highly critical of the social performance of the product they are paid to produce by the media corporations.

Only so will there be any counterbalance to the economic weight of the multinationals and the mercantile approach of the media corporations. There are few alternatives for assuring journalistic independence in Quebec short of legally creating a formal profession which would establish a code of ethics separate from that espoused by media corporations. Such an ethic designed for professionals will provide a foundation for sorting out and defending the meaning of the right to free expression in a democratic society. Historically this has meant more than publishing just any opinion, however immoral, stupid or simply in bad taste. It has included the idea that the major task of journalists is to disseminate the kind of information which illuminates collective choices.

Only in such a broader democratic political framework can other ethical issues of journalism practice be sorted out. Chief among these are conflicts of interest, relations with sources, protection of privacy, responsibilities toward the police and the legal system and cooperation with colleagues. The "good employee's" ethic is silent on these and other issues of public concern such as sensationalism, concentration of ownership and the social role of journalist associations.

We have covered much terrain, and have touched on some ethical problems–more are dealt with in a previous book of mine, *Prodigal Press*–but the battle against propaganda requires additional emphasis. Christians need to distinguish between being on the Lord's side, by sticking as closely as we can to His revealed Word, and being the servant of any person or group of people, no matter how distinguished. Put no confidence in princes is good advice for everyone and *especially* for journalists, whom princes readily try to influence. And yet, the tendency to confuse journalism with public relations is a common failing among Christian magazines and newspapers. God-respecting and self-respecting editors should not run pieces puffing particular organizations, *especially* those that offer incentives to do so.

One of the most telling signs of the generally low level of Christian journalism at the end of the twentieth century is the expectation of many publicists that Christian magazines and newspapers will do their bidding. Some Christian groups express irritation at *World* for publishing anything negative about them, even generally positive reports that contain a critical paragraph. Sometimes, organizations tell us not that the material we have gathered about them is inaccurate, but that we should drop an inquiry because its results could embarrass them. Allies also propose to us what appear to be the customary deals of our era: You publish a favorable piece about us, and we will be of special help to you. A firm no surprises them. Given the pressures to puff, it is no surprise that journalists are bought and sold, and that many Christian publications act in worldly ways. But Christians have already been bought with a price far greater than anything cash can match.

Ideological pressures may also pile up. Some readers want Christian conservative magazines to be hard-nosed about liberal hypocrisy but blind to that among some conservatives. The temptation to have a double standard is present because, biblical Christians are fighting alongside conservatives on many issues–but a publication, to receive (and be worthy of) reader trust, should treat facts as facts. Early Christian journalists such as Marchamont Nedham emphasized the importance of covering the defeats of our own side. In this connection, there is no conflict of interest for a Christian publication staffer to be engaged in pro-life work on the side: Every Christian should be strongly pro-life. However, if you are reporting on political candidates, you should not be writing materials for a particular candidate, even if he embraces pro-life principles: Putting no confidence in princes, you need to be free to report the failures of all candidates, including your favourite.

The fear of the Lord and of violating God's law by lying (even in a good cause) is the beginning of good reporting. Accuracy, accuracy, accuracy: Observing God's world lackadaisically shows disrespect for his creation. This is the world that God has made; rejoicing and being glad in it means not coveting an alternative world. An editor's demand for specific detail should also be more than a utilitarian cry to increase reader interest. Just as Rembrandt, Franz Hals, and other great Dutch painters of their era showed Reformational understanding by painstakingly portraying humans on earth, not floating off the ground, so a search for descriptive material is moral as well as mechanical. A lack of precise detail often reflects a murkiness of observation and thought, but it also contributes to a tendency to scream. *World* has never run anything as loaded as the following, but here is the beginning of one lead story from a Christian newspaper:

Ordinary Americans are increasingly living in a fantasy world created by a mendacious and cavalier oligarchy of would-be rulers. . . a haughty association of self-proclaimed demigods whose control of great wealth has provided them the means to suborn, use and manipulate morally weak human beings. Through these chattels they are creating a never-never world of Alice in Wonderland mind-boggling madness where down is up, no is yes and wrong is right.. . .

That is an extreme example, but it is easy to fall into the trap of offering hysteria, not history. As you research and write a story, you should ask yourself: Am I teaching readers to be resolute in biblical application but calm in the face of anti-Christian aggression, or am I fostering panic? For example, a story on the homosexual lifestyle could inspire us to fiery denunciations–but better to keep a grip on our feelings and present the facts of the hunt for stimulation, as the San Francisco article excerpt earlier did. Sentences like, "Dan White sated the gay community's demand for blood by killing himself in 1985," should be deleted. You need to exercise special caution when sensational facts that fit well with your political attitudes are revealed.

For example, since the editors of *World* are not fans of Bill Clinton, coverage of the Paula Jones accusations that surfaced early in 1994 posed challenges. Biblical accusations demand the testimony of at least two witnesses, but Ms. Jones and Mr. Clinton were the only two individuals in the room when the alleged sexual harassment took place. Ms. Jones did tell a half-dozen people about the incident shortly after it occurred, but she did not cry out during the event and physical evidence was lacking–so there was only one witness on the record, and we did not run a story. What became interesting after that was the difference between media handling of Ms. Jones's accusations and those made by Anita Hill. Ms. Hill's complaint concerned words, not physical exposure, and was not made until a decade had gone by.

Yet the *Washington Post* and other mainline media outlets that had lionized Ms. Hill ignored Ms. Jones; the *Post* even suspended without pay for two weeks a reporter who wrote a story about the harassment charge and was angry when the *Post* refused to publish it. When feminist groups that had supported Anita Hill sneered at Paula Jones, and when the *Post*'s suppression of the story became an issue, *World* assigned a reporter to write a cover story not so much on Paula Jones's allegations as on the media and feminist inconsistencies. The article, which ran on April 30, 1994 (the Post finally ran a story on May 4, and other media came through on May 6 when Ms. Jones filed a sexual-harassment lawsuit), also had to be sensitive to reader sensitivities concerning sexual explicitness.

Paula Jones was 23 years old in May 1991, working at a conference Gov. Clinton was attending; according to her sworn testimony, a state trooper approached her and said the governor wanted to see her in his room. Being a new state employee, she complied. She entered the room and found him alone, she attests, and he began making sexual advances. He asked her to perform a sex act that wouldn't require her to remove her clothes, she says. She left the room, shocked and crying, and immediately told a co-worker, her mother, her fiancee, her two sisters, and a close friend. Reporting such charges and others does not show a lack of respect for those in authority: The only way to maintain respect for the presidency may be to disrespect pretenders in the Oval Office. "Honoring the king" means honoring Richard the Lion-Hearted, not John who usurped the throne; in 1776, Americans realized that they could no longer obey a king, George III, who acted like a dog. Compassion does not mean overlooking the sins of others, but confronting them and suffering with them as they struggle to change–and confronting our own sins as well.

Overall, Christian publications that wish to practice biblically directed journalism should stand firm against propaganda in five ways: They should not pretend that all is well with Christian organizations that are having problems; they should be willing to criticize political allies; they should be willing to praise opponents who act rightly in particular circumstances; they should not place above criticism even great church leaders; and they should not cover up embarrassments that befall even strong organizations. Let us look briefly at some examples of those practices of nonpropagandistic journalism. First, an honest publication needs to be willing to report on hard times for allies, as in a *World* story headlined, "Rescue Me," and subtitled, "Stung by Federal Law and the High Court, 'Operation Rescue' Is in Need of Rescue–or Reinvention":

By the time Operation Rescue National director Flip Benham and Wendy Wright, ORN communications director, arrived at the Little Rock "com centre" the day after the Fourth of July, they had been beaten up by the media's questions and by the oppressive 100-degree heat, and beaten down by the reception the group had received so far in the Arkansas capital.

Com centers in operations past have been wide, busy rooms filled with phone banks and volunteers and a sense of carefully aimed anarchy. The Little Rock com centre was an empty office, 8-feet-by-20-feet, with an answering machine and only one telephone that seemed to work.. . .

By Wednesday afternoon hardcore activists from the three participating groups (ORN, Rescue America, and the Pro-Life Action Network) were showing up for the three-day "Summer of Justice" event, but whether any Arkansans would turn out remained to be seen. Miss Wright said she was keeping her expectations low; "Maybe I'll be surprised."

She wasn't.. . .

Second, there should be a willingness to oppose associates when biblical principles warrant. For example, *World* favored most of Newt Gingrich's agenda in 1995, but still was critical at times. Achilles' heel number one is the tendency of the new leadership to imply that economic issues are the only ones that really matter in America today. No better proof of that has been offered than the decision by Mr. Gingrich to select New Jersey Gov. Christine Todd Whitman for the high profile job of responding to President Clinton's State of the Union address last week. Economics is about the only thing Gov. Whitman has in common with the highly energized Republican masses who rose up on Nov. 8 to call for new directions in Washington and throughout the country. Granted, economics is a big part of that call–and was a dominant theme in the "Contract with America" that propelled Mr. Gingrich to the

Speaker's chair and so many of his Republican majority into office. But economics was by no means the only fuel in that noisy engine. Mrs. Whitman is little more than a Democrat in Republican's clothing–and the disguise is shabby at that. Beyond her Johnny-come-lately commitment to tax-cutting, she shares little with the Republican platform of recent years.. . . She favored abortionists by proclaiming Freedom of Choice Day in New Jersey; she endorsed condom distribution in the schools; and she wrote an open letter praising the state's "gay, lesbian, and bisexual community." The point is that Speaker Gingrich reached all too deliberately in Gov. Whitman's direction. "We want to show how broad a base the Republican Party has," he explained pointedly when he asked Mrs. Whitman to take the important speaking job. How could Mr. Gingrich have said more specifically that the economic revolution matters, but the social revolution doesn't?

For tens of thousands of footsoldiers, that message doesn't settle in very comfortably. If the new Republican leadership thinks it can reshape America simply by restructuring fiscal issues, just by realigning taxes and downloading some tasks to the states, then its analysis of things isn't ultimately much different from Marxism. Its methods are different–and far preferable–to those of Marx, but its bottom-line message is that human beings will in the end respond to economic factors more than to any other. Such an analysis is repulsive to earnest Christians. Third, a publication that hopes to report and teach rather than propagandize is always aware that leaders who consistently have done evil can do good once in a while. Such surprises need to be reported, in the way that *World* reported favorably the initiative of one ardently liberal senator.

Sen. Howard Metzenbaum (D-Ohio) reportedly was infuriated in 1989 by a Cincinnati, Ohio, case in which a black child was quickly taken from white, Christian, foster parents after they expressed a desire to adopt. The reason: The child allegedly needed a black home. The child was killed not long after by an abusive black adoptive couple in upstate New York. As a result, Metzenbaum last summer crafted the Multiethnic Adoption Act, which originally was designed to fight discrimination against couples seeking to adopt transracially.. . . Fourth, an honest publication should be willing to criticize even great church leaders, for all have sinned and fallen short of the glory of God. One *World* article that generated considerable comment, pro and con, was the cover story headlined, "Silence of the Shepherds," and subtitled, "As the Preborn Death Toll Mounts, Pro-lifers Are Asking: Where Is the Pastoral Leadership in Opposition to Abortion?"

The article, supportively quoted pro-life leaders who criticized Billy Graham's quiet concerning abortion. Some readers were shocked by *World's* implicit critique of a tremendous leader, even though it was respectfully couched. And yet, Christian journalists should always be willing to speak up sadly if the facts warrant. Fifth, embarrassments must not be covered up, or else Christian journalism is embarrassed. The New Era foundation scandal in 1995 was big news, but one Christian news organization did not publish any stories about the affair because its parent organization was itself involved in the financial collapse, and the parents did not want bad publicity. Here, once again, it is important to remember the great cloud of Christian journalistic witnesses: Were some of our predecessors tortured and killed so that we can live lives of fear under much less intimidating circumstances?

A commitment to avoid covering up mistakes should begin in a publication's own letters-to-the-editor page. Some publications fill such pages with letters praising their efforts or offering minor additions to stories, but a Christian publication with spunk will receive letters that strongly criticize its stands; the publication should print them even when all the staffers believe that the letters are misguided. There is even an ulterior motive in doing so; as publisher Joel Belz wrote in *World*:

We aren't thrilled when people point out that we dropped the ball in a certain instance. But we still are committed to provide a regular opportunity for people to make just those points for a very simple reason: It adds to our overall credibility.

Oddly, many Christians (and the leaders of too many Christian organizations) believe an open forum for criticism injures their credibility. So they sit on the facts and suppress discussion. They clam up and shut off the information flow. Such folks forget, however, that light always trumps darkness. Truth, by God's order of things, always beats out ignorance. That tendency toward occasional self-examination, combined with a confidence in God's providence, is not found in the liberal press these days, particularly as pressure toward political correctness makes deviations career-shortening. God saves [sinners, but] for many leaders of the liberal press there is no sin, just faults in the system of things. For many there is no personal salvation, just social restructuring. Maybe there could be a God in such a system, but he would have nothing to do.

The technological change since then has been so remarkable that there is no need to remark on it here. What is striking, though, is that amidst all the material upsurge the spiritual draught has remained. The essential combination of ideas in place among intellectual and media leaders ever since the progressive upsurge early in this century–a new, government-centered gospel–has remained standard. Muckraker Lincoln Steffens was one of the prime molders in this regard. Modern journalism began in 1517 with the sound of Martin Luther's hammering on the cathedral door, but in 1917 Steffens baptized the newborn Russian Revolution, writing of how Petrograd mobs made him "think of the mobs that followed Jesus about." For centuries much of American journalism had emphasized *restraint*, but Steffens set the tone for twentieth-century journalism by praising radicals who were willing to "lay out consciously and carry through ruthlessly [a programme] to arrange the conditions of social living. . . to adjust the forces of economic life." Other journalists have shied away from the extremes of ruthlessness, but the emphasis on using government power to adjust economic forces has been a constant. Earlier journalists had pointed readers to the Bible, but after 1917 leading editors such as Oswald Garrison Villard argued that, "There are plain masses seeking a journalistic Moses to clarify their minds, to give them a programme of reconstruction." Decade after decade, in line with such thinking, leading newspapers and magazines from the 1920s to the present have portrayed man as possessing unlimited potential that a strong and benevolent state could help to liberate, if only journalistic influence were brought to bear on the side of perceived righteousness.

The story of the past seven decades is one of muckraking become common, and mainstream journalists claiming that they are for liberty but in practice promoting new forms of oppression. In doing so, they often neglected the sacrifices of their courageous predecessors and genuflected before a future that claimed to work. American journalism, which had developed as an antiestablishment force, became part of a new establishment that did not have the self-understanding to recognize itself as one. Mainline journalists considered themselves the watchdogs of government, but many went from keeping watch over government to keeping watch over their ideological interests. In the 1920s, when liberal educators tried to install evolution as the established religion in public schools, reporters at the Scopes trial in Tennessee refused to take seriously opposing views and cast William Jennings Bryan as a redneck menace. In the 1930s, many correspondents in Moscow, believing that they had a greater purpose than accurate reporting, became shills for Stalin and launched scurrilous attacks against those few who were determined to tell the truth.

Every decade has brought with it notorious examples not only of journalistic intolerance but also heroism: There always will be members of the great cloud of journalistic witnesses. Perhaps the most outstanding of these in twentieth-century America was Whittaker Chambers, a Communist Party member and spy during the 1930s who went through two major life changes at the end of that decade and the beginning of the next: He became a Christian, and he became a superb writer for *Time* magazine at a time when it was not the vehicle for the left that it has since become. In the late 1940s, with the cold war and concern about Soviet espionage growing, Chambers was called to testify about the Communist Party's work for the Soviet Union and did so, bringing out facts about former State Department official Alger Hiss that Hiss denied.

A jury eventually found Hiss guilty of perjury, but newspapers such as the *Washington Post* were not happy. (One reporter told Hiss, "Do you want to know the verdict of the press? Not guilty–in fifteen minutes.") Chambers received extreme abuse, but his Christian faith enabled him to persevere; in

1951 he wrote a best-selling book, *Witness*, that is still well worth reading. He died ten years later. Archives from the former Soviet Union support Chambers's reports and suggest Hiss's guilt. The courage of Chambers and others slowed down the journalistic rush to the left, and during the 1950s the press bent to a generally conservative era; during the 1960s, however, a new stampede began. Pride in shaping the news was everywhere; by 1965, correspondents were noting that they did not write stories unless they could include "analysis and interpretation." For a long time newspaper home offices had held the reins on Washington reporters who tended to favour more centralized power, but by the mid-1960s a typical correspondent was able to say, concerning his relationship with editors, "I make a hundred decisions where they make one."

The long-range journalistic triumph of Horace Greeley and Lincoln Steffens became evident in many areas of coverage; for example, as reporter Robert Elegant has noted, his colleagues in Vietnam during the 1960s overlooked the record of Communism and, attracted by the vision, saw the North Vietnamese as "righteous, magnanimous, and just." The herd mentality was in evidence as most correspondents spent most of their time at a comfortable Saigon hotel and, in Elegant's words, talked "chiefly to other correspondents to confirm their own mythical vision of the war." Some reporters did get out in the field, where they practiced a new objectivity. *New York Times* correspondent Gloria Emerson has written about how she accompanied four Vietnamese "students" on their mission to firebomb an American vehicle and burn to death the American soldiers inside; she figured that since she had gone along on U.S. patrols she should go with the other side as well. The plan was for one member of the ambush team to race into a busy intersection and wave his arms until a jeep stopped; then a second member would throw in a plastic bag full of gasoline, and a third member would toss in a lit match.

Emerson and the ambushers waited for twenty minutes; in an autobiographical account, *Winners and Losers*, she wrote about "warning myself over and over again to stay out of it and not to interfere, not to remember the crusts and the smell of burned men I had already seen in hospitals." When an American jeep came by, "There was that second when I could have screamed, yelled, rushed forward to warn him, given the plan away." But she did not. Providentially, one of the "students" had bad aim: His bag of gasoline splashed against the windshield, and the GI escaped. But the incident nevertheless was a defining moment for a new journalistic ethic: Since reporters had gone out on ambush-setting by U.S. soldiers, not to go to the other side's ambush would be a biased act. American reporters were not Americans but citizens of the world, superior to the morality by which their fellow citizens lived. William Randolph Hearst in 1898 succeeded in his plan to use press sensationalism to push the United States into conflict with Spain.

He had sent Frederick Remington to Cuba to draw victims of Spanish atrocities; when Remington cabled from Havana that he could not fulfill the assignment because the facts did not support the allegations, Hearst purportedly cabled back, "You furnish the pictures, I'll furnish the war." In Vietnam, reporters tried to sucker servicemen into incidents that would show American brutality, such as cutting the ears off of a corpse or throwing a body from a plane. Journalists learned to "falsify with credibility," according to Elegant. They furnished the pictures, and America abandoned Indochina.

The result was truly gruesome, and unexpected by reporters who, brought up to believe in the natural goodness of man, found it difficult to gauge depths of depravity. Sydney Schanberg of the *New York Times* wrote from Cambodia in 1975, just before the Khmer Rouge took power, that for "the ordinary people of Indochina. . . [it] is difficult to imagine how their lives could be anything but better with the Americans gone." His failure of imagination was corrected too late: On May 9, 1975, he wrote about the "maniacal behaviour" of the Khmer Rouge, but by then there was nothing the United States could do to save several million Cambodians from execution. On May 3, 1976, Schanberg received the Pulitzer Prize for international reporting.

The search for foreign heroes of the left continued into the 1980s. Karen de Young, foreign editor of the *Washington Post*, acknowledged that "Most journalists now, most Western journalists at least, are very eager to seek out guerilla groups, leftist groups, because you assume they must be the good guys." In Nicaragua, *La Prensa* editor Pablo Antonio Cuadra wrote that he was "forced to endure for nine years of the Sandinista regime the almost daily visits of American journalists. They always ask the same questions–almost all of them fervent admirers of what the Sandinistas have told them. . . after the questions and answers, the result is always the same: a total lack of comprehension."

In domestic politics as well, reporters over time (as journalist-professor William Rivers noted) became "prime promoters or offstage prompters of the Congressional hearings, legislative battles and other events they are chronicling, theoretically with detachment." One *Washington Post* editor described the practice of "not only getting it from the horse's mouth but being inside his mouth." Another *Post* editor, Philip Foisie, described how staffers at meetings had agreed on the key issues for the 1970s and 1980s–establishing limits on resources and growth, and other aspects of the liberal agenda–and would "use these trends more methodically to line up our sights on the news. We should reach out more for the news, and not wait until it comes to our doorstep, until it 'happens.'. . ."

That degree of editorial self-consciousness was unusual; most journalists simply and unthinkingly fit the bits and pieces of daily events into a grid that excludes God. Benjamin Harris in 1690 saw every story as a piece of the heaven-designed quilt; latter-day liberal reporters of 1995 see a feminist triumph in Vermont or the establishment of a day-care centre in Texas as part of a progressive etching-in-progress. Cotton Mather's report on a New England earthquake in the 1720s began, "The glorious God has roared out of Zion." Mather surely did not have to ask himself, before composing his report, how the earthquake fit into his worldview. Similarly, experienced reporters rarely stop to think about the way a particular event fits within their larger understanding; they know that it does.

If mainline (or should they be called oldline?) newspapers continue in their ideological cheerleading, the function of biblically directed journalists will become even more significant–and not just for Christians, but for any who desire alternative voices. Twenty years ago many cities boasted feisty "alternative" news voices: They were criticizing liberalism from the left, but at least they were able to perceive some of the emperor's nakedness. In 1994, however, the *Washington Post* reported that, "what began as the alternative press has been completely assimilated now." Christians have always resisted assimilation. Today, those who are bold and courageous can stand with the great cloud of witnesses, made up of Christians who spent their lives and sometimes gave them up in the pursuit of God directed writing and teaching. Directed reporting, based on faith in the Triune God and not in man, is a lever for toppling modern journalism's idols and bringing readers back to a Christ-centered press. Every Christian journalist should look in the mirror and ask: Will I stand with John Foxe, John Stubbes, Alexander Leighton, John Twyn, Increase Mather, John Peter Zenger, Samuel Adams, and many more, or will I follow the ways of the world?

There will be opposition, but–as the writer of Hebrews begins chapter 12–"Therefore, since we are surrounded by such a great cloud of witnesses, let us throw off everything that hinders and the sin that so easily entangles, and let us run with perseverance the race marked out for us. Let us fix our eyes on Jesus, the author and perfecter of our faith, who for the joy set before him endured the cross, scorning its shame, and sat down at the right hand of the throne of God. Consider him who endured such opposition from sinful men, so that you will not grow weary and lose heart".

The *Washington Post* article on the seventeenth annual convention of the Association of Alternative Newsweeklies was filled with mournful quotations. "I look at these papers and detect a lack of passion," one radical editor commented. "No one is on the ramparts because they're not sure what they should be fighting for. Do we have an ideology other than being pro-choice, pro-gay rights and pro-Grateful Dead?" No, the passionless alternatives do not, but passionate disciples of Christ's passion do, out of gratitude for the sacrifice that transcends the daily news, because it lasts for eternity.

Journalism, ethics and codes of conduct -why journalists need a 'conscience clause':

- The delicate task of making journalism more ethical without damaging its freedoms is one that has so far eluded policy makers.

The period since the first Royal Commission into the press and the establishment of the first Press Council has demonstrated that voluntary codes of conduct have little or no impact against the far more powerful pressure of circulation increase and profit maximisation. Editors are after all employed for their ability to get people to read the paper. Sex, scandal and celebrity, sells newspapers as does the ancient art of whipping up prejudice and stirring dissent.

- Any attempt to legislate a fairer and more considered journalism runs into the problem of implementation. Laws that seek to protect one group of people will always be used by others, whose behaviour really should come under scrutiny, but who have the power and the money to use the courts to protect them.
- The journalists themselves could perhaps effect change and re-focus the news media on the fundamental tasks of informing citizens and encouraging debate, but only if they are given the power within their news organisations to act according to their own consciences, rather than always to follow editorial orders.
- In debates about ethics the role of the ordinary journalist is too often subsumed within that of the editors and proprietors as though those people who work for the news media always have exactly the same interests, and the same power to protect their interests, as do those who employ and direct them. This fundamental error applies to the teaching of ethics on journalism courses in colleges and universities just as much as it has always applied to the policy makers who have attempted to legislate or regulate the media.
- The reality is that journalists are what Bourdieu refers to as "weakly autonomous". As individuals, their autonomy is circumscribed by a steeply hierarchical employment structure, with an editor at the top who is under constant pressure to chase audience ratings or circulation.
- The degree of autonomy experienced by the individual journalist varies according to the type of publication or broadcasting outlet and the level of their own influence (cultural capital). Those journalists working for the 'elite' press have more autonomy than those who are at the mass-market end.
- Amongst mass market journalists it would probably be true to say that only the highly paid columnists, who are rarely chosen for their ethical standards, have any real autonomy – and they are subject to summary termination of contract if they should displease.
- Ordinary working journalists are subject to the orders of editors and can expect to find that their work is heavily re-written by sub-editors under instructions from editors. Those who find, and write, exclusive stories, which fit well within the ethos of the news

organisation, will be preferred over those who stick to bread and butter, diary stories.

- Successful journalists are those who, over a period of time, internalize the requirements of the editors and who then move into more powerful and more (apparently) autonomous positions – the rest move on into other jobs.
- Those working in television have more protection from these pressures due to regulations requiring 'balance and/or impartiality' which counteract, to some extent, the pressures to maximisc profit that are experienced in newspapers.
- How then can these 'weakly' autonomous agents be the key to improving ethical standards?
- Some have suggested making them responsible for their work by embedding ethical codes into their contracts of employment. But this would be like holding private soldiers responsible for the direction of a war. Nothing gets into the paper without the say-so of an editor and nothing gets onto the front page of a daily tabloid without the active involvement of the editor. The bi-line over an article may not indicate who is responsible for the slant and emphasis (and often it is the slant and emphasis which creates the ethical problem).
- Making individual journalists legally responsible for what goes out in their name would often be unfair and would almost certainly have the effect of decreasing autonomy and giving editors an opportunity for scapegoating individuals when more often it is editorial decisions which are at fault.
- A more useful strategy would be to increase the autonomy of journalists by giving them some recourse against editorial edicts.
- Journalists at the Daily Express provided an object lesson in how much, on the one hand, their work is directed and controlled by editors and how little, on the other hand, they are supported if they decide to act ethically.
- On two occasions, in 2001 and 2004, journalists at the Express complained collectively to the Press Complaints Commission about being forced to write what they believed to be 'racist' articles. Having failed with their first attempt to get a PCC ruling, the journalists then took a different tack: "The chapel wrote to the PCC asking it to insert a 'conscience clause' into its code of practice, whereby journalists who refused unethical assignments would be protected from disciplinary action or dismissal."
- The idea of a conscience clause is something that the National Union of Journalists raised when giving evidence to the Commons Select Committee on Privacy and Media Intrusion in 2003. The committee

recommended such a clause but it was rejected out of hand by the PCC.

- Robert Pinker, acting Chairman of the Press Complaints Commission, defending this position at an NUJ conference said: "It is not our job to be involved in disputes between employers and staff." He also suggested that such a clause would affect sales by making newspapers: "So sanitised people will not want to read them".
- This view underlines the difficulties faced by journalists who wish to speak out against what they see as unethical standards. On the one hand they are assumed to have the power to act ethically, on the other hand they are denied, by the very body which is there to police ethics, the right to act autonomously.
- To act ethically absolutely requires the exercise of autonomy. As things stand, the only realistic recourse open to a journalist who disagrees with an editorial decision, is to leave. This is not a decision that a young journalist, with a reputation to build, is likely to take lightly. Nor, on the other hand, would such a person be likely vexatiously to report editorial decisions to the PCC because that would also impact on their careers.
- A conscience clause might not often be used but it would operate as a means of providing journalists with a small degree of individual power. It would also serve to remind both ordinary journalists and editors that individual conscience remains a very useful steer in a world in which maximising profits has become the over-arching goal. It would certainly make a lot more sense to those who teach journalism if they could say to their students; "Commit the code of conduct to memory because it will protect you from being forced to do something you believe to be wrong." That small safe guard alone would be worth having.

4

Professionalization and Journalistic Education

The composite culture of India incorporates Mass Communication and Journalism in all its languages and regions. Education in this field made its advent through western influences via English colonial efforts. Mass Communication and Journalism education assumes new significance in the age of globalization and communication. There is considerable potential for national initiative and co-operation in the production of educational materials and development of qualitative learning methods by those who are working at various universities, colleges and professional organizations or other institutions involved in Mass Communication and Journalism education.

Mass Communication educators, media professionals and policy makers are required to debate upon serious issues, challenges and responsibilities involved in Mass Communication education in India and provide necessary policy inputs in order to make Mass Communication education result oriented and purposeful. More exchanges, interactions and inputs at various levels are required to further consolidate the core areas on which actions need to be taken. In India, about 45,000 newspapers, journals and periodicals are now brought out in 105 languages and dialects. There are over 4000 daily newspapers and magazines. India also produces the largest number o feature films and newsreels in the world. All India Radio is known as the largest radio network in the world. It runs 195 radio stations (including 183 full-fledged stations) and has 302 transmitters (144 MW, 55 SW and 103 FM channels). All India Radio covers 90% of the geographical area and 97.3% of the country's populace.

Doordarshan, state-supported television, has grown over the years as a promising broadcasting network. It has 83 HPTs, 600 LPTs, 19 VLPTs and 18 Transposers. Doordarshan covers 72% of the geographical areas and 87% of the country's populace. India has become a global leader in software industry. India has also become one of the few advanced countries in the field of satellite communication. India has also achieved tremendous progress in the field of telecommunication. The media industry in India has grown enormously and earned global appreciation.

STATUS OF MASS COMMUNICATION AND JOURNALISM EDUCATION

In the Indian sub-continent, Punjab University of Lahore was the first to offer a journalism course. In India, education and training in Mass Communication and Journalism is about 60 years old. Media education in India has not received proper recognition from the government as well as media. In India at present some 60 Universities, 25 agricultural universities and 100 private institutions annually train about 2000 students in various aspects of Mass Communication and Journalism including reporting, editing, photography, videography, printing, designing, advertising, public relations and so on. Especially agricultural universities are imparting training on farm communication, extension education and development communication. Most of the universities and colleges have provided infrastructural facilities and manpower in audio-visual communication field also to some extent.

However, Mass Communication and Journalism teaching, training, research and extension activities are not properly organized on sound footing of resources and systematic management. Especially the teaching of communication skills and crafts in almost all Indian languages has been haphazard. The Press Commissions (1954&1984) have recognized the importance of Mass Communication and Journalism training in the country. However, the second Press Commission headed by Justice K K Mathew has made only a passing reference in this regard. Sound Mass Communication and Journalism training in English and regional languages are very essential in order to develop media systems, professionals and activities vigorously.

Currently, the country's mass media pattern is almost the same in all developing countries including Southeast Asia. The Indian universities and other institutions have expanded educational services in accordance with the needs of the media industry. Mass Communication and Journalism being the multi-faceted discipline and multi-pronged profession, planned, deliberate and specialized training in English and Indian languages is of great significance in a developing country like ours. There is an all round progress in the mass media system in the country in the post independence era.

Today, Mass Communication and Journalism education is taken for granted especially by the policy makers. Most of the universities have not updated the syllabi in accordance with the changing media scenario. Adequate faculty members who are specialists in various aspects of Communication and Journalism are not recruited because of policy constraints and financial constraints. The faculty members are not given adequate opportunities to develop higher specialization, skill and competence. In reality, fellowships, scholarships and other facilities are not extended to the faculty members adequately in order to ensure advanced studies, research and professional growth. The students are taught history, theory, research, extension and a broad array of other aspects of Mass Communication and Journalism.

Educators with advanced degrees and diplomas are not available in plenty. Those who have not experienced the real practical problems, challenges and opportunities are not in a position to handle the subjects judiciously. There are sizeable number of Mass Communication and Journalism departments in the country, which are managed by one or two teachers and couple of part timers. This is indeed a pathetic situation with respect to Mass Communication teaching in the country. The private managements have taken the teachers for granted. They are not encouraged by these private managements to acquire specialized knowledge and experience. Those who are qualified and competent professionally and otherwise are not encouraged with judicious pay, allowances, promotions and other benefits.

Media practitioners and scholars often find themselves on different paths. There are very few centers of learning where the citadel of Mass Communication education is directed at professional competence. Even now there is no agreement on what Mass Communication education should be in India. The question of whether universities should teach Mass Communication and Journalism has not been answered decisively. Especially the private coaching institutions are not conducting the courses on sound agenda and grounds. Even now there is dearth of qualified and competent teachers especially in regard to training the students in the fields of New Communication Technologies, Broadcasting Journalism, Film Journalism, Advertising, Public Relations, Media Laws, Media Management and so on.

A good deal of theoretical inputs is made available instead of adequate practically relevant components and inputs. In the absence of practically relevant training the graduates are found in a helpless situation when they join the media organizations. Lack of trained teachers, infrastructural facilities and upgraded syllabi are the major hurdles in the way of sound Mass Communication teaching. Most of the departments are not getting latest books and professional journals due to financial constraints. They do not have well equipped audio-visual lab, computer lab, photo lab, close circuit television, Internet facility, departmental library and allied facilities. A major drawback of Mass Communication and Journalism education in India is the lack of locally relevant textbooks, professional journals and advanced reading materials.

Many scholars have identified this glaring gap with concern. Senior media professionals and teachers are not encouraged to contribute their mite in this regard. Publishers also show lukewarm interest in producing books which fit into Indian context mainly due to marketing and sales limitations. The government, UGC, universities and publishing houses has not come forward to bridge this gap. There is utter lack of locally relevant reading materials especially in Indian languages. The libraries also have fewer books and professional journals. The policy makers in the government, UGC, universities and other bodies have not accorded a place of pride to Mass Communication and Journalism education even though there are gainful employment opportunities to the students in the modern society.

Lot of funds are made available to medical, engineering, management and other professional courses in universities and private institutions. Unfortunately Mass Communication and Journalism departments are hunting for funds from several quarters. These factors are largely responsible for the sorry state of affairs in journalism training. The less said the better about the current state of journalism education in the Indian languages. Mass Communication and Journalism training programmes in India are not planned as an integrated development programme. Even now universities, governments, UGC and media organizations have not come forward to work in unison. Many scholars have also criticized the utter callousness and hostility on the part of media organizations in regard to journalism education in our country.

LACK OF LEARNING PERSPECTIVE

There is no consensus with respect to syllabi in this age of communication revolution. Many scholars have rightly felt that general instructions and classroom lectures particularly in universities and colleges are bookish, bereft of practical demonstration or explanation on the part of faculty. Many have not worked in the print, audio-visual and new media organizations. The latest techniques such as desktop printing, video display terminals, facsimile editions, videography, photography and so on are not fully and properly understood by the faculty, mainly due to lack of exposure and job-oriented training facilities.

Media institutions have become industrial centres. We come across information industry, knowledge industry, entertainment industry, advertising industry and other kinds of media industries. The expectations of these media industries are not properly understood by our policy makers and educationists. What is Mass Communication and Journalism? What are the expectations of the media industry? How to train our students? What should these students do in the media organizations? These questions have to be answered by our policy makers and teachers in order to facilitate need-based training and make students worthy communicators of our times. The purpose of Mass Communication education is more than understanding theory and practice, though communication skill development and communicators' capacity building are very essential. Its purpose should go beyond these things.

Prof Dua suggests: "In fact eminent media persons should give constant advice on updating the course content. The courses in all languages could be split into two general areas – (i) core and (ii) general, or optionals. The core courses should include – (a) subject orientation, (b) inter-disciplinary back ground, (c) theoretical research and field survey, (d) basic and applied skills in all spheres of media- print, film and broadcasting including television and video, public relations and advertising, (e) compulsory media internship and production of professional assignments to be judged by senior media executives." He has also suggested the constitution of a regulatory body called Indian Council for Journalism/Mass Communication Education, Research and Training on the lines of Indian Council of Medical Education, Bar Council of India or Institute of Chartered Accountants. This could be made responsible for standardization of course curricular, contents of training, quality of research, monitoring job opportunities and also collaborating with advanced Journalism/Communication bodies in abroad.

The ultimate purpose of Mass Communication training is to build a band of conscious, committed, competitive, courageous and compassionate professionals and nation builders. The educational institutions should contribute champions of professionalism and public interest. The media owners should look forward to recruiting such worthy graduates. However, they should not be indifferent to these qualities of graduates. It would simply mar the profession of Mass Communication and Journalism. These aspects need proper introspections by the policy makers in the universities and colleges. These aspects should be adequately covered in the syllabi at various levels of Mass Communication and Journalism training.

The great task for Mass Communication educators is to equip their students with a firm sense of professionalism. Mass Communication and Journalism training institutions and programmes should become centers of excellence where these ideals are translated into realities. The teachers and trainees cannot confine themselves to the classroom. The best foundation for a career in Mass Communication is in the field setting (newsroom in print media, studio in electronic media, film making settings in film media, computer room in software setting etc,). Practical exposure is indispensable. Otherwise, trainees remain malnourished practically and otherwise. The media owners can no more remain under the age-old impression that 'Mass Communicators are born'. They must encourage well-qualified, trained, skilled and competent work force in order to enhance professional excellence, accountability and social responsibility.

Mass Communication training programmes are not designed in tune with the changing media trends and expectations. The programmes lack professional depth, seriousness and quality. The need for involvement of media professionals in the training programmes is not felt by the policy makers. The teachers are not deputed to media institutions in order to gain professional skill and outlook. The students do not get opportunities frequently to gain familiarity with the diverse media systems and operations. They do not personally understand the media environment along with social, economic, political and cultural needs and aspirations due to lack of frequent interactions.

The students are not enabled to acquire practical skills and operational competence on regular basis during their study period. The standard of teaching, research, extension and publication activities is not periodically assessed in order to make necessary changes and improvements. The critics have termed Mass Communication training programmes as 'hog-wash'. Teachers, professionals and policy makers do not work together toward making Mass Communication and Journalism education purposeful.

Therefore, showing concern to the improvement of qualitative learning methods becomes very essential in the present times. Such deliberations and resolutions through programme of this kind would go a long way in facilitating qualitative learning methods in Mass Communication education. In this age of competitiveness, earnest efforts should be made toward elevating learning methods. Inter-disciplinary teaching, innovative multi-media programmes, collaborative exercises, training sessions in the media organizations, periodic practical assignments and university-industry collaboration would enrich Mass Communication teaching in this competitive times.

SUGGESTIONS

Mass Communication and Journalism education in India has made considerable progress during the last three decades. In reality, a majority of Mass Communication and Journalism departments are ill equipped in terms of manpower, equipments, literature and allied resources. By and large, training in this sector is not imparted on the basis of sound vision, expertise, recognition and patronage. In particular, the vernacular Mass Communication and Journalism education is absolutely unplanned and disorganized. Keeping in view of the relevance of the present topic of national seminar and the imperativeness of enhancing qualitative learning methods, the following suggestions are made for consideration. They include:

- Mass Communication and Journalism education should be planned as an integrated development programme taking it to account the present trends like globalization, liberalization and privatization. The changing media scenario should be properly understood by the policy makers and that factors like manpower, resources, technologies, equipments, literature, research and extensions should be taken into account while redesigning education system in general and enriching qualitative learning methods in particular.
- Standardization of Mass Communication and Journalism training should be ensured in order to make training in this sector absolutely result oriented. A national level regulatory body consisting of policy makers, scholars, specialists, professionals and bureaucrats should be set up to streamline admission procedure, course contents, recruitment norms, training methods and evaluation techniques. This

body should be empowered to govern the process of Mass Communication and Journalism training in the country.

- The Departments of Mass Communication and Journalism should be equipped with the state of art facilities and competent manpower.
- The course contents should be modified in order to keep pace with changing needs of media industry in particular and national and international environment in general. There should be meaningful combination of basic and applied Mass Communication and Journalism. The ratio of theory and practice should be 25:75 in order to enable the students acquire necessary professional skill and competence. There should be simultaneous teaching in the classroom and internship in the media organizations.
- There should be a regular scheme of special lectures to strengthen the process of training since all departments cannot afford to recruit and maintain large number of specialists as trainers. UGC, Publications Division, National Book Trust, Research and Reference Division, Universities and other publishing houses should produce teaching materials which fit into national and regional contexts adequately.
- The teachers should also be trained very frequently in order to keep pace with the changing needs of media industry as well as teaching profession.

Multi-ethnicity, multi-culture and multi-language are the hallmarks of India. The dichotomy between rural and urban population has complicated the media scenario further. Many courses are offered in Mass Communication and Journalism at different levels with different nomenclatures. They range from certificates to doctoral programmes. Though most of the institutions offer only English as the instructional medium, students can write examinations in the regional language. Even doctoral research is encouraged in vernacular Mass Communication and Journalism.

The educational scenario depicts series of drawbacks with respect to qualitative learning methods. Suitable networks have to be created at local, regional and national levels to facilitate integrated development of Mass Communication and Journalism education in India. The Departments of Mass Communication and Journalism will have to devote their time, energy and resources in this direction. Recent evidence has come to light that indicates the originators of the concept of a school of journalism came before either Joseph Pulitzer or Walter Williams. The importance of an earlier starting date for journalism education lies in the fact that many historians link the start of journalism education in the twentieth century with a broad journalistic effort to professionalize journalism, which was said to have begun at the same time. Thus, pushing back the start date of journalism education efforts would raise the possibility that journalistic professionalization began much earlier than current journalism histories assert. The purpose of this article is to present a new perspective of journalism education history based on primary sources from the mid-nineteenth century. This challenges traditional claims that Pulitzer originated the concept of university journalism education and emphasizes the link between the development of journalistic education and journalists' efforts to professionalize. In attempting to gain a more complete picture of what some journalists thought about journalism education in the mid-nineteenth century, this study has utilized the first ten years of minutes of the Missouri Press Association (MPA) from 1867 to 1876. These minutes indicate Missouri journalists in the mid-nineteenth century were already advocating professional university education.

One might ask why Missouri editors were apparently particularly interested in journalistic education. There may have been several reasons. An influential MPA member was one possibility. Founding MPA member John Marmaduke was interested in higher education and later was a member of the University Of Missouri Board Of Curators. His interest in education and journalism appears to have influenced him to advocate journalism education. Another possibility was the time period. The mid-nineteenth century was a time when professions were becoming popular, and education was one rung in the ladder toward achieving that end. MPA members saw education as concomitant to turning journalism into a profession.

It is also possible that the Missouri frontier climate encouraged an interest in professionalism. Rural publishers might have seen professionalism as an attractive, if self-serving, way to raise their status. Conversely, metropolitan publishers with larger circulations might have seen professionalism as a danger to the bottom line. Missouri publishers also may have felt more of a need to elevate their status than did their counterparts in more settled parts of the country. Perhaps professionalization was seen as the easiest path to journalistic prestige.

"THE CLUBS ARE SOCIAL GATHERINGS"

But were the mid-nineteenth century press clubs professional associations? Traditional journalism texts have focused on mid-nineteenth century press clubs as being social clubs or business-oriented clubs. In Frederic Hudson's 1873 book, *Journalism in the United States,* he characterized the New York Press Club meetings as unimportant, remarking: "We don't suppose its [the New York Press Club] dinners, or its speeches, or the intercourse of its members improved the tone of the Press.... They continued to criticize and abuse each other, as they always did and always will." Hudson further indicated the non-professional nature of the meetings when he commented, "The Clubs are social gatherings.... None of these social circles are destined for long life but they are useful while they last." Augustus Maverick in 1870 also saw the New York Press Clubs as social in nature. He stated they formed for "the purpose of cultivating the social graces" and criticized them for not maintaining a professional association such as those maintained by doctors, lawyers, and the clergy. Gerald Baldasty is book, *The Commercialization of News in the Nineteenth Century*, characterized the meetings as almost entirely based on business interest. He said:

State and regional publishers and editors organized the earliest newspaper trade associations. The founders of the Ohio Editorial Association, begun in 1849, touted it as a nonpartisan business organization. The first meeting of the Wisconsin Press Association, in 1853, dealt with advance payment of subscriptions, increased rates for legal printing, state printing contracts, and uniform prices for job work. In 1857, the Wisconsin Press Association attempted to set guidelines for advertising rates for member newspapers and to get the legislature to raise rates for printing state laws. One of the founders of the New York Press Association had established this organization mainly to try to set uniform advertising rates and, thus, to present a united front to advertisers.

This business perspective is supposed to represent the entire landscape of press associations during the mid-nineteenth century, but in reality it was the exact opposite of the MPA membersí attitudes. While the goal of the New York Press Association may have been to set uniform advertising rates, the Missouri Press Associationís 1867 constitution prohibited the association from attempting such actions: "This association shall not have power to regulate prices of advertising." Thus, the MPA was different from the start.

HONORING THE PROFESSION

This presents an interesting question. Why was the MPA a strong group that sought a more educated class for its editors? One reference notes that the MPA met to honour the profession in which they served. Other references indicate the MPA formed to promote journalism as a profession. However this does not answer the underlying question of what motivated MPA members to feel this way. Context may provide a clue. The MPA formed shortly after the Civil War, and it is possible that publishers felt they needed to form a professional organization to overcome residual bitterness.

Another contributing factor may have been the background of prominent Missouri publishers at the time. Quite a few had backgrounds in the traditional professions, and three of the members who exerted great influence in the starting of the MPA had professional backgrounds. Norman J. Colman, editor and publisher of the *Rural World* (still in existence today as the *Missouri Ruralist*), was MPA Recording Secretary in 1868 and chaired the MPA Committee on Arrangements in 1869. In 1868, he had been appointed by the governor to the University Of Missouri Board Of Curators and later that same year made an unsuccessful bid for lieutenant governor of the state. Several years later Colman was appointed the first Secretary of the United States

Department of Agriculture. In regard to professional training, he received his teaching license at sixteen and was licensed to practice law a number of years later. He also helped organize the State Historical Society, the St. Louis Historical Society, and the St. Louis Fair Association.

Then, there was Marmaduke. According to one history, "[His] scholarship in all branches of learning was surpassed by few men in the service of the Southern Confederacy." His background included a father who was governor of Missouri in 1844, a mother who was the daughter of a prominent physician, and an education that included classes at both Harvard and Yale. His interest in education would continue when he became governor of Missouri in 1885. Furthermore, historical accounts reveal influential MPA member J. C. Moore had a diverse professional career, including serving in the Confederate Army as a colonel under Major General Marmaduke. By the time Moore joined the MPA, he was licensed to practice law, had served in the Colorado legislature, was the first mayor of Denver, had worked at the *St. Louis Times* and had co-founded the *Kansas City Times*.

However, despite evidence to the contrary, many traditional histories paint the nineteenth-century journalistic landscape as one where journalism education was universally scorned by serious journalists. When journalistic education was discussed, the prevailing opinion tended to be that the university was not considered the place for it, and discussion of professional education, as practiced by doctors, lawyers and the clergy, was largely absent. Albert Sutton, in *Education for Journalism in the United States From Its Beginning to 1940*, contended that it was not until the twentieth century that "state press associations began to lend active support to the movement in some localities."

According to journalism historian Willard Bleyer in his 1927 book, *Main Currents in the History of American Journalism*, although there had been efforts at journalistic education before the twentieth century, it was not until the twentieth century that journalistic education took a "tangible form." Before the twentieth century an apprentice system had taught reporters the basics of reporting, and many journalists in the nineteenth century favored this system, even ridiculing the concept of formalized education.

Alfred McClung Lee's *The Daily Newspaper in America* credited Civil War General Robert E. Lee with some of the first efforts in journalistic education in the nineteenth century. As president of Washington College, he authorized the first courses in journalism in 1869 in an effort to curb the journalistic excesses that he had witnessed during the war. Lee, however, did not experience smooth sailing in his endeavors. Historian Sidney Kobre described Lee's efforts in this manner: "On all sides, General Lee's school had met opposition, ridicule and scorn from newspapermen." Historian Alfred McClung Lee described the response to Lee's school as "feeble" and noted that the programme only survived until 1878, closing less than a decade after its inception. There is no evidence to suggest that any notable students emerged from the experiment, according to scholar Douglas Birkhead. Maurine Beasley and Kathryn Theus point out that a journalism school for women was started in Detroit during this period. However, according to historian Frank Luther Mott, this was a period when "education for journalism remained only an idea, laughed at by most observers." For instance, Whitelaw Reid of the *New York Tribune* favored the concept of training but not institutional education. In 1873 he wrote:

Such an establishment as the *New York Herald*, or *Tribune*, or *Times* is the true college for newspaper students. Professor James Gordon Bennett or Professor Horace Greeley would turn out more real genuine journalists in one year than the Harvards, the Yales, and the Dartmouths could produce in a generation.... The genius for the work is in them [the journalists themselves]. It is not to be acquired at a college in Virginia or Massachusetts.

During this time some universities began teaching courses in printing and editing. However, the interest in professional university education, not merely the offering of one or two courses on printing or editing, was not evident in these initiatives.

The traditional perspective on journalism education places Joseph Pulitzer as the key figure in founding university journalism education, a fact evident in Kobre's 1959 book *Modern American Journalism* in which he stated: "Although Pulitzer was the first to propose and initiate the movement for a journalism school, the first one became a reality in April, 1908 when the Missouri legislature voted the necessary funds to establish a School of Journalism at the University of Missouri." William F. May expressed a similar opinion that Pulitzer was the force behind the concept of a university journalism education in the 1986 article "Professional Ethics, The University and The Journalist." He stated: "The general turnaround occurred in the early twentieth century. By 1904 Joseph Pulitzer had endowed the Columbia School of journalism... and by 1913 the Columbia School of Journalism had opened its doors."

Pulitzer was the original author of the view that university journalism education was his idea. In 1910, he commented, "I have long had an idea. It has been called impossible, ridiculous, fantastic. But I have finally persuaded the trustees of Columbia University that it is not as farfetched as it sounds and they are ready to accept it." In 1891 Pulitzer had made a proposal to officials at Columbia College for a school of journalism, but he was turned down. However, in 1903 he told a friend: "Before the century closes schools of journalism will be generally accepted as a feature of specialized higher education, like schools of law or medicine." Pulitzer's reference to the classical professions of law and medicine was not an accident. He saw journalism education as a means of professionalizing. Yet was Pulitzer the originator of the idea to professionalize journalism through university education? Evidence indicates much earlier roots.

The MPA minutes from the May 19, 1869, convention contained a strong argument in favour of schools of journalism. The speaker, publisher Colman, specifically cited the need for education as part of the pattern set up by the classical professions. As mentioned previously, he had been appointed a University of Missouri curator in the previous year, had a certificate to teach and a license to practice law, and had worked with clergy at a seminary. With his background in three classical professions, Colman pled:

The Teacher, the Physician, the Lawyer, and the Divine, must each undergo a thorough prefatory course, before being permitted to enter his chosen career.... But any particular training, or course of study, or lectures, or schools, or colleges to prepare young men for the most important of all professions—the Editorial—have never been heard of. Those institutions of this kind could be established, and would be attended with the most beneficial results, can scarcely be doubted. Each member of the profession has now to learn for himself all of the duties devolving upon him.

Perhaps the most significant part of this passage was the mention of the need for education in the pattern set by teachers, doctors, lawyers and the clergy, the last three of which were classical professions. Colman justified such professional education by commenting, "Other professions have been greatly benefited by special preparation and such preparation is a wise provision for proper qualification and special excellence." In 1874 MPA member Milo Blair closed an address to the MPA convention with another plea for journalism education in which he said: "In conclusion, I would say that the destiny of our country depends greatly on the influence the press henceforward shall exert, and that influence will rest immeasurably on the kind of education and training which the editor has and may still receive."

At still another meeting in 1879, MPA member William F. Switzler specifically referred to university education for journalists:

I think there are many cogent reasons in support of the conviction, long entertained and often propounded by myself, that editing newspapers is as much a profession as practicing law or medicine, and that a department of journalism ought to be established, and I have no doubt at no distant day will be established, in our own and other Universities. University journalism education might not exist today without the early efforts of the MPA. Colman advocated such edution in 1869, not only before Pulitzer but even before Robert E. Lee started the first formal journalism education at Washington College. In 1873 the University of Missouri held a first of its kind lecture series on journalism, some believe due to Colman's influence. William F. Switzler's impassioned plea in 1879 reinforced the view. This was also the year that the University of Missouri carried its first course in journalism taught by David R. McAnally, Jr., entitled, "History of Journalism—Lectures with Practical Explanations of Daily Newspaper Life." The MPA members, however, apparently were not content merely to talk about journalistic education. The minutes indicate they used the meetings as educational training sessions as well. MPA members saw the meetings as a vehicle to teach the members both the history and principles of journalism, part of informal continuing education. In an oral essay by Milo Blair, he defined the use of MPA annual addresses: "I see before me those... whose ability to teach more practically, than myself, none can question." In fact, most, if not all, of the annual addresses during the MPA's first decade were of an informal educational nature. Switzler made it clear that these early essays were designed as enlightenment for MPA members. The topics included journalism history, journalism theory and journalism ethics. He even compared the MPA in its educational function to the University of Missouri when he said in 1879, "Each [the University of Missouri and the MPA] is working out the problem of human progress, of higher civilization and of wiser and more wholesome government. Each is an educator."

In a 1917 unpublished historical overview of the MPA, for the MPA's fiftieth anniversary, historian Floyd Shoemaker described the MPA's informal education function as part of its purpose: The first school of Journalism in Missouri was not founded in 1906 or 1908, nor was it located in Columbia. Forty years before in St. Louis was this institution truly founded. More accurate would be the name, a school of journalists, [than] that of journalism, for this was the Missouri Press Association. During an existence of half a century, it reveals many of the features of an educational institution. Instruction was provided by the lectures of the deans, professors and teachers in the world of newspapers.... It stands today as it has for half a century, the Great Educator of Missouri Editors.

HE continued this theme of the MPA as the informal educational institution of Missouri journalists. As an Educator, the MPA has been a teacher of the purely intellectual and social—a liberalizer.... The face to face conversation, the floor debates for hours, the sittings side by side at banquet tables—these furnished another kind of Education.... The means at hand for the function of the Association as an Educator were legion and well has it served its purpose. Shoemaker even gave a description of the curriculum. That the Association has well furnished this kind of instruction is obvious.... Not only in the fields of editorial writing, news gathering, reporting, cartooning, advertising, feature writing, and a score of related subjects, but also in type, ink, paper, wages, circulation, rates, dead-heading, and a hundred other topics has the Association been an instructor to Missouri editors.

THE NEWSPAPER BUSINESS

The MPA continued to see education as important to journalism professionalization throughout the nineteenth century as is evidenced by the comments of MPA member and *Mexico Ledger* publisher R.W. White, who said in 1893: "The newspaper business is a distinguished profession and there should be a chair of journalism in our colleges so that young men could have an opportunity to educate themselves for newspaper work." The MPA proposed this to the Missouri legislature in 1895, but the resolution failed. The journalism school was finally established in 1908 directly due to pressure from the MPA, and the Columbia School of Journalism opened its doors soon after in 1912.

Such schools were manifestations of professionalization. Those interested in professionalization of journalism at the turn of the century knew formal education was necessary if journalism was to achieve the professional status accorded to doctors and lawyers. This was evident from the words of Walter Williams, the first dean of the school of journalism at the University of Missouri, who wrote in 1910, "The new education for journalism differs from the old in its recognition of journalism as a profession, as law and medicine are professions." Non-journalists also recognized that professionalization efforts were resulting in schools of journalism.

Visiting Missouri in 1908, United States presidential aspirant William Jennings Bryan stressed the importance of professional training by the University of Missouri journalism school. "I think that men can be taught to be journalists just as men can be taught to be lawyers, doctors, or engineers," he commented. This was an important aspect because the MPA was formed as a professional association and promoted professional goals such as education, association and codes of ethics. Colman stated:

Doubtless one of the leading objects [the founders] had in view in the organization of this association was to bring the members of the Press of this state into a closer and more intimate relationship with one another, that those social and professional courtesies might be cultivated that should exist among members of an honorable profession.

This link of education to professionalization may help explain why the professionally minded Missouri Press Association advocated journalism education at a time when it was not popular among other journalists. In 1869 when Colman was advocating university journalism education Pulitzer had just been hired for his first reporting job after driving a mule team, had not yet learned to write in English and had not settled on a career in journalism. Because the MPA promoted journalism education long before Pulitzer, it is possible Pulitzer borrowed the concept from the MPA. It would not have been the first time he had appropriated another's idea for himself.

In the late nineteenth century, he took the idea for a typesetting machine invented by Ottmar Mergenthaler and called it the Rogers Typograph. A court issued a permanent injunction against Pulitzer using this machine on the basis that it was merely a modification of Mergenthaler's Linotype typesetting machine. He also took credit for inventing the "New Journalism," an honour more deserving of his *New York World* managing editor John Cockerill. Pulitzer might have had access to the MPA's perspective on journalistic professionalization early in his life since he learned to write in English under MPA member and *St. Louis Times* editor Stilson Hutchins. Perhaps Hutchins also taught Pulitzer a respect for the professionalization of journalism.

He was an active MPA member and was even scheduled to deliver the annual address in 1870. Pulitzer would eventually become Hutchinsí close friend when both moved east—Hutchins founding the *Washington Post* and Pulitzer purchased the *New York World*. While at the *St. Louis Times* Pulitzer also may have worked with prominent MPA member and orator J.C. Moore, who was an editor at the *St. Louis Times* before founding the *Kansas CityTimes*. Thus, Pulitzer might have had access to the ideas of professionalization and journalistic education proposed by the MPA, as well as the MPA members who supported them. There is some indication that some MPA members in Missouri had little respect for Pulitzer, however. In 1890 MPA president J.W. Goodwin noted, "Joe Pulitzer never was a great writer."

This is not to say that the MPA members totally originated the idea; they may have become interested in it through the efforts of Robert E. Lee. While northern journalists scoffed at Lee's efforts to professionalize, MPA members embraced his concept of journalistic education, perhaps because of an admiration for him. Prominent MPA member Switzler was on record as having a great admiration for Lee, delivering a eulogy for him in 1870, and Hutchins admired Lee so much that he named his son after Lee. Therefore, it may not be a coincidence that Colman advocated journalistic education at the May 19, 1869, MPA meeting just three months before Lee announced on August 19 a plan for journalism education at Washington College. On the other hand, Pulitzer may not have had the same love for Lee since Pulitzer had been a soldier in Philip Sheridan's army that forced Lee's surrender during the Civil War.

The implications of recognizing an earlier start date for the concept of journalism education is that it underscores the apparent interest in professionalization fostered by members of the MPA. It should be noted that the MPA members were involved in other aspects of professionalization: they referred to themselves as professionals and to journalism as a profession twenty-five times in the 1867-76 minutes; they compared themselves to the traditional professions of doctors, lawyers and the clergy; and they proposed a code of ethics in 1876.

If one looks at professionalization as a gradual scale, as sociologist Wilbert Moore has suggested, the call for university education in the mid-nineteenth century would be a benchmark in the professionalization process that culminated during the first part of the twentieth century. This does not mean the contributions of Pulitzer and Williams were not significant benchmarks of professionalization as well, but it does cast light on earlier journalists whose contributions have never been publicized and presents a new perspective on journalistic professionalization.

After 80 years of experience with university-level programs journalism educators still find themselves caught between the often opposing pulls of industry and the academy. Recent attempts to "re-invent" journalism education, however, demonstrate that there exists a solid tradition upon which educators can build. We may be more restrained than the early 19th Century English Whigs who drank this toast, but we are probably just as convinced that the quality of our lives depends to a very great extent on the quality of our media. Knowledge is not only power; today-in the so-called Information Age—it is the fountain of the good life and the source of most of the things we treasure. And as the quality of the information we need in our increasingly complex society takes on ever greater importance, so does the competence of the people who provide us with that information.

We need to be able to trust our sources of information; we want our journalists to be thoroughly competent and responsible. Such an insight was partially at the root of Joseph Pulitzer's proposal in 1892 to the trustees of Columbia University in New York City that he endow a university programme in journalism education. Pulitzer, who knew h m experience how easy it was LO let market considerations dominate news judgment, hoped that a university education would be the antidote. But equally important to him was raising the status of the profession. "My idea is to recognize that journalism is, or ought to be, one of the great and intellectual professions; to encourage, elevate and educate in a practical way the present, and still more, future members of that profession, exactly as if it were the profession of law or medicine".

With the memory of the Pulitzer-Hearst yellow journalism battles undimmed, the trustees of Columbia were reluctant to accept Pulitzer's offer. Journalism was not an entirely reputable calling. It smacked of bohemianism and adventurism, and respectable people, following Queen Victoria's lead, were not inclined to receive journalists socially. Pulitzer's plan was interpreted in some quarters as being akin to a proposal to launder dirty money. However, $2 million canies a convincing argument and Columbia's guardians were eventually persuaded that a professional school of journalism might indeed be a good thing. Because of all the foot dragging, Columbia was not the first university to institute a school of journalism. When it finally opened its doors in 1912, the University of Missouri had had a school in place for four years.

UNRIVALLED PRESTIGE

Columbia, however, set the tone of journalism education for years to come. For example, when Canada's first schools, at Carleton and the University of Western Ontario, were established in the mid-1940s both followed Columbia's lead. As an Ivy League school in the media capital of the world, Columbia's prestige was unrivalled. And it seemed to take to heart the university ethos, pledging its allegiance, not to the industry, but to the public interest It seemed a foregone conclusion that journalists would acquire the cachet of the university-trained professional man (Pulitzer had no use for higher education for women) and journalism itself would move out of the realm of trade schools to the more lofty heights of medicine, theology and law.

Toexpedite this process, Columbia in 1935 became a graduate school offering only professional training. Meanwhile, other schools began offering graduate courses in journalism that emphasized a more traditional scholarly orientation, thereby sowing the seeds for endless future debates about the nature of journalism education. At the same time as journalists were making these efforts to raise the status of their calling, doctors and lawyers were engaged in a similar process of professionalization-but their efforts were met with a much greater degree of success.

Today, nobody disputes the right of doctors and lawyers to call themselves professionals, and their schools and faculties enjoy nearly unanimous social and academic prestige. Journalists, however, are still not recognized as [illegible] professionals and their academic institutions are often stigmatized as trade schools. As if to add insult to injury, the media industry itself often joins in that chorus of dam- nation. Journalism education, to the eternal lament of its practitioners and advocates, has ended up as neither fish nor fowl; it feels itself unloved by the industry and tolerated, barely, by the academy.

It is little wonder then that journalism educators these days are going through yet another round of the intense navel- gazing that has characterized the profession from the beginning. Everette Dennis, the executive director of the Gannett Centre for Media Studies at Columbia University, four years ago headed a task force that took the most comprehensive look yet at journalism education. As he sees it, "journalism education still falls uncomfortably between two stools-the university and the industry". That is an awkward position at best, and in the end, anyone attempting to occupy that space is bound to fail. No one can serve two masters without earning the contempt of both, and that, in a nutshell, is what seems to have happened. It is time, says Dennis, to reinvent journalism education.

THE QUEBEC EXPERIENCE

One attempt at reinvention was made not too long ago in Quebec, when journalism educators began looking into the possibility of consolidating the three French-language university-level journalism programs into one central institute of journalism education. They were dissatisfied with a state of affairs which, they felt, scattered already scarce resources, allowing nobody to do an adequate job. The existing programs were all 30-credit minor options within other departments, where, lacking a power base of their own, they were grossly underfunded and understaffed. At the Universite de Montreal, the programme was part of the evening extension department and was staffed almost entirely by part-time instructors. At Laval and UQAM, the programs were located within the communications studies departments, which had other priorities and orientations. For the most part, the journalism educators were professional journalists who moved easily between media jobs and the university. The communications professors tended to be full-time academics with little or no media experience. There was a strong suggestion of two solitudes in these camps, a classic example of the industry-university cleavage Dennis finds so problematical in the United States. Meanwhile, in English Canada, journalism programs seemed to be enjoying considerably more autonomy and prestige.

None of the seven university-level programs was a minor appendage of a communications studies department, and two, Carleton and Western, were constituted as free-standing professional schools with comparatively large budgets and faculties. Even relations with the industry seemed better. Graduates of the English-language programme seemed to find jobs more easily, perhaps because the vocational side of their training was more intensive and more attuned to industry needs. As these differences became more apparent, especially after the establishment of a nation-wide association of directors of journalism schools in 1983, the conviction grew that the system had to change if journalism education in French was to make any serious impact in Quebec. As one educator put it: "English graduates are gradually taking over everywhere, but the French schools are significant." Hence the proposal for a central institute of journalism education which would draw in all the interested parties-the professionals and the academics, the industry and the university. Meetings were organized to examine and compare the merits of the journalism education systems in English Canada, the United States and Europe. Nothing concrete was decided, but a preference seemed to be arising for an institute modelled somewhat along the lines of the Centre de formation professionnelle des journalistes in Paris, which offered graduate-level professional and vocational training. The bubble burst, however, when the Bourassa Government, presumably after sounding out the industry, declined to underwrite a feasibility study for the venture.

Laval's Jacques Guay was understandably upset by the decision. It means, he wrote, that the training of journalists will remain dispersed and disorganized since no one school has the necessary resources, and it will be carried out without any meaningful contact with the industry. But that seems to be the way the industry prefers it, As a senior editor at a Quebec City daily newspaper recently asked: "Why do we need it?"

ON-THE-JOB 'LKAINING

The prevailing attitude seems to be that things are all right as they are. Editors are content to hire political science and sociology graduates with passable writing styles. Whatever polishing they need can be done on the job. According to one young francophone graduate of a journalism programme: "There is still the feeling that the best education is on-the-job training and that you learn so much more hanging around bars and drinking with old pros".

The only problem with that philosophy is that few media organizations have their own braining programs these days. Most do hire students for summer internships, but these cannot be counted as true braining programs inasmuch as the students are expected to be competent from day one and usually replace vacationing staff. There are some programs, such as the one at La Presse, which are supervised by an editor who provides pointers and feedback to the cub reporters, but even in such cases there is little training beyond matters of style. Laval journalism professor Florian Sauvageau is one of those who woes that the emphasis on a grammatically precise and literary style tends to be at the expense of reporting skills. "To have a beautiful wrapping and nothing inside is only manipulation".

That feeling is shared by UQAM's Jacques Larue-Langlois, who would like to double the amount of time journalism students spend learning their craft. The training process for journalists, he says, has to be carried out methodically by experienced educators whose horizons are not blocked or blinkered by industry needs and who are receptive to new developments in both theory and practice. "Some of the professionals, who may have many years of experience, but have never taken a journalism course, imagine there is nothing further to learn," says Lame-Langlois.

DIALOGUE OF THE DEAF

Between the journalism schools and the industry, it's a dialogue of the deaf, sums up Alain Rajotte, a student journalist at UQAM. Similar attitudes, of course exist outside French-language newsrooms, too. When today's senior journalists were entering the ranks 20 or 30 years ago, journalism education was the exception rather than the rule. For many, the only schooling they received was in the school of hard knocks. Quite a few, as a result, are convinced that universities are ivory tower institutions for pointy-headed social misfits who can't make any contribution to journalism until all the airy-fairy ideas they have acquired in their misspent university years are knocked out of their systems by a year or two of on-the-job training.

These old-line journalists, some of whom are not necessarily old-timers, seem to reserve their bitterest vituperation for journalism schools and educators. The schools only exist so that "failed journalists can get jobs," one Anglophone editor of a daily newspaper said recently. Another believes strongly that the only use of journalism schools is to "train PR types and bureaucrats". And more than a few working journalists, it seems, are suspicious of journalism education on the grounds that its main purpose, as one editor put it, is to get "control of the agenda". In an industry that is extremely sensitive in the name of press freedom-to any centralizing or regulating tendency, journalism education may well seem to point in that direction.

And for many in the media industry, the kind of certification of competency that professional training implies is only a step away from the licensing of journalists. This, of course, is a legitimate concern, especially since the movement to professionalization in this century has always tended towards such exclusiveness. The issue is not one that is likely to go away in the foreseeable future. The industry's concern has to be seen in the light of nearly 500 years of press history, during which time there has been an almost constant effort to subvert press freedom on the part of governments and special interest groups everywhere.

We wouldn't countenance it if the government denied anyone, consumer or contributor, access to the press; and it is surely just as much a violation of press Mom if access is denied by a special interest group such as a professional body. This may well be the best reason for journalism to avoid entrenchment as a profession with its own admissions standards, procedures and disciplinary body.

ACADEMIC SCRUTINY

The industry is quick to perceive this kind of threat, perhaps because it is equally a threat to its autonomy, but it is somewhat slower off the mark when it comes to criticism that the industry itself has become a special interest group. The movement to newspaper monopolies, cross-media ownership, concentration of ownership and conglomeration, for example, has not been wholly in the public interest, as the Kent Royal Commission and other studies have pointed out. Much of this kind of scrutiny and critique of the media has come from the academy and has not endeared journalism educators to the industry. Nevertheless, the industry has gradually come to realize that it is to a certain extent dependent on journalism schools for filling its job vacancies.

As Montreal Gazette publisher Clark Davey said some years ago: "What the academic com- munity sets great store in are two things: publication of learned papers and the academic degrees that the faculty has. I don't think that either of these aspects is nearly as important as maintaining a much closer relationship with the industry. If journalism is seen to be a poor relation somehow academically at some universities, that doesn't concern me as much as the fact that some journalism courses are seen to be irrelevant by the journalism business."

Davey, himself a graduate of Western's journalism programme, has been one of the staunchest supporters of journalism education in Canada, and his newspaper's owners, the Southam chain, have also been more supportive than most. But as with so many things, the future is being invented in the United States and it is there that one sees the full extent of the industry-university connection.

Even a quick flypast confirms that virtually every significant media owner in the U.S. has ended up with his name emblazoned over the portals of some school. And equally large sums of money have been given to endow scholarships and academic chairs and to support research.

CLOSE TIES

These connections have not been without their attendant problems, and Canadian educators who envy such close ties and, especially, the financial support, would do well to reflect upon the experience of Kurt Lang, former director of the School of Communications at the University of Washington. In 1986, the Allied Daily Newspapers, an association of 55 regional dailies in the Pacific Northwest, proposed a programme to improve co-operation between the industry and area journalism schools, citing concern about the quality of journalism graduates and "the overemphasis at some institutions on theoretical re- search". Allied established an ad hoc committee for journalism education and proposed to distribute questionnaires to the schools and follow these up with campus visits. Schools that ended up with a "recommended" status after this scrutiny would receive financial aid and scholarships and would be eligible to participate in a wide array of professional programs sponsored by Allied.

Although several educators spoke out against the coercive nature of the programme, only the faculty at the University of Washington flatly rejected it as a "thoroughly bad idea." Lang, who had spearheaded the opposition to Allied's plan, was dismissed from his post some months later, ostensibly in a routine personnel shuffle. What Allied was basically attempting to establish, dangling its largesse as a carrot, was an accreditation system which it could manipulate for its own ends, and no matter how legitimate those ends might be in their eyes, such interference is a threat to the academic freedom that is basic to the university tradition, and by extension, to the public interest. It should be noted, however, that there is an official "Accrediting Council on Education in Journalism and Mass Communications" in the United States which certifies colleges that "have measured up to high standards set by leaders in education and the professional media."

The 89 colleges that currently make up this list are known as the "Journalism Ivys" and include many of the best-known journalism programs in the country. Still, nearly three-quarters of the 343 schools which offer at least a bachelor's degree in journalism or mass communications are not participants in the programme, and not always because they do not measure up. Some have questioned the relevance of the criteria used for accreditation and others have wondered whether such a process may not in fact interfere with academic freedom since it gives an outside interest, namely the media industry, a say in curricular decisions.

Some are also opposed to what they see as a standardizing mechanism in journalism education. Truth, as John Milton pointed out so many years ago, seldom appears whole or in one guise. It has to be pieced together from diverse sources, using diverse Reinventing Journalism Education. If journalism educators are to take their task seriously, it can be argued, they have to resist centralizing and homogenizing tendencies.

ACCREDITATION

Advocates of accreditation see the issue very differently. For them, it is purely a matter of ensuring that minimal standards of competency are met. Interestingly enough, it was the diversity of programs and the "pretty arbitrary" range of elective courses that led Prof. Jason Zasursky, dean of the school of journalism at Moscow University, to make a similar criticism of American journalism schools: "A certain flexibility in the choice of subjects is all very well, but it does not, unfortunately, provide the necessary basic level of knowledge. It doesn't provide for a standard which in the given context, should not be thought of as a levelling process, but as a required level of training". Prof. Zasursky's 1,256 students, for what it's worth, are required to take half of their core courses in political theory and ideology.

Another trend in the United States that may have a lesson for Canadian journalism educators is the movement to establish ever larger and more all-inclusive communications schools. Some of these monster schools now have nearly 4,000 students, with almost half of them enrolled in non-journalism courses such as public relations and advertising. Some observers, however, are not at all convinced that, apart from bringing in more state funding through per capita grants, this trend is good for journalism education. Purists are concerned that a journalism ethic dedicated to the pursuit of truth cannot flourish side by side with endeavours oriented towards commercial advantage. The fear is that, instead of leading to a potent cross-fertilization of fields that would expedite the generation of knowledge, the welter of conflicting value systems, theories and practices will end up rendering journalism studies into cacophonous impotence.

INTELLECTUAL STRANGERS

Already, as a recent survey indicates, U.S. journalism and mass communications faculties are "divided into several cultures of intellectual strangers" bout 30 cent, the survey found, are "industry isolates", oriented almost exclusively to industry interests and activities; 20 per cent are "academic isolates", with little or no contact with the industry; 40 per cent are "electics", relating to both sectors; and about 10 per cent are "outliers" who relate to neither sector. The dialogue of the deaf clearly extends into the academy. The fear that some of these developments have run away from themselves is patently behind Everette Dennis's call for a re-invention of journalism studies. And insofar as there is a need for an overhaul of the structures and cumcula of some programs, he is right, but it seems to me that it would be hard to find a better guiding light are better bedrock of principles- for journalism education than James Carey's 1979 exposition of the "university tradition".

Carey, dean of the College of Communications at the University of Illinois (Urbana), took dead aim at the professionalization of journalism he saw taking place around him. In his analysis, which he shares with Ivan Illich and Christopher Lasch among others, the trend to professionalism in general is seen as inimical to human freedom and development. Not only has professionalization eroded the moral basis of society, but it has fostered a set of social practices that are "thoroughly anti-intellectual and anti ethical.

"The great danger in modem journalism," he says, "is one of a professional orientation to an audience: the belief, usually implicit, that the audience is there to be informed, to be educated, to be filled with the vital information and knowledge whose nature, production and control rests with a professional class. This knowledge is defined, identified, presented based upon canons of professional expertise over which the audience exercises no real judgment or control. And in this new client-professional relationship that emerges the same structures of dependency are developed that typify the relations of doctors, lawyers and social workers to their clients".

THE UNIVERSITY TRADITION

The antidote to this menace, he says, is "to extirpate much of the professional spirit of our curricula. We must do that in order to re-assert the university tradition, in order to reassert the general ethical and intellectual point of view against all the claims of specialism that would overwhelm it". It is encouraging that a recent proposal for an integrated journalism curriculum by G. Stuart Adam, finds its major inspiration in Carey's orbit. Like Carey, Adam wants journalism education to be a preparation for enlightened and responsible citizenship. He wants it to show individuals "how to know and benefit from the great works of thought and art so that their private lives will become rich and their acts of citizenship informed.

The vocational aims, which are also a part of the university's mission, should be ancillary and dependent on the success with which the other two aims are achieved". Equally satisfying is Adam's recognition that journalism must be organized and developed as an academic discipline in its own right, not as an appendage to communications studies. As noted already, the source of much of the diffuseness and many of the divisions in journalism education has been its inclusion, side by side with the conflicting value systems of theorists, PR practitioners and popular culture addicts, as a sub-field of communications. Journalists must, indeed, learn about communications theories and the media systems and contexts in which they will practise their profession, just as they should know something about media history, media law, media ethics, etc., but that is not reason enough for Journalism to be subsumed holus-bolus as a sub-field of any of these discipline or vice versa.

There is something rather fanciful, thus, in Adam's reasoning that major chunks of communications studies are more properly a sub-field of journalism, one of five along with philosophy of journalism, professional practice or "operations", criticism and methodology. Adam's primary intention, however, is not to provoke jurisdictional quarrels, but to bring journalism studies into the academic culture by incorporating the "university's methods of classifying, analyzing and communicating knowledge". It's not so much a question of re-invention as of repackaging, because, as he admits, all of the elements that would constitute his integrated field of journalism studies already exist in a kind of "oral tradition" and need only to be formalized?

ACADEMIC CULTURE

Journalism, of course, has already made valiant attempts to be accepted by the academic culture. For the better part of the last *two* decades, journalism educators and researchers in the academy have churned out boxcar loads of publications based on arcane and abstruse social sciences methodologies, many of which were little more than ritualistic articulations of the self-evident Academic culture, in case it needs to be spelled out, can be just as much an introverted dead-end as professionalism, especially if it is not informed by any- thing other than its own narrow specialisms. Adam's orienting of journalism studies towards the humanities-i.e. Carey's "university tradition-is therefore of signal importance. One major issue that Adam begs in his "re-invention" of the field, is that of the appropriate level at which journalism studies should be situated.

The implication in what he says, however, is that as a unified discipline at the heart of the university tradition, it must have a strong presence at all levels, just like Literature, History or Political Science. These other fields, however, are not involved in professional or vocational training, at least not in any direct way. Journalism education, on the other hand, would not make any sense without its vocational aspects. If journalism education is implemented at the undergraduate level, it has to include vocational training and that fact by itself is the source of countless problems. What, for example, should be the ratio of "academic" to "workshop" courses so that students are not shortchanged in the quality of their general education or vice versa? Can we, in fact, devise an integrated field of journalism, as Adam sets out to do, which serves all the ends of a general education as well as of professional training?

GRADUATE PROGRAMS

However, such issues-and most of the other problems of journalism education as well-become much less relevant when journalism is situated at the graduate level, after students have already acquired their basic education. Students at that level are generally more mature, better informed and better motivated. Because they already possess a degree in one of the many disciplines now found in the university, they will bring to bear on their journalism studies a diversity of insights, methods and values which will discourage homogenization of practices and encourage independent thinking. Graduate students are free of other academic commitments and can devote their full attention to journalism. In this way, they can (and do) easily cover the equivalent of three years of undergraduate courses in just three terms-and at a higher level to boot.

For graduate students who are vocationally inclined, such a programme would enable them to enter the job market. For those who wish to work at a higher level, to conduct research or to teach, there should be a second tier of courses leading to a Ph.D. degree. There has already been considerable movement in this direction in Canada, with virtually all of the university-level journalism programs instituting graduate courses leading to a "fust professional degree."

In fact, one school, The University of Western Ontario, like Columbia, did away entirely with its undergraduate programme, and another, Carleton, has taken steps to implement second-tier graduate programs of a more scholarly bent. On the whole, the experience with graduate programs has been very successful-for all the reasons stated above-and the industry has welcomed the change as a significant improvement in journalism education.

And inspired by the proliferation and success of MBA programs, some journalism educators are already predicting that the trend to graduate schools offering first professional degrees will be the saving of journalism education. Everette Dennis, for one envisages journalism graduate schools with the high profile and power of Ivy League MBA schools. However, such forecasts and aspirations should be tempered with at least a modicum of caution. Graduate schools of journalism are a good thing but they do not provide all the answers. Just as there can be no one standard of journalism, there should not be only one approach to journalism education. As long as journalism educators can keep sight of that fact they will remain where the public interest demands that they be-within the orbit of Carey's "university tradition."

5

Freedom of Speech and Press

Freedom of speech is the freedom to speak freely without censorship or limitation. The synonymous term freedom of expression is sometimes used to denote not only freedom of verbal speech but any act of seeking, receiving and imparting information or ideas, regardless of the medium used. Freedom of speech and freedom of expression are closely related to, yet distinct from, the concept of freedom of thought. In practice, the right to freedom of speech is not absolute in any country and the right is commonly subject to limitations, such as on "hate speech".

The right to freedom of speech is recognized as a human right under Article 19 of the Universal Declaration of Human Rights and recognized in international human rights law in the International Covenant on Civil and Political Rights (ICCPR). The ICCPR recognizes the right to freedom of speech as "the right to hold opinions without interference. Everyone shall have the right to freedom of expression". Furthermore freedom of speech is recognized in European, inter-American and African regional human rights law.

THE RIGHT TO FREEDOM OF SPEECH AND EXPRESSION

Freedom of speech, or the freedom of expression, is recognized in international and regional human rights law. The right is enshrined in Article 19 of the International Covenant on Civil and Political Rights, Article 10 of the European Convention on Human Rights, Article 13 of the American Convention on Human Rights, Article 9 of the African Charter on Human and Peoples' Rights, and the First Amendment to the United States Constitution. The freedom of speech can be found in early human rights documents, such as the British Magna Carta (1215) and The Declaration of the Rights of Man (1789), a key document of the French Revolution. Based on John Stuart Mill's arguments, freedom of speech today is understood as a multi-faceted right that includes not only the right to express, or disseminate, information and ideas, but three further distinct aspects:

- The right to seek information and ideas;
- The right to receive information and ideas;
- The right to impart information and ideas.

International, regional and national standards also recognize that freedom of speech, as the freedom of expression, includes any medium, be it orally, in written, in print, through the Internet or through art forms. This means that the protection of freedom of speech as a right includes not only the content, but also the means of expression.

RELATIONSHIP TO OTHER RIGHTS

The right to freedom of speech is closely related to other rights, and may be limited when conflicting with other rights. The right to freedom of speech is particularly important for media, which plays a special role as the bearer of the general right to freedom of expression for all.

ORIGINS AND ACADEMIC FREEDOM

Freedom of speech and expression has a long history that predates modern international human rights instruments. In Islamic ethics freedom of speech was first declared in the Rashidun period by the caliph Umar in the 7th century. In the Abbasid Caliphate period, freedom of speech was also declared by al-Hashimi (a cousin of Caliph al-Ma'mun) in a letter to one of the religious opponents he was attempting to convert through reason.

According to George Makdisi and Hugh Goddard, "the idea of academic freedom" in universities was "modelled on Islamic custom" as practiced in the medieval Madrasah system from the 9th century. Islamic influence was "certainly discernible in the foundation of the first deliberately-planned university" in Europe, the University of Naples Federico II founded by Frederick II, Holy Roman Emperor in 1224.

FREEDOM OF SPEECH AND TRUTH

One of the earliest Western defences of freedom of expression is *Areopagitica* (1644) by the English poet and political writer John Milton. Milton wrote in reaction to an attempt by the English republican parliament to prevent "seditious, unreliable, unreasonable and unlicensed pamphlets". Milton advanced a number of arguments in defence of freedom of speech: a nation's unity is created through blending individual differences rather than imposing homogeneity from above; that the ability to explore the fullest range of ideas on a given issue was essential to any learning process and truth cannot be arrived upon unless all points of view are first considered; and that by considering free thought, censorship acts to the detriment of material progress.

Milton also argued that if the facts are laid bare, truth will defeat falsehood in open competition, but this cannot be left for a single individual to determine. According to Milton, it is up to each individual to uncover their own truth; no one is wise enough to act as a censor for all individuals. Noam Chomsky states that: "If you believe in freedom of speech, you believe in freedom of speech for views you don't like. Stalin and Hitler, for example, were dictators in favour of freedom of speech for views they liked only. If you're in favour of freedom of speech, that means you're in favour of freedom of speech precisely for views you despise."

An often cited quote that describes the principle of freedom of speech comes from Evelyn Beatrice Hall (often mis-attributed to Voltaire) "I disapprove of what you say, but I will defend to the death your right to say it," as an illustration of Voltaire's beliefs. Professor Lee Bollinger argues that "the free speech principle involves a special act of carving out one area of social interaction for extraordinary self-restraint, the purpose of which is to develop and demonstrate a social capacity to control feelings evoked by a host of social encounters." As said by Bollinger, tolerance is a desirable value, if not essential. However, critics argue that society should also be concerned by those who directly deny, for example, a great social harm, such as a genocide. From this point of view, it could sometime be more important to prevent memories from a great sentimental hurt..

DEMOCRACY

One of the most notable proponents of the link between freedom of speech and democracy is Alexander Meiklejohn. He argues that the concept of democracy is that of self-government by the people. For such a system to work an informed electorate is necessary. In order to be appropriately knowledgeable, there must be no constraints on the free flow of information and ideas. According to Meiklejohn, democracy will not be true to its essential ideal if those in power are able to manipulate the electorate by withholding information and stifling criticism. Meiklejohn acknowledges that the desire to manipulate opinion can stem from the motive of seeking to benefit society. However, he argues, choosing manipulation negates, in its means, the democratic ideal. Eric Barendt has called the defence of free speech on the grounds of democracy "probably the most attractive and certainly the most fashionable free speech theory in modern Western democracies".

Thomas I. Emerson expanded on this defence when he argued that freedom of speech helps to provide a good balance between stability and change. Freedom of speech acts as a "safety valve" to let off steam when people might otherwise be bent on revolution. He argues that "The principle of open discussion is a method of achieving a moral adaptable and at the same time more stable community, of maintaining the precarious balance between healthy cleavage and necessary consensus." Emerson furthermore maintains that "Opposition serves a vital social function in offsetting or ameliorating (the) normal process of bureaucratic decay."

Research undertaken by the Worldwide Governance Indicators project at the World Bank, indicates that freedom of speech, and the process of accountability that follows it, have a significant impact in the quality of governance of a country. "Voice and Accountability" within a country, defined as "the extent to which a country's citizens are able to participate in selecting their government, as well as freedom of expression, freedom of association, and free media" is one of the six dimensions of governance that the Worldwide Governance Indicators measure for more than 200 countries.

SOCIAL INTERACTION AND COMMUNITY

Richard Moon has developed the argument that the value of freedom of speech and freedom of expression lies with social interactions. Moon writes that "by communicating an individual forms relationships and associations with others - family, friends, co-workers, church congregation, and countrymen. By entering into discussion with others an individual participates in the development of knowledge and in the direction of the community."

LIMITATIONS ON FREEDOM OF SPEECH

According to the Freedom Forum Organization, legal systems, and society at large, recognize limits on the freedom of speech, particularly when freedom of speech conflicts with other values or rights. Limitations to freedom of speech may follow the "harm principle" or the "offense principle", for example in the case of pornography or "hate speech". Limitations to freedom of speech may occur through legal sanction and/or social disapprobation.

In "On Liberty" (1859) John Stuart Mill argued that "...there ought to exist the fullest liberty of professing and discussing, as a matter of ethical conviction, any doctrine, however immoral it may be considered." Mill argues that the fullest liberty of expression is required to push arguments to their logical limits, rather than the limits of social embarrassment. However, Mill also introduced what is known as the harm principle, in placing the following limitation on free expression: "the only purpose for which power can be rightfully exercised over any member of a civilized community, against his will, is to prevent harm to others.

In 1985 Joel Feinberg introduced what is known as the "offence principle", arguing that Mill's harm principle does not provide sufficient protection against the wrongful behaviours of others. Feinberg wrote "It is always a good reason in support of a proposed criminal prohibition that it would probably be an effective way of preventing serious offense (as opposed to injury or harm) to persons other than the actor, and that it is probably a necessary means to that end." Hence Feinberg argues that the harm principle sets the bar too high and that some forms of expression can be legitimately prohibited by law because they are very offensive. But, as offending someone is less serious than harming someone, the penalties imposed should be higher for causing harm.

In contrast Mill does not support legal penalties unless they are based on the harm principle. Because the degree to which people may take offense varies, or may be the result of unjustified prejudice, Feinberg suggests that a number of factors need to be taken into account when applying the offense principle, including: the extent, duration and social value of the speech, the ease with which it can be avoided, the motives of the speaker, the number of people offended, the intensity of the offense, and the general interest of the community at large.

THE INTERNET

International, national and regional standards recognise that freedom of speech, as one form of freedom of expression, applies to any medium, including the Internet.

FREEDOM OF INFORMATION

Jo Glanville, editor of the Index on Censorship, states that "the Internet has been a revolution for censorship as much as for free speech". Freedom of information is an extension of freedom of speech where the medium of expression is the Internet. Freedom of information may also refer to the right to privacy in the context of the Internet and information technology. As with the right to freedom of expression, the right to privacy is a recognised human right and freedom of information acts as an extension to this right. Freedom of information may also concern censorship in an information technology context, i.e. the ability to access Web content, without censorship or restrictions.

The World Summit on the Information Society (WSIS) Declaration of Principles adopted in 2003 reaffirms democracy and the universality, indivisibility and interdependence of all human rights and fundamental freedoms. The Declaration also makes specific reference to the importance of the right to freedom of expression for the "Information Society" in stating:

"We reaffirm, as an essential foundation of the Information Society, and as outlined in Article 19 of the Universal Declaration of Human Rights, that everyone has the right to freedom of opinion and expression; that this right includes freedom to hold opinions without interference and to seek, receive and impart information and ideas through any media and regardless of frontiers. Communication is a fundamental social process, a basic human need and the foundation of all social organisation. It is central to the Information Society. Everyone, everywhere should have the opportunity to participate and no one should be excluded from the benefits of the Information Society offers."

The Internet opens new possibilities for exercising freedom of speech. The pseudonymity of the Internet allows people to communicate. Data havens (such as Freenet) and gripe sites allow free speech by guaranteeing that material cannot be removed (censored).

INTERNET CENSORSHIP

The concept of freedom of information has emerged in response to state sponsored censorship, monitoring and surveillance of the internet. Internet censorship includes the control or suppression of the publishing or accessing of information on the Internet. The Electronic Frontier Foundation (EFF) is an organization dedicated to protecting freedom of speech on the Internet. The Open Net Initiative (ONI) is a collaboration between the Citizen Lab at the Munk Centre for International Studies, the University of Toronto, the Berkman Centre for Internet & Society at Harvard Law School, the Advanced Network Research Group at the Cambridge Security Programme (University of Cambridge), and the Oxford Internet Institute, at Oxford University which aims to investigate, expose, and analyse Internet filtering and surveillance practices in a credible and non-partisan fashion. Groups such as the Global Internet Freedom Consortium advocate for freedom of information for what they term "closed societies".

According to the Reporters without Borders (RSF) "internet enemy list" the following states engage in pervasive internet censorship: Cuba, Iran, Maldives, Myanmar/Burma, North Korea, Syria, Tunisia, Uzbekistan and Vietnam. A widely publicised example is the "Great Firewall of China" (in reference both to its role as a network firewall and to the ancient Great Wall of China). The system blocks content by preventing IP addresses from being routed through and consist of standard firewall and proxy servers at the Internet gateways.

The system also selectively engages in DNS poisoning when particular sites are requested. The government does not appear to be systematically examining Internet content, as this appears to be technically impractical. Internet censorship in the People's Republic of China is conducted under a wide variety of laws and administrative regulations. In accordance with these laws, more than sixty Internet regulations have been made by the People's Republic of China (PRC) government, and censorship systems are vigorously implemented by provincial branches of state-owned ISPs, business companies, and organizations.

Freedom of the press consists of constitutional or statutory protections pertaining to the media and published materials. With respect to governmental information, any government distinguishes which materials are public or protected from disclosure to the public based on classification of information as sensitive, classified or secret and being otherwise protected from disclosure due to relevance of the information to protecting the national interest. Many governments are also subject to sunshine laws or freedom of information legislation that are used to define the ambit of national interest.

BASIC PRINCIPLES AND CRITERIA

"I fear the newspapers more than a hundred thousand bayonets." — *Napoleon Bonaparte* The Universal Declaration of Human Rights states: *"Everyone has the right to freedom of opinion and expression; this right includes freedom to hold opinions without interference, and impart information and ideas through any media regardless of frontiers"*

This philosophy is usually accompanied by legislation ensuring various degrees of freedom of scientific research (known as scientific freedom), publishing, press and printing the depth to which these laws are entrenched in a country's legal system can go as far down as its constitution. The concept of freedom of speech is often covered by the same laws as freedom of the press, thereby giving equal treatment to media and individuals.

Besides legal definitions, some non-governmental organizations use other criteria to judge the level of press freedom around the world:

- Reporters Without Borders considers the number of journalists murdered, expelled or harassed, and the existence of a state monopoly on TV and radio, as well as the existence of censorship and self-censorship in the media, and the overall independence of media as well as the difficulties that foreign reporters may face.
- The Committee to Protect Journalists (CPJ) uses the tools of journalism to help journalists by tracking press freedom issues through independent research, fact-finding missions, and firsthand contacts in the field, including local working journalists in countries around the world. CPJ shares information on breaking cases with other press freedom organizations worldwide through the International Freedom of Expression Exchange, a global e-mail network. CPJ also tracks journalist deaths and detentions. CPJ staff applies strict criteria for each case; researchers independently investigate and verify the circumstances behind each death or imprisonment.
- Freedom House likewise studies the more general political and economic environments of each nation in order to determine whether relationships of dependence exist that limit in practice the level of press freedom that might exist in theory. So the concept of independence of the press is one closely linked with the concept of press freedom.

STATUS OF PRESS FREEDOM WORLDWIDE

WORLDWIDE PRESS FREEDOM INDEX

Every year, Reporters without Borders establishes a ranking of countries in terms of their freedom of the press. The Worldwide press freedom index list is based on responses to surveys sent to journalists that are members of partner organisations of the RWB, as well as related specialists such as researchers, jurists and human rights activists. The survey asks questions about direct attacks on journalists and the media as well as other indirect sources of pressure against the free press, such as pressure on journalists by non-governmental groups. RWB is careful to note that the index only deals with press freedom, and does not measure the quality of journalism.

In 2003, the countries where press was the most free were Finland, Iceland, the Netherlands In 2004, apart from the above countries, Denmark, Ireland, Slovakia, Portugal and Switzerland were tied at the top of the list, followed by New Zealand and Latvia. The country with the least degree of press freedom was North Korea, followed by Burma, Turkmenistan, People's Republic of China (mainland only), Vietnam, Nepal, and Iran.

NON-DEMOCRATIC STATES

According to Reporters Without Borders, more than a third of the world's people live in countries where there is no press freedom. Overwhelmingly, these people live in countries where there is no system of democracy or where there are serious deficiencies in the democratic process.Freedom of the press is an extremely problematic problem/concept for most non-democratic systems of government since, in the modern age, strict control of access to information is critical to the existence of most non-democratic governments and their associated control systems and security apparatus. To this end, most non-democratic societies employ state-run news organizations to promote the propaganda critical to maintaining an existing political power base and suppress (often very brutally, through the use of police, military, or intelligence agencies) any significant attempts by the media or individual journalists to challenge the approved "government line" on contentious issues. In such countries, journalists operating on the fringes of what is deemed to be acceptable will very often find themselves the subject of considerable intimidation by agents of the state. This can range from simple threats to their professional careers (firing, professional blacklisting) to death threats, kidnapping, torture, and assassination. Reporters Without Borders reports that, in 2003, 42 journalists lost their lives pursuing their profession and that, in the same year, at least 130 journalists were in prison as a result of their occupational activities. In 2005, 63 journalists and 5 media assistants were killed worldwide.

- The Lira Baysetova case in Kazakhstan.
- In Nepal, Eritrea and China (mainland only), journalists may spend years in jail simply for using the "wrong" word or photo.
- The Georgiy R. Gongadze case in Ukraine (information needed, spammer removed information)

According to the Press Freedom Index for 2007, Iran ranked 166th out of 169 nations. Only three other countries - Eritrea, North Korea and Turkmenistan - had more restrictions on news media freedom than Iran. The government of Ali Khamenei and the Supreme National Security Council had imprisoned 50 journalists in 2007 and had all but eliminated press freedom. Reporters Without Borders (RWB) has dubbed Iran the "Middle East's biggest prison for journalists."

Poland

Freedom of Press laws are first passed in the Commonwealth in 1532.

Sweden

The world's first Freedom of the Press Act was introduced in Sweden in 1766.

Denmark-Norway

Between September 4, 1770 and October 7, 1771 the kingdom of Denmark-Norway had the most unrestricted freedom of press of any country in Europe. This occurred during the regime of Johann Friedrich Struensee, whose first act was to abolish the old censorship laws. However, due to the great amount of mostly anonymous pamphlets published that was critical and often slanderous towards Struensees own regime, he reinstated some restrictions regarding the freedom of press a year later, October 7 1771.

England

The Glorious Revolution of 1688 in England established parliamentary sovereignty over the Crown and, above all, the right of revolution. A major contributor to Western liberal theory was John Locke. Locke argued in *Two Treatises of Government* that the individual placed some of his rights present in the state of nature in trusteeship with the sovereign (government) in return for protection of certain natural individual rights. A social contract was entered into by the people.

Until 1694, England had an elaborate system of licensing. No publication was allowed without the accompaniment of a government-granted license. Fifty years earlier, at a time of civil war, John Milton wrote his pamphlet *Areopagitica*. In this work Milton argued forcefully against this form of government censorship and parodied the idea, writing "when as debtors and delinquents may walk abroad without a keeper, but unoffensive books must not stir forth without a visible jailer in their title." Although at the time it did little to halt the practice of licensing it would be viewed later a significant milestone in press freedom.

Milton's central argument was that the individual is capable of using reason and distinguishing right from wrong, good from bad. In order to be able to exercise this ration right, the individual must have unlimited access to the ideas of his fellow men in "a free and open encounter." From Milton's writings developed the concept of the open marketplace of ideas, the idea that when people argue against each other, the good arguments will prevail. One form of speech that was widely restricted in England was seditious libel, and laws were in place that made criticizing the government a crime. The King was above public criticism and statements critical of the government were forbidden, according to the English Court of the Star Chamber. Truth was not a defence to seditious libel because the goal was to prevent and punish all condemnation of the government.

John Stuart Mill approached the problem of authority versus liberty from the viewpoint of a 19th century utilitarian: The individual has the right of expressing himself so long as he does not harm other individuals. The good society is one in which the greatest number of persons enjoy the greatest possible amount of happiness. Applying these general principles of liberty to freedom of expression, Mill states that if we silence an opinion, we may silence the truth. The individual freedom of expression is therefore essential to the well-being of society.

Mill's application of the general principles of liberty is expressed in his book On Liberty: "If all mankind minus one, were of one opinion, and one, and only one person were of the contrary opinion, mankind would be no more justified in silencing that one person, than he, if he had the power, would be justified in silencing mankind".

Nazi Germany

The dictatorship of Adolf Hitler largely suppressed freedom of the press through Joseph Goebbels' Ministry of Public Enlightenment and Propaganda. As the Ministry's name implies, propaganda did not carry the negative connotations that it does today (or did in the Allied countries); how-to manuals were openly distributed by that same ministry explaining the craft of effective propaganda. The Ministry also acted as a central control-point for all media, issuing orders as to what stories could be run and what stories would be suppressed. Anyone involved in the film industry — from directors to the lowliest assistant — had to sign an oath of loyalty to the Nazi Party, due to opinion-changing power Goebbels perceived movies to have. (Goebbels himself maintained some personal control over every single film made in Nazi Europe.) Journalists who crossed the Propaganda Ministry were routinely imprisoned or shot as traitors.

India

The Indian Constitution, while not mentioning the word "press", provides for *"the right to freedom of speech and expression"* (Article 19(1) a). However this right is subject to restrictions under sub clause (2), whereby this freedom can be restricted for reasons of "sovereignty and integrity of India, the security of the State, friendly relations with foreign States, public order, preserving decency, preserving morality, in relation to contempt, court, defamation, or incitement to an offense". Laws such as the Official Secrets Act and Prevention of Terrorism Act (PoTA) have been used to limit press freedom. Under PoTA, person could be detained for up to six months for being in contact with a terrorist or terrorist group. PoTA was repealed in 2006, but the Official Secrets Act 1923 continues. For the first half-century of independence, media control by the state was the major constraint on press freedom. Indira Gandhi famously stated in 1975 that All India Radio is "a Government organ, it is going to remain a Government organ..." With the liberalization starting in the 1990s, private control of media has burgeoned, leading to increasing independence and greater scrutiny of government. Organizations like Tehelka and NDTV have been particularly influential, e.g. in bringing about the resignation of powerful Haryana minister Venod Sharma however this freedom of speech and expression is automatically canceled during emergency. The word Reasonable was not present in the original article 19(1)(a. But this was later on added to this article, and presently in India there are number of organizations who are really influential.

IMPLICATIONS OF NEW TECHNOLOGIES

Many of the traditional means of delivering information are being slowly superseded by the increasing pace of modern technological advance. Almost every conventional mode of media and information dissemination has a modern counterpart that offers significant potential advantages to journalists seeking to maintain and enhance their 'freedom of speech'. A few simple examples of such phenomena include:

- Terrestrial television versus satellite television: Whilst terrestrial television is relatively easy to manage and manipulate, satellite television is much more difficult to control as journalistic content can easily be broadcast from other jurisdictions beyond the control of individual governments. An example of this in the Middle East is the satellite broadcaster Al Jazeera. This Arabic language media channel operates out of the 'relatively liberal' state of Qatar, and often presents views and content that are problematic to a number of governments in the region and beyond. However, because of the increased affordability and miniaturisation of satellite technology (e.g. dishes and receivers) it is simply not practicable for most states to control popular access to the channel.
- Web-based publishing (e.g., blogging) vs. traditional publishing: Traditional magazines and newspapers rely on physical resources (e.g. offices, printing presses) that can easily be targeted and forced to close down. Web-based publishing systems can be run using ubiquitous and inexpensive equipment and can operate from any global jurisdiction. To get control over web publications, nations and organisations are using Geolocation and Geolocation software.
- Voice over Internet protocol (VOIP) vs. conventional telephony: Although conventional telephony systems are easily tapped and recorded, modern VOIP technology can employ sophisticated encryption systems to evade central monitoring systems. As VOIP and similar technologies become more widespread they are likely to make the effective monitoring of journalists (and their contacts and activities) a very difficult task for governments.

Naturally, governments are responding to the challenges posed by new media technologies by deploying increasingly sophisticated technology of their own (a notable example being China's attempts to impose control through a state run internet service provider that controls access to the Internet) but it seems that this will becomes an ever increasingly difficult task as journalists continue to find new ways to exploit technology and stay one step ahead of the generally slower moving government institutions that attempt to censor them.

The First Amendment to the United States Constitution provides that "Congress shall make no law... abridging the freedom of speech, or of the press...." This language restricts government both more and less than it would if it were applied literally. It restricts government more in that it applies not only to Congress, but to all branches of the federal government, and to all branches of state and local government. It restricts government less in that it provides no protection to some types of speech and only limited protection to others.

This report provides an overview of the major exceptions to the First Amendment — of the ways that the Supreme Court has interpreted the guarantee of freedom of speech and press to provide no protection or only limited protection for some types of speech. For example, the Court has decided that the First Amendment provides no protection to obscenity, child pornography, or speech that constitutes "advocacy of the use of force or of law violation... where such advocacy is directed to inciting or producing imminent lawless action and is likely to incite or produce such action."

The Court has also decided that the First Amendment provides less than full protection to commercial speech, defamation (libel and slander), speech that maybe harmful to children, speech broadcast on radio and television, and public employees' speech. Even speech that enjoys the most extensive First Amendment protection may be subject to "regulations of the time, place, and manner of expression which are content-neutral, are narrowly tailored to serve a significant government interest, and leave open ample alternative channels of communication." And, even speech that enjoys the most extensive First Amendment protection may be restricted on the basis of its content if the restriction passes "strict scrutiny," i.e., if the government shows that the restriction serves "to promote a compelling interest" and is "the least restrictive means to further the articulated interest."

OBSCENITY

Obscenity apparently is unique in being the only type of speech to which the Supreme Court has denied First Amendment protection without regard to whether it is harmful to individuals. According to the Court, there is evidence that, at the time of the adoption of the First Amendment, obscenity "was outside the protection intended for speech and press." Consequently, obscenity may be banned simply because a legislature concludes that banning it protects "the social interest in order and morality." No actual harm, let alone compelling governmental interest, need be shown in order to ban it. What is obscenity? It is not synonymous with pornography, as most pornography is not legally obscene; i.e., most pornography is protected by the First Amendment.

To be obscene, pornography must, at a minimum, "depict or describe patently offensive 'hard core' sexual conduct." The Supreme Court has created a three-part test, known as the Miller test, to determine whether a work is obscene. The Miller test asks: (a) whether the "average person applying contemporary community standards" would find that the work, taken as a whole, appeals to the prurient interest; (b) whether the work depicts or describes, in a patently offensive way, sexual conduct specifically defined by the applicable state law; and (c) whether the work, taken as a whole, lacks serious literary, artistic, political, or scientific value.

The Supreme Court has clarified that only "the first and second prongs of the Millertest — appeal to prurient interest and patent offensiveness — are issues of fact for the jury to determine applying contemporary community standards." As for the third prong, "[t]he proper inquiry is not whether an ordinary member of any given

CHILD PORNOGRAPHY

Child pornography is material that visually depicts sexual conduct by children. It is unprotected by the First Amendment even when it is not obscene; i.e., child pornography need not meet the Miller test to be banned. Because of the legislative interest in destroying the market for the exploitative use of children, there is no constitutional right to possess child pornography even in the privacy of one's own home. In 1996, Congress enacted the Child Pornography Protection Act (CPPA), which defined "child pornography" to include visual depictions that appear to be of a minor, even if no minor is actually used.

The Supreme Court, however, declared the CPPA unconstitutional to the extent that it prohibited pictures that are produced without actual minors. Pornography that uses actual children may be banned because laws against it target "[t]he production of the work, not its content"; the CPPA, by contrast, targeted the content, not the production. The government "may not prohibit speech because it increases the chance an unlawful act will be committed 'at some indefinite future time.'"

In 2003, Congress responded by enacting Title V of the PROTECT Act, P.L. 108-21, which prohibits any "digital image, computer image, or computer-generated image that is, or is indistinguishable from, that of a minor engaging in sexually explicit conduct." It also prohibits "a visual depiction of any kind, including a drawing, cartoon, sculpture, or painting, that... depicts a minor engaging in sexually explicit conduct," and is obscene or lacks serious literary, artistic, political, or scientific value.

CONTENT-BASED RESTRICTIONS

Justice Holmes, in one of his most famous opinions, wrote: The most stringent protection of free speech would not protect a man in falsely shouting fire in a theater and causing a panic.... The question in every case is whether the words used... create a clear and present danger.... In its current formulation of this principle, the Supreme Court held that "advocacy of the use of force or of law violation" is protected unless "such advocacy is directed to inciting or producing imminent lawless action and is likely to incite or produce such action." Similarly, the Court held that a statute prohibiting threats against the life of the President could be applied only against speech that constitutes a "true threat," and not against mere "political hyperbole."

In cases of content-based restrictions of speech other than advocacy or threats, the Supreme Court generally applies "strict scrutiny," which means that it will uphold a content-based restriction only if it is necessary "to promote a compelling interest," and is "the least restrictive means to further the articulated interest." Thus, it is ordinarily unconstitutional for a state to proscribe a newspaper from publishing the name of a rape victim, lawfully obtained.

By contrast, "[n]o one would question but that a government might prevent actual obstruction to its recruiting service or the publication of the sailing dates of transports or the number and location of troops." Similarly, the government may proscribe "'fighting' words — those which by their very utterance inflict injury or tend to incite an immediate breach of the peace." Here the Court was referring to utterances that constitute "epithets or personal abuse" that "are no essential part of any exposition of ideas," as opposed to, for example, flag burning, which is discussed below, under "Symbolic Speech."

NON-CONTENT-BASED RESTRICTIONS

If the government limits speech, but its purpose in doing so is not based on the content of the speech, then the limitation on speech may still violate the First Amendment, but it is less likely than a content-based restriction to do so. This is because the Supreme Court applies less than "strict scrutiny" to non-content-based restrictions. With respect to non-content-based restrictions, the Court requires that the governmental interest be "significant" or "substantial" or "important," but not necessarily, as with content-based restrictions, "compelling."

And, in the case of non-content-based restrictions, the Court requires that the restriction be narrowly tailored, but not, as with content-based restrictions, that it be the least restrictive means to advance the governmental interest. Two types of speech restrictions that receive this "intermediate" scrutiny are (1) time, place, or manner restrictions, and (2) incidental restrictions, which are restrictions aimed at conduct other than speech, but that incidentally restrict speech. This report includes separate sections on these two types of restrictions. In addition, restrictions on commercial speech, though content-based, are subject to similar intermediate scrutiny; this report also includes a separate section on commercial speech.

PRIOR RESTRAINT

There are two ways in which the government may attempt to restrict speech. The more common way is to make a particular category of speech, such as obscenity or defamation, subject to criminal prosecution or civil suit, and then, if someone engages in the proscribed category of speech, to hold a trial and impose sanctions if appropriate. The second way is by prior restraint, which may occur in two ways. First, a statute may require that a person submit the speech that he wishes to disseminate — a movie, for example — to a governmental body for a license to disseminate it — e.g., to show the movie. Second, a court may issue a temporary restraining order or an injunction against engaging in particular speech — publishing the Pentagon Papers, for example.

With respect to both these types of prior restraint, the Supreme Court has written that"[a]ny system of prior restraint of expression comes to this Court bearing a heavy presumption against its constitutional validity." Prior restraints, it has held, are the most serious and least tolerable infringement on First Amendment rights.... A prior restraint... by definition, has an immediate and irreversible sanction. If it can be said that a threat of criminal or civil sanctions after publication "chills" speech, prior restraint "freezes" it at least for the time. The damage can be particularly great when the prior restraint falls upon the communication of news and commentary on current events.

The Supreme Court has written that "[t]he special vice of a prior restraint is that communication will be suppressed... before an adequate determination that it is unprotected by the First Amendment." The prohibition on prior restraint, thus, is essentially a limitation on restraints until a final judicial determination that the restricted speech is not protected by the First Amendment. It is a limitation, for example, against temporary restraining orders and preliminary injunctions pending final judgment, not against permanent injunctions after a final judgment is made that the restricted speech is not protected by the First Amendment. In the case of a statute that imposes prior restraint, "a prescreening arrangement can pass constitutional muster if it includes adequate procedural safeguards."

These procedural safeguards, the Court wrote, include that "the burden of proving that the film is unprotected expression must rest on the censor," and "that the censor will, within a specified brief period, either issue a license or go to court to restrain showing the film." In the case of time, place, or manner restrictions (and presumably other forms of speech that do not receive full First Amendment protection), lesser procedural safeguards are adequate. Prior restraints are permitted in some circumstances.

The Supreme Court has written, in dictum, "that traditional prior restraint doctrine may not apply to [commercial speech]," and the Court has not ruled whether it does. "The vast majority of [federal] circuits... do not apply the doctrine of prior restraint to commercial speech." "Some circuits [however] have explicitly indicated that the requirement of procedural safeguards in the context of a prior restraint indeed applies to commercial speech." Furthermore, "only content-based injunctions are subject to prior restraint analysis."

COMMERCIAL SPEECH

"The Constitution... affords a lesser protection to commercial speech than to other constitutionally guaranteed expression." Commercial speech is "speech that proposes a commercial transaction." That books and films are published and sold for profit does not make them commercial speech; i.e., it does not "prevent them from being a form of expression whose liberty is safeguarded [to the maximum extent] by the First Amendment." Commercial speech, however, may be banned if it is false or misleading, or if it advertises an illegal product or service. Even if fits in none of these categories, the government may regulate it more than it may regulate fully protected speech. In addition, the government may generally require disclosures to be included in commercial speech; see the section on "Compelled Speech," below. The Supreme Court has prescribed the four-prong Central Hudson test to determine whether a governmental regulation of commercial speech is constitutional. This test asks initially (1) whether the commercial speech at issue is protected by the First Amendment (that is, whether it concerns a lawful activity and is not misleading) and (2) whether the asserted governmental interest in restricting it is substantial. "If both inquiries yield positive answers," then to be constitutional the restriction must (3) "directly advance the governmental interest asserted," and (4) be "not more extensive than is necessary to serve that interest."

The Supreme Court has held that, in applying the third prong of the Central Hudson test, the courts should consider whether the regulation, in its general application, directly advances the governmental interest asserted. If it does, then it need not advance the governmental interest as applied to the particular person or entity challenging it. Its application to the particular person or entity challenging it is relevant in applying the fourth Central Hudson factor, although this factor too is to be viewed in terms of "the relation it bears to the overall problem the government seeks to correct."

The fourth prong is not to be interpreted "strictly" to require the legislature to use the "least restrictive means" available to accomplish its purpose. Instead, the Court has held, legislation regulating commercial speech satisfies the fourth prong if there is a reasonable "fit" between the legislature's ends and the means chosen to accomplish those ends.

The Supreme Court has applied the Central Hudson test in all the commercial speech cases it has decided since Central Hudson, and we discuss the ten most recent below, in chronological order. In nine of these cases, the Court struck down the challenged speech restriction; it has not upheld a commercial speech restriction since 1993.

In its most recent commercial speech case, Thompson v. Western States Medical Centre, the Court noted that "several Members of the Court have expressed doubts about the Central Hudson analysis and whether it should apply in particular cases." These justices believe that the test does not provide adequate protection to commercial speech, but the Court has found it unnecessary to consider whether to abandon the test, because it has been striking down the statutes in question anyway. In Cincinnati v. Discovery Network, Inc., the Court struck down a Cincinnati regulation that banned news racks on public property if they distributed commercial publications, but not if they distributed news publications.

As for the first two prongs of the Central Hudson test, the Court found that the commercial publications at issue were not unlawful or misleading, and that the asserted governmental interest in safety and esthetics was substantial. As for the third and fourth prongs, although banning commercial newsracks presumably advances the asserted governmental interests, the distinction between commercial and noncommercial speech "bears no relationship whatsoever to the particular interests that the city has asserted."

The city, therefore, did not establish "the 'fit' between its goals and its chosen means that is required by our opinion in Fox." In Edenfield v. Fane, the Court struck down a Florida ban on solicitation by certified public accountants, even though the Court had previously, in Ohralik v. upheld a ban on solicitation by attorneys. The Court found that the government had substantial interests in the ban, including the prevention of fraud, the protection of privacy, and the need to maintain CPA independence and to guard against conflicts of interest.

However, the Court found no evidence that the ban directly advanced these interests, and noted, among other things, that, "[u]nlike a lawyer, a CPA is not 'a professional trained in the art of persuasion,'" and "[t]he typical client of a CPA is far less susceptible to manipulation than the young accident victim in Ohralik." The Court added, more generally, that the government's burden in justifying a restriction on commercial speech "is not satisfied by mere speculation or conjecture; rather, a governmental body seeking to sustain a restriction on commercial speech must demonstrate that the harms it recites are real and that its restriction will in fact alleviate them to a material degree."

In United States v. Edge Broadcasting Co., the Court upheld "federal statutes that prohibit the broadcast of lottery advertising by a broadcaster licensed to a State that does not allow lotteries, while allowing such broadcasting by a broadcaster licensed to a State that sponsors a lottery...."

The governmental interest in the statutes was to balance the interests of states that prohibit lotteries and states that operate lotteries. The broadcaster that challenged the statutes was licensed in North Carolina, which does not allow lotteries, but broadcasted from only three miles from the Virginia border, which does allow lotteries.

The broadcaster claimed that prohibiting it from broadcasting advertisements for the Virginia lottery did not advance the governmental interest or represent a "reasonable fit" because North Carolina radio listeners in its area were already inundated with advertisements from Virginia stations advertising the Virginia lottery and because most of the broadcaster's listeners were in Virginia. The Supreme Court upheld the statutes because, even if they did not advance the governmental interest or represent a reasonable fit as applied to the particular broadcaster, they did as applied to the overall problem the government sought to address.

The Court found sufficiently substantial to satisfy the second prong of the *Central Hudson* test the government's interest in curbing "strength wars" by beer brewers who might seek to compete for customers on the basis of alcohol content. However, it concluded that the ban "cannot directly and materially advance" this "interest because of the overall irrationality of the Government's regulatory scheme." This irrationality is evidenced by the fact that the ban does not apply to beer advertisements, and by the fact that the statute *requires* the disclosure of alcohol content on the labels of wines and spirits. In *Florida Bar v. Went For It, Inc.*, the Court upheld a rule of the Florida Bar that prohibited personal injury lawyers from sending targeted direct-mail solicitations to victims and their relatives for 30 days following an accident or disaster.

The Bar argued "that it has a substantial interest in protecting the privacy and tranquility of personal injury victims and their loved ones against intrusive, unsolicited contact by lawyers," and the Court found that "[t]he anecdotal record mustered by the Bar" to demonstrate that its rule would advance this interest in a direct and material way was "noteworthy for its breadth and detail"; it was not "mere speculation and conjecture." Therefore, the rule passed what the Court called the second prong of the *Central Hudson* test.

As for the final prong, the Court found the Bar's rule to be "reasonably well tailored to its stated objective...." In a subsequent case, the Court wrote that, in *Florida Bar v. Went For It, Inc.*, it had "upheld a 30-dayprohibition against a certain form of legal solicitation largely because it left so many channels of communication open to Florida lawyers." In *44 Liquormart, Inc. v. Rhode Island*, the Court, struck down a state statute that prohibited disclosure of retail prices in advertisements for alcoholic beverages. In the process, it increased the protection that the *Central Hudson* test guarantees to commercial speech by making clear that a total prohibition on "the dissemination of truthful, non misleading commercial messages for reasons unrelated to the preservation of a fair bargaining process" will be subject to a stricter review by the courts than a regulation designed "to protect consumers from misleading, deceptive, or aggressive sales practices." The Court added: "The First Amendment directs us to be especially skeptical of regulations that seek to keep people in the dark for what the government perceives to be their own good."

It concluded "that the price advertising ban cannot survive the more stringent constitutional review that *Central Hudson* itself concluded was appropriate for the complete suppression of truthful, non misleading commercial speech." In *Greater New Orleans Broadcasting Association, Inc. v. United States,* the Court applied the *Central Hudson* test to strike down, as applied to advertisements of private casino gambling that are broadcast by radio or television stations located in Louisiana, where such gambling is legal, the same federal statute it had upheld in as applied to broadcast advertising of Virginia's lottery by a radio station located in North Carolina, where no such lottery was authorized.

The Court emphasized the interrelatedness of the four parts of the *Central Hudson* test; e.g., though the government has a substantial interest in reducing the social costs of gambling, the fact that the Congress has simultaneously encouraged gambling, because of its economic benefits, makes it more difficult for the government to demonstrate that its restriction on commercial speech materially advances its asserted interest and constitutes a reasonable "fit."

In this case, "[t]he operation of [18 U.S.C.] 1304 and its attendant regulatory regime is so pierced by exemptions and inconsistencies that the Government cannot hope to exonerate it.... [T]he regulation distinguishes among the indistinct, permitting a variety of speech that poses the same risks the Government purports to fear, while banning messages unlikely to cause any harm at all." In *Lorillard Tobacco Co. v. Reilly,* the Supreme Court applied the *Central Hudson* test to strike down most of the Massachusetts Attorney General's regulations governing the advertising and sale of cigarettes, smokeless tobacco, and cigars.

The Court first found the "outdoor and point-of-sale advertising regulations targeting cigarettes" to be preempted by the Federal Cigarette Labeling and Advertising Act, 15 U.S.C. 1331-1341. By its terms, however, this statute's preemption provision applies only to cigarettes, so the Court considered the smokeless tobacco and cigar petitioners' First Amendment challenges to the outdoor and point-of-sale advertising regulations. Further, the cigarette petitioners did not raise a preemption challenge to Massachusetts' sales practices regulations (regulations, described below, other than outdoor and point-of-sale advertising regulations), so the Court considered the cigarette as well as the smokeless tobacco and cigar petitioners' claim that these regulations violate the First Amendment.

The Court struck down the outdoor advertising regulations under the fourth prong of the *Central Hudson* test, finding that the prohibition of any advertising within 1,000 feet of schools or playgrounds "prohibit[ed] advertising in a substantial portion of the major metropolitan areas of Massachusetts," and that such a burden on speech did not constitute a reasonable fit between the means and ends of the regulatory scheme. "Similarly, a ban on all signs of any size seems ill suited to target the problem of highly visible billboards, as opposed to smaller signs." The Court found "that the point-of-sale advertising regulations fail both the third and fourth steps of the *Central Hudson* analysis."

The prohibition on advertising "placed lower than five feet from the floor of any retail establishment which is located within a one thousand foot radius of" any school or playground did not advance the goal of preventing minors from using tobacco products because "[n]ot all children are less than 5 feet tall, and those who are certainly have the ability to look up and take in their surroundings." The Court, however, upheld the sales practices regulations that "bar the use of self-service displays and require that tobacco products be placed out of the reach of all consumers in a location accessible only to salespersons."

These regulations, though they "regulate conduct that may have a communicative component," do so "for reasons unrelated to the communications of ideas." The Court therefore applied the *O'Brien* test for incidental restrictions of speech and concluded "that the State has demonstrated a substantial interest in preventing access to tobacco products by minors and has adopted an appropriately narrow means of advancing that interest." In *Thompson v. Western States Medical Centre*, the Court struck down section 503A of the Food, Drug, and Cosmetic Act, 21 U.S.C. § 353a, which "exempts 'compounded drugs' from the Food and Drug Administration's standard drug approval requirements as long as the providers of those drugs abide by several restrictions, including that they refrain from advertising or promoting particular compounded drugs."

"Drug compounding," the Court explained, "is a process by which a pharmacist or doctor combines, mixes, or alters ingredients to create a medication tailored to the needs of an individual patient." The Court found that the speech restriction in this case served "important" governmental interests, but that, "[e]ven assuming" that it directly advances these interests, it failed the fourth prong of the *Central Hudson* test. In considering the fourth prong, the Court wrote that "the Government has failed to demonstrate that the speech restrictions are 'not more extensive than is necessary to serve'" the governmental interests, as "[s]everal non- speech-related means [of serving those interests] might be possible here."

"If the First Amendment means anything," the Court added, "it means that regulating speech must be a last — not first — resort. Yet here it seems to have been the first strategy the Government thought to try." The Court noted that it had "rejected the notion that the Government has an interest in preventing the dissemination of truthful commercial information in order to prevent members of the public from making bad decisions with the information."

In saying that the government failed to demonstrate that the speech restrictions were "not more extensive than is necessary to serve" the governmental interests, the Court was quoting from the fourth prong of the *Central Hudson* test, but nowhere in *Thompson* did it note that it had previously modified the fourth prong to require merely a reasonable "fit" between the legislature's ends and means, and not use of the least restrictive means to serve the governmental interests. Rather, it wrote: "In previous cases addressing this final prong of the *Central Hudson* test, we have made clear that if the Government could achieve its interests in a manner that does not restrict speech, or that restricts less speech, the Government must do so." Yet the Court did not state that it intended to overrule its reasonable "fit" construction of the fourth prong.

DEFAMATION

Defamation (libel is written defamation; slander is oral defamation) is the intentional communication of a falsehood about a person, to someone other than that person, that injures the person's reputation. The injured person may sue and recover damages under state law, unless state law makes the defamation privileged (for example, a statement made in a judicial, legislative, executive, or administrative proceeding is ordinarily privileged). Being required to pay damages for a defamatory statement restricts one's freedom of speech; defamation, therefore, constitutes an exception to the First Amendment.

The Supreme Court, however, has granted limited First Amendment protection to defamation. The Court has held that public officials and public figures may not recover damages for defamation unless they prove, with "convincing clarity," that the defamatory statement was made with "'actual malice' — that is, with knowledge that it was false or with reckless disregard of whether it was false or not."

The Court has also held that a private figure who sues a media defendant for defamation may not recover without some showing of fault, although not necessarily of actual malice (unless the relevant state law requires it). However, if a defamatory falsehood involves a matter of public concern, then even a private figure must show actual malice in order to recover presumed damages (i.e., not actual financial damages) or punitive damages.

SPEECH HARMFUL TO CHILDREN

Speech that is otherwise fully protected by the First Amendment may be restricted in order to protect children. This is because the Court has "recognized that there is a compelling interest in protecting the physical and psychological well-being of minors." However, any restriction must be accomplished "'by narrowly drawn regulations without unnecessarily interfering with First Amendment freedoms.'

It is not enough to show that the government's ends are compelling; the means must be carefully tailored to achieve those ends." Thus, the government may prohibit the sale to minors of material that it deems "harmful to minors" ("so called 'girlie' magazines"), whether or not they are not obscene as to adults. It may prohibit the broadcast of "indecent" language on radio and television during hours when children are likely to be in the audience, but it may not ban it around the clock unless it is obscene.

Similarly, Congress may not ban dial-a-porn, but it may prohibit it from being made available to minors or to persons who have not previously requested it in writing. In *Reno v. American Civil Liberties Union*, the Supreme Court declared unconstitutional two provisions of the Communications Decency Act (CDA) that prohibited indecent communications to minors on the Internet. The Court held that the CDA's "burden on adult speech is unacceptable if less restrictive alternatives would be at least as effective in achieving the legitimate purpose that the statute was enacted to serve." "[T]he governmental interest in protecting children from harmful materials... does not justify an unnecessarily broad suppression of speech addressed to adults.

As we have explained, the Government may not 'reduc[e] the adult population... to... only what is fit for children.'" The Court distinguished the Internet from radio and television because (1) "[t]he CDA's broad categorical prohibitions are not limited to particular times and are not dependent on any evaluation by an agency familiar with the unique characteristics of the Internet," (2) the CDA imposes criminal penalties, and the Court has never decided whether indecent broadcasts "would justify a criminal prosecution," and (3) radio and television, unlike the Internet, have, "as a matter of history... 'received the most limited First Amendment protection... in large part because warnings could not adequately protect the listener from unexpected programme content.... [On the Internet], the risk of encountering indecent material by accident is remote because a series of affirmative steps is required to access specific material."

In 1998, Congress enacted the Child Online Protection Act (COPA), P.L. 105- 277, title XIV, to replace the CDA. COPA differs from the CDA in two main respects: (1) it prohibits communication to minors only of "material that is harmful to minors," rather than material that is indecent, and (2) it applies only to communications for commercial purposes on publicly accessible websites. COPA has not taken effect, because a constitutional challenge was brought and the district court, finding a likelihood that the plaintiffs would prevail, issued a preliminary injunction against enforcement of the statute, pending a trial on the merits.

The Third Circuit affirmed, but, in 2002, in *Ashcroft v. American Civil Liberties Union*, the Supreme Court held that COPA's use of community standards to define "material that is harmful to minors" does not by itself render the statute unconstitutional. The Supreme Court, however, did not remove the preliminary injunction against enforcement of the statute, and remanded the case to the Third Circuit to consider whether it is unconstitutional nonetheless. In2003, the Third Circuit again found the plaintiffs likely to prevail and affirmed the preliminary injunction.

In 2004, the Supreme Court affirmed the preliminary injunction because it found that the government had failed to show that filtering prohibited material would not be as effective in accomplishing Congress's goals. It remanded the case for trial, however, and did not foreclose the district court from concluding otherwise. On March 22, 2007, the district court found COPA unconstitutional and issued a permanent injunction against its enforcement.

The grounds for its decision were that "COPA is not narrowly tailored to Congress' compelling interest," the Attorney General "failed to meet his burden of showing that COPA is the least restrictive, most effective alternative in achieving the compelling interest," and "COPA is impermissibly vague and overbroad."

CHILDREN'S FIRST AMENDMENT RIGHTS

In a case upholding high school students' right to wear black arm bands to protest the war in Vietnam, the Supreme Court held that public school students do not "shed their constitutional rights to freedom of speech or expression at the schoolhouse gate." They do, however, shed them to some extent. The Supreme Court has upheld the suspension of a student for using a sexual metaphor in a speech nominating another student for a student office. It has upheld censorship of a student newspaper produced as part of the school curriculum. (Lower courts have indicated that non-school-sponsored student writings may not be censored.)

A plurality of the justices found that a school board must be permitted "to establish and apply their curriculum in such away as to transmit community values," but that it may not remove school library books in order to deny access to ideas with Board of Education, Island Trees School District v. Pico, 457 U.S. 853, 864 (1982). The Court noted that "nothing in our decision today affects in any way the discretion of a local school board to choose books to *add* to the libraries of their schools."

The Supreme Court has also held that Congress may not prohibit people 17 or younger from making contributions to political candidates and contributions or donations to political parties. Most recently, in *Morse v. Frederick*, the Court held that a school could punish a pupil for displaying a banner that read, "BONG HiTS 4 JESUS," because these words could reasonably be interpreted as "promoting illegal drug use."

The Court indicated that it might have reached a different result if the banner had addressed the issue of "the criminalization of drug use or possession." Justice Alito, joined by Justice Kennedy, wrote a concurring opinion stating that they had joined the majority opinion "on the understanding that

- It goes no further than to hold that a public school may restrict speech that a reasonable observer would interpret as advocating illegal drug use and
- It provides no support for any restriction on speech that can plausibly be interpreted as commenting on any political or social issue, including speech on issues such as 'the wisdom of the war on drugs or of legalizing marijuana for medicinal use.'"

As *Morse v. Frederick* was a 5-to-4 decision, Justices Alito's and Kennedy's votes were necessary for a majority and therefore should be read as limiting the majority opinion with respect to future cases.

TIME, PLACE, AND MANNER RESTRICTIONS

Even speech that enjoys the most extensive First Amendment protection may be subject to "regulations of the time, place, and manner of expression which are content-neutral, are narrowly tailored to serve a significant government interest, and leave open ample alternative channels of communication." In the case in which this language appears, the Supreme Court allowed a city ordinance that banned picketing "before or about" any residence to be enforced to prevent picketing outside the residence of a doctor who performed abortions, even though the picketing occurred on a public street. The Court noted that"[t]he First Amendment permits the government to prohibit offensive speech as intrusive when the 'captive' audience cannot avoid the objectionable speech."

Other significant governmental interests, besides protection of captive audiences, may justify content-neutral time, place, and manner restrictions. For example, in order to prevent crime and maintain property values, a city may place zoning restrictions on "adult" theaters and bookstores. And, in order to maintain the orderly movements of crowds at a state fair, a state may limit the distribution of literature to assigned locations. However, a time, place, and manner restriction will not be upheld in the absence of sufficient justification or if it is not narrowly tailored. Thus, the Court held unconstitutional a total restriction on displaying flags or banners on public sidewalks surrounding the Supreme Court.

And a time, place, and manner restriction will not be upheld if it fails to "leave open ample alternative channels for communication." Thus, the Court held unconstitutional an ordinance that prohibited the display of signs from residences, because "[d]isplaying a sign from one's own residence often carries a message quite distinct from placing the same sign someplace else...." When a court issues an *injunction* that restricts the time, place, or manner of a particular form of expression, because prior restraint occurs, "a somewhat more stringent application of general First Amendment principles" is required than is required in the case of a generally applicable statute or ordinance that restricts the time, place, or manner of speech.

Instead of asking whether the restrictions are "narrowly tailored to serve a significant governmental interest," a court must ask "whether the challenged provisions of the injunction burden no more speech than necessary to serve a significant government interest." Applying this standard, the Supreme Court, in *Madsen v. Women's Health Centre, Inc.*, upheld a state court injunction that had ordered the establishment of a 36-foot buffer zone on a public street outside a particular health clinic that performed abortions. The Court in this case also upheld an injunction against noise during particular hours, but found that a "broad prohibition on all 'images observable' burdens speech more than necessary to achieve the purpose of limiting threats to clinic patients or their families."

It also struck down a prohibition on all uninvited approaches of persons seeking the services of the clinic, and a prohibition against picketing, within 300 feet of the residences of clinic staff. The Court distinguished the 300-foot restriction from the ordinance it had previously upheld that banned picketing "before or about" any residence. In *Schenck v. Pro-Choice Network of Western New York*, the Court applied *Madsen* to another injunction that placed restrictions on demonstrating outside an abortion clinic.

The Court upheld the portion of the injunction that banned "demonstrating within fifteen feet from either side or edge of, or in front of, doorways or doorway entrances, parking lot entrances, driveways and driveway entrances of such facilities" — what the Court called "fixed buffer zones." It struck down a prohibition against demonstrating "within fifteen feet of any person or vehicles seeking access to or leaving such facilities" — what it called "floating buffer zones." The Court cited "public safety and order" in upholding the fixed buffer zones, but it found that the floating buffer zones "burden more speech than is necessary to serve the relevant governmental interests" because they make it "quite difficult for a protester who wishes to engage in peaceful expressive activity to know how to remain in compliance with the injunction."

The Court also upheld a "provision, specifying that once sidewalk counselors who had entered the buffer zones were required to 'cease and desist' their counseling, they had to retreat 15 feet from the people they had been counseling and had to remain outside the boundaries of the buffer zones." In *Hill v. Colorado*, the Court upheld a Colorado statute that makes it unlawful, within 100 feet of the entrance to any health care facility, to "knowingly approach" within eight feet of another person, without that person's consent, "for the purpose of passing a leaflet or handbill to, displaying a sign to, or engaging in oral protest, education, or counseling with such other person."

This decision is significant because it upheld a statute that applies to everyone, and not, as in *Madsen* and *Schenck*, merely an injunction directed to particular parties.

The Court found the statute to be a content-neutral time, place, and manner regulation of speech that "reflects an acceptable balance between the constitutionally protected rights of law- abiding speakers and the interests of unwilling listeners...." The restrictions are content-neutral because they regulate only the places where some speech may occur, and because they apply equally to all demonstrators, regardless of viewpoint. Although the restrictions do not apply to all speech, the "kind of cursory examination" that might be required to distinguish casual conversation from protest, education, or counseling is not "problematic."

The law is "narrowly tailored" to achieve the state's interests. The eight-foot restriction does not significantly impair the ability to convey messages by signs, and ordinarily allows speakers to come within a normal conversational distance of their targets. Because the statute allows the speaker to remain in one place, persons who wish to hand out leaflets may position themselves beside entrances near the path of oncoming pedestrians, and consequently are not deprived of the opportunity to get the attention of persons entering a clinic.

INCIDENTAL RESTRICTIONS

Some laws are not designed to limit freedom of expression, but nevertheless can have that effect. For example, when a National Park Service regulation prohibiting camping in certain parks was applied to prohibit demonstrators, who were attempting to call attention to the plight of the homeless, from sleeping in certain Washington, D.C. parks, it had the effect of limiting the demonstrators' freedom of expression. Nevertheless, the Court found that application of the regulation did not violate the First Amendment because the regulation was content-neutral and was narrowly focused on a substantial governmental interest in maintaining parks "in an attractive and intact condition."

The Supreme Court has said that an incidental restriction on speech is constitutional if it is not "greater than necessary to further a substantial governmental interest." However, the Court has made clear that an incidental restriction, unlike a content-based restriction, "need not be the least restrictive or least intrusive means" of furthering a governmental interest. Rather, the restriction must be "narrowly tailored," and "the requirement of narrow tailoring is satisfied 'so long as the... regulation promotes a substantial governmental interest that would be achieved less effectively absent the regulation.'" The Court has noted that the standard for determining the constitutionality of an incidental restriction "in the last analysis is little, if any, different from the standard applied to time, place, or manner restrictions." Thus, the restriction on camping may be viewed as a restriction on conduct that only incidentally affects speech, or, if one views sleeping in connection with a demonstration as expressive conduct, then the restriction may be viewed as a time, place, and manner restriction on expressive conduct. In either case, as long as the restriction is content-neutral, the same standard for assessing its constitutionality will apply.

In 1991, the Supreme Court held that the First Amendment does not prevent the government from requiring that dancers wear "pasties" and a "G-string" when they dance (non-obscenely) in "adult" entertainment establishments. Indiana sought to enforce a state statute prohibiting public nudity against two such establishments, which asserted First Amendment protection. The Court found that the statute proscribed public nudity across the board, not nude dancing as such, and therefore imposed only an incidental restriction on expression. In 2000, the Supreme Court again upheld the application of a statute prohibiting public nudity to an "adult" entertainment establishment. It found that the statute was intended "to combat harmful secondary effects," such as "prostitution and other criminal activity."

In a 1994 case, the Supreme Court apparently put more teeth into the test for incidental restrictions by remanding the case for further proceedings rather than deferring to Congress's judgment as to the necessity for the "must-carry" provisions of the Cable Television Consumer Protection and Competition Act of 1992. To justify an incidental restriction of speech, the Court wrote, the government "must demonstrate that the recited harms are real, not merely conjectural, and that the regulation will in fact alleviate these harms in a direct and material way." The Court added that its obligation to exercise independent judgment when First Amendment rights are implicated is not a license to reweigh the evidence *de novo*, or to replace Congress' factual predictions with our own. Rather, it is to assure that, in formulating its judgments, Congress has drawn reasonable inferences based on substantial evidence.

SYMBOLIC SPEECH

"The First Amendment literally forbids the abridgment only of 'speech,' but we have long recognized that its protection does not end at the spoken or written word." Thus wrote the Supreme Court when it held that a statute prohibiting flag desecration violated the First Amendment. Such a statute is not content-neutral if it is designed to protect "a perceived need to preserve the flag's status as a symbol of our Nation and certain national ideals."

By contrast, the Court upheld a federal statute that made it a crime to burn a draft card, finding that the statute served "the Government's substantial interest in assuring the continuing availability of issued Selective Service certificates," and imposed only an "appropriately narrow" incidental restriction of speech. Even if Congress's purpose in enacting the statute had been to suppress freedom of speech, "this Court will not strike down an otherwise constitutional statute on the basis of an alleged illicit legislative motive."

In 1992, in *R.A.V. v. City of St. Paul*, the Supreme Court struck down an ordinance that prohibited the placing on public or private property of a symbol, such as "a burning cross or Nazi swastika, which one knows or has reasonable grounds to know arouses anger, alarm or resentment in others, on the basis of race, colour, creed, religion or gender." Read literally, this ordinance would clearly violate the First Amendment, because, "[i]f there is a bedrock principle underlying the First Amendment, it is that the Government may not prohibit the expression of an idea simply because society finds the idea itself offensive or disagreeable."

In this case, however, the Minnesota Supreme Court had construed the ordinance to apply only to conduct that amounted to fighting words. Therefore, the question for the Supreme Court was whether the ordinance, construed to apply only to fighting words, was constitutional. The Court held that it was not, because, although fighting words may be proscribed "*because of their constitutionally proscribable content*," they may not "be made the vehicles for content discrimination unrelated to their distinctively proscribable content."

Thus, the government may proscribe fighting words, but it may not make the further content discrimination of proscribing particular fighting words on the basis of hostility "towards the underlying message expressed." In this case, the ordinance banned fighting words that insult "on the basis of race, colour, religion or gender," but not "for example, on the basis of political affiliation, union membership, or homosexuality.... The First Amendment does not permit St. Paul to impose special prohibitions on those speakers who express views on disfavored subjects."

This decision does not, of course, preclude prosecution for illegal conduct that may accompany cross burning, such as trespass, arson, or threats. As the Court put it: "St. Paul has sufficient means at its disposal to prevent such behaviour without adding the First Amendment to the fire." In a subsequent case, the Supreme Court held that its opinion in *R.A.V.* did not mean that statutes that impose additional penalties for crimes that are motivated by racial hatred are unconstitutional. Such statutes imposed enhanced sentences not for bigoted thought, but for the commission of crimes that can inflict greater and individual and societal harm because of their bias-inspired motivation.

A defendant's motive has always been a factor in sentencing, and even in defining crimes; "Title VII[of the Civil Rights Act of 1964], for example, makes it unlawful for an employer to discriminate against an employee '*because of* such individual's race, colour, religion, sex, or national origin.'" In *Virginia v. Black*, the Court held that its opinion in *R.A.V.* did not make it unconstitutional for a state to prohibit burning a cross with the intent of intimidating any person or group of persons. Such a prohibition does not discriminate on the basis of a defendant's beliefs — "as a factual matter it is not true that cross burners direct their intimidating conduct solely to racial or religious minorities....

The First Amendment permits Virginia to outlaw cross burning done with the intent to intimidate because burning a cross is a particularly virulent form of intimidation. Instead of prohibiting all intimidating messages, Virginia may choose to regulate this subset of intimidating messages...."

COMPELLED SPEECH

On occasion, the government attempts to compel speech rather than to restrict it. For example, in *Riley v. National Federation of the Blind of North Carolina, Inc.*, a North Carolina statute required professional fundraisers for charities to disclose to potential donors the gross percentage of revenues retained in prior charitable solicitations.

The Supreme Court held this unconstitutional, writing. In the commercial speech context, by contrast, the Supreme Court held, in *Zauderer v. Office of Disciplinary Counsel*, that an advertiser's constitutionally protected interest in *not* providing any particular factual information in his advertising is minimal.... [A]n advertiser's rights are reasonably protected as long as disclosure requirements are reasonably related to the State's interest in preventing deception of consumers.... The right of a commercial speaker not to divulge accurate information regarding his services is not... a fundamental right.

In *Zauderer*, the Supreme Court upheld an Ohio requirement that advertisements by lawyers that mention contingent-fee rates disclose whether percentages are computed before or after deduction of court costs and expenses. In *Meese v. Keene*, however, the Court upheld compelled disclosure in a noncommercial context. This case involved a provision of the Foreign Agents Registration Act of 1938, which requires that, when an agent of a foreign principal seeks to disseminate foreign "political propaganda," he must label such material with certain information, including his identity, the principal's identity, and the fact that he has registered with the Department of Justice. The material need not state that it is "political propaganda," but one agent objected to the statute's designating material by that term, which he considered pejorative.

The agent wished to exhibit, without the required labels, three Canadian films on nuclear war and acid rain that the Justice Department had determined were "political propaganda." In *Meese v. Keene*, the Supreme Court upheld the statute's use of the term, essentially because it considered the term not necessarily pejorative. On the subject of compelled disclosure, the Court wrote: Congress did not prohibit, edit, or restrain the distribution of advocacy materials.... To the contrary, Congress simply required the disseminators of such material to make additional disclosures that would better enable the public to evaluate the import of the propaganda.

One might infer from this that compelled disclosure, in a noncommercial context, gives rise to no serious First Amendment issue, and nothing in the Court's opinion would seem to refute this inference. Thus, it seems impossible to reconcile this opinion with the Court's holding a year later in *Riley* (which did not mention *Meese v. Keene*) that, in a noncommercial context, there is no difference of constitutional significance between compelled speech and compelled silence. In *Meese v. Keene,* the Court did not mention earlier cases in which it had struck down laws compelling speech in a noncommercial context.

In *Wooley v. Maynard,* the Court struck down a New Hampshire statute requiring motorists to leave visible on their license plates the motto "Live Free or Die." In *West Virginia State Board of Education v. Barnette,* the Court held that a state may not require children to pledge allegiance to the United States. In *Miami Herald Publishing Co. v. Tornillo,* the Court struck down a Florida statute that required newspapers to grant political candidates equal space to reply to the newspapers' criticism and attacks on their record. The Court decided two cases in its 1994-1995 term involving compelled speech.

In *McIntyrev. Ohio Elections Commission,* the Court, applying strict scrutiny, struck down a compelled disclosure requirement by holding unconstitutional a state statute that prohibited the distribution of anonymous campaign literature. "The State," the Court wrote, "may, and does, punish fraud directly. But it cannot seek to punish fraud indirectly by indiscriminately outlawing a category of speech, based on its content, with no necessary relationship to the danger sought to be prevented." In *Hurley v. Irish-American Gay Group of Boston,* the Court held that Massachusetts could not require private citizens who organize a parade to include among the marchers a group imparting a message — in this case support for gay rights — that the organizers do not wish to convey.

Massachusetts had attempted to apply its statute prohibiting discrimination on the basis of sexual orientation in any place of public accommodations, but the Court held that parades are a form of expression, and the state's "[d]isapproval of a private speaker's statement does not legitimatize use of the Commonwealth's power to compel the speaker to alter the message by including one more acceptable to others." In *Glickman v. Wileman Brothers &Elliott, Inc.,* the Supreme Court upheld the constitutionality of marketing orders promulgated by the Secretary of Agriculture that imposed assessments on fruit growers to cover the cost of generic advertising of fruits.

The First Amendment, the Court held, does not preclude the government from "compel[ling] financial contributions that are used to fund advertising," provided that such contributions do not finance "political or ideological" views. In *United States v. United Foods, Inc.,* the Court struck down a federal statute that mandated assessments on handlers of fresh mushrooms to fund advertising for the product. The Court did not apply the *Central Hudson* commercial speech test, but rather found "that the mandated support is contrary to First Amendment principles set forth in cases involving expression by groups which include persons who object to the speech, but who, nevertheless, must remain members of the group bylaw or necessity."

It distinguished *Glickman* on the ground that "[i]n *Glickman* the mandated assessments for speech were ancillary to a more comprehensive programme restricting marketing authority. Here, for all practical purposes, the advertising itself, far from being ancillary, is the principal object of the regulatory scheme." In *Johanns v. Livestock Marketing Association,* the Supreme Court upheld a federal statute that directed the Secretary of Agriculture to use funds raised by an assessment on cattle sales and importation to promote the marketing and consumption of beef and beef products.

The Court found that, unlike in *Glickman* and *United Foods,* where "the speech was, or was presumed to be, that of an entity other than the government itself," in *Johanns* the promotional campaign constituted the government's own speech and therefore was "exempt from First Amendment scrutiny."

It did not matter "whether the funds for the promotions are raised by In *Action for Children's Television v. Federal Communications Commission* (ACT III), 58 F.3d 654, 660 (D.C. Cir. 1995) (en banc), *cert. denied,* 516 U.S. 1043 (1996), the court of appeals, in upholding a ban on indecent broadcasts from 6 a.m. to 10 p.m., wrote: "While we apply strict scrutiny to regulations of this kind regardless of the medium affected by them, our assessment of whether section 16(a) survives that scrutiny must necessarily take into account the unique context of the broadcast media."

As for the plaintiffs' contention "that crediting the advertising to 'America's Beef Producers'" attributes the speech to them, the Court found that, because the statute does not *require* such attribution, it does not violate the First Amendment, but the plaintiffs' contention might form the basis for challenging the manner in which the statute is applied.

RADIO AND TELEVISION

Radio and television broadcasting has more limited First Amendment protection than other media. In *Red Lion Broadcasting Co. v. Federal Communications Commission,* the Supreme Court invoked what has become known as the "scarcity rationale" to justify this discrimination: Where there are substantially more individuals who want to broadcast than there are frequencies to allocate, it is idle to posit an unabridgeable First Amendment right to broadcast comparable to the right of every individual to speak, write, or publish.

The Court made this statement in upholding the constitutionality of the Federal Communication Commission's "fairness doctrine," which required broadcast media licensees to provide coverage of controversial issues of interest to the community and to provide a reasonable opportunity for the presentation of contrasting viewpoints on such issues. Later, in *Federal Communications Commission v. Pacifica Foundation,* the Court upheld the power of the FCC "to regulate a radio broadcast that is indecent but not obscene."

The Court cited two distinctions between broadcasting and other media: "First, the broadcast media have established a uniquely pervasive presence in the lives of all Americans... confront[ing] the citizen, not only in public, but also in the privacy of the home," and "Second, broadcasting is uniquely accessible to children." In *Turner Broadcasting System, Inc. v. Federal Communications Commission*, the Court declined to question the continuing validity of the scarcity rationale, but held that "application of the more relaxed standard of scrutiny adopted in *Red Lion.*

On remand, the lower court upheld the must-carry rules, and the Supreme Court affirmed, finding "that the must-carry provisions further important governmental interests; and... do not burden substantially more speech than necessary to further those interests." Turner Broadcasting System, Inc. v. Federal Communications Commission, 520 U.S. 180, 185 (1997) and other broadcast cases is inapt when determining the First Amendment validity of cable regulation."

In *Turner*, however, the Court found the "must-carry" provisions of the Cable Television Consumer Protection and Competition Act of 1992, which require cable television systems to devote a portion of their channels to the transmission of local broadcast television stations, to be content-neutral in application and subject only to the test for incidental restrictions on speech. Attempting to apply this test, however, the Court found "genuine issues of material fact still to be resolved" as to whether "broadcast television is in jeopardy" and as to "the actual effects of must-carry on the speech of cable operators and cable programmers."

It therefore remanded the case for further proceedings. In *Denver Area Educational Telecommunications Consortium, Inc. v. Federal Communications Commission*, a plurality of the Supreme Court (four justices) apparently retreated from the Court's position in *Turner* that cable television is entitled to full First Amendment protection. In Part II of its opinion, the plurality upheld 10(a) of the Cable Television Consumer Protection and Competition Act of 1992, 47 U.S.C. 532(h), which permits cable operators to prohibit indecent material on leased access channels.

In upholding § 10(a), the Court, citing *Pacifica*, noted that cable television "is as 'accessible to children' as over-the-air broadcasting," has also "established a uniquely pervasive presence in the lives of all Americans," and can also "'confron[t] the citizen' in 'the privacy of the home,'... with little or no prior warning." It also noted that its "distinction in *Turner*... between cable and broadcast television, relied on the inapplicability of the spectrum scarcity problem to cable," but that that distinction "has little to do with a case that involves the effects of television viewing on children."

Applying something less than strict scrutiny, the Court concluded "that 10(a) is a sufficiently tailored response to an extraordinarily important problem." In Part III of *Denver Area*, a majority of the Court (six justices) struck down § 10(b) of the 1992 Act, 47 U.S.C. 532(j), which required cable operators, if they do not prohibit such programming on leased access channels, to segregate it on a single channel and block that channel unless the subscriber requests access to it in writing. In this part of the opinion, the Court seemed to apply strict scrutiny, finding "that protection of children is a 'compelling interest,'" but "that, not only is it not a 'least restrictive alternative,' and is not 'narrowly tailored' to meet its legitimate objective, it also seems considerably 'more extensive than necessary.'"

In Part IV, which only three justices joined, the Court struck down 10(c), 42 U.S.C. 531 note, which permitted cable operators to prohibit indecent material on public access channels. Without specifying the level of scrutiny they were applying, the justices concluded "that the Government cannot sustain its burden of showing that § 10(c) is necessary to protect children or that it is appropriately tailored to secure that end." In *United States v. Playboy Entertainment Group, Inc.*, the Supreme Court made clear, as it had not in *Denver Consortium*, that strict scrutiny applies to content-based speech restriction on cable television.

The Court struck down a federal statute designed to "shield children from hearing or seeing images resulting from signal bleed," which refers to blurred images or sounds that come through to non- subscribers. The statute required cable operators, on channels primarily dedicated to sexually oriented programming, either to fully scramble or otherwise fully block such channels, or to not provide such programming when a significant number of children are likely to be viewing it, which, under an FCC regulation meant to transmit the programming only from 10 p.m. to 6 a.m.

The Court apparently assumed that the government had a compelling interest in protecting children from sexually oriented signal bleed, but found that Congress had not used the least restrictive means to do so. Congress in fact had enacted another provision that was less restrictive and that served the government's purpose. This other provision requires that, upon request by a cable subscriber, a cable operator, without charge, fully scramble or fully block any channel to which a subscriber does not subscribe.

FREEDOM OF SPEECH AND GOVERNMENT FUNDING

The Supreme Court has held that Congress, incident to its power to provide for the general welfare, may attach conditions on the receipt of federal funds, and has repeatedly employed the power "to further broad policy objectives by conditioning receipt of federal moneys upon compliance with federal statutory and administrative directives."... The breadth of this power was made clear in *United States v. Butler*, 297 U.S. 1, 66 (1936), where the Court... determined that "the power of Congress to authorize expenditure of public moneys for public purposes is not limited by the direct grants of legislative power found in the Constitution."

This means that Congress may regulate matters by attaching conditions to the receipt of federal funds that it might lack the power to regulate directly. However, the Court added, "other constitutional provisions may provide an independent bar to the conditional grant of federal funds." One of these other constitutional provisions is the First Amendment. The Court has held, in fact, that the government "may not deny a benefit to a person on a basis that infringes his constitutionally protected interests — especially, his interest in freedom of speech."

Similarly, in *Federal Communications Commission v. League of Women Voters*, the Court declared unconstitutional a federal statute that prohibited noncommercial television and radio stations that accepted federal funds from engaging in editorializing, even with nonfederal funds. Congress would have the authority to prohibit television and radio stations from using the federal funds they accept to engage in editorializing, as the Court would view Congress in that case not as limiting speech, but as choosing to fund one activity to the exclusion of another.

"A refusal to fund protected activity [i.e., speech], without more, cannot be equated with the imposition of a 'penalty' on that activity." In *Rust v. Sullivan*, the case in which this quotation appears, the Court upheld a "gag order" that prohibited family planning clinics that accept federal funds from engaging in abortion counseling or referrals. The Court found that, in this case, "the government is not denying a benefit to anyone, but is instead simply insisting that public funds be spent for purposes for which they were authorized."

In *Rust v. Sullivan*, the Court also indicated that it will allow Congress to condition the receipt of federal funds on acceptance of a limitation on the use of nonfederal funds as well as of federal funds, but apparently will not allow Congress to limit the use of nonfederal funds outside the project that accepts the federal funds. Justice Blackmun, dissenting, feared that, "[u]nder the majority's reasoning, the First Amendment could be read to tolerate *any* governmental restriction upon an employee's speech so long as that restriction is limited to the funded workplace."

The Court also "recognized that the university is a traditional sphere of free expression so fundamental to the functioning of our society that the Government's ability to control speech within that sphere by means of conditions attached to the expenditure of Government funds is restricted by the vagueness and over breadth doctrines of the First Amendment." In *National Endowment for the Arts v. Finley*, the Supreme Court upheld the constitutionality of a federal statute requiring the NEA, in awarding grants, to "take into consideration general standards of decency and respect for the diverse beliefs and values of the American public."

The Court acknowledged that, if the statute were "applied in a manner that raises concern about the suppression of disfavored viewpoints," 191 then such application might be unconstitutional. The statute on its face, however, is constitutional because it "imposes no categorical requirement," being merely "advisory." "Any content- based considerations that may be taken into account in the grant-making process are a consequence of the nature of arts funding.... The 'very assumption' of the NEA is that grants will be awarded according to the 'artistic worth of competing applications,' and absolute neutrality is simply 'inconceivable.'"

The Court also found that the terms of the statute, "if they appeared in a criminal statute or regulatory scheme... could raise substantial vagueness concerns.... But when the Government is acting as patron rather than as sovereign, the consequences of imprecision are not constitutionally severe." In *Legal Services Corporation v. Velazquez,* the Court struck down a provision of the Legal Services Corporation Act that prohibited recipients of Legal Services Corporation (LSC) funds (i.e., legal-aid organizations that provide lawyers to the poor in civil matters) from representing a client who seeks "to amend or otherwise challenge existing [welfare] law."

This meant that, even with non-federal funds, a recipient of federal funds could not argue that a state welfare statute violated a federal statute or that a state or federal welfare law violated the U.S. Constitution. If a case was underway when such a challenge became apparent, the attorney had to withdraw. The Supreme Court distinguished this situation from that in *Rust v. Sullivan* on the ground "that the counseling activities of the doctors under Title X amounted to governmental speech," whereas "an LSC-funded attorney speaks on behalf of the client in a claim against the government for welfare benefits."

Furthermore, the restriction in this cases "distorts the legal system" by prohibiting "speech and expression upon which courts must depend for the proper exercise of the judicial power," and thereby is "inconsistent with accepted separation-of-powers principles." In *United States v. American Library Association,* the Supreme Court followed *Rust v. Sullivan,* and upheld the Children's Internet Protection Act, which requires schools and libraries that accept federal funds to purchase computers used to access the Internet to block or filter minors' Internet access to visual depictions that are obscene, child pornography, or "harmful to minors"; and to block or filter adults' Internet access to visual depictions that are obscene or child pornography. Blocking or filtering technology may be disabled, however, "to enable access for bona fide research or other lawful purpose."

The plurality noted that "Congress may not 'induce' the recipient [of federal funds] 'to engage in activities that would themselves be unconstitutional.'" The plurality therefore viewed the question before the Court as "whether public libraries would violate the First Amendment by employing the filtering software that CIPA requires." Does CIPA, in other words, effectively violate library *patrons* rights? The plurality concluded that it does not, as "Internet access in public libraries is neither a 'traditional' or a 'designated' public forum," and that therefore it would not be appropriate to apply strict scrutiny to determine whether the filtering requirements are constitutional.

But the plurality also considered whether CIPA imposes an unconstitutional condition on the receipt of federal assistance — in other words, does it violate public *libraries'* rights by requiring them to limit their freedom of speech if they accept federal funds? The plurality found that, assuming that government entities have First Amendment rights (it did not decide the question), CIPA does not infringe them. This is because CIPA does not deny a benefit to libraries that do not agree to use filters; rather, as in *Rust v. Sullivan*, the statute "simply insists[s] that public funds be spent for the purposes for which they were authorized." "CIPA does not 'penalize' libraries that choose not to install such software, or deny them the right to provide their patrons with unfiltered Internet access.

Rather, CIPA simply reflects Congress' decision not to subsidize their doing so." The Court distinguished *Velazquez* on the ground that public libraries have no role comparable to that of legal aid attorneys "that pits them *against* the Government, and there is no comparable assumption that they must be free of any conditions that their benefactors might attach to the use of donated funds or other assistance." In *Rumsfeld v. Forum for Academic and Institutional Rights, Inc.*, the Supreme Court upheld the Solomon Amendment, which provides that, in the Court's summary, "if any part of an institution of higher education denies military recruiters access equal to that provided other recruiters, the entire institution would lose certain federal funds."

FAIR, the group that challenged the Solomon Amendment, is an association of law schools that barred military recruiting on their campuses because of the military's discrimination against homosexuals. FAIR challenged the Solomon Amendment as violating the First Amendment because it forced schools to choose between enforcing their nondiscrimination policy against military recruiters and continuing to receive specified federal funding. The Court first rejected an interpretation of the Solomon Amendment that would have avoided the constitutional issue; under this interpretation, "a school excluding military recruiters would comply with the Solomon Amendment so long as it also excluded any other employer that violates its nondiscrimination policy."

The Court instead construed the Solomon Amendment to require schools to allow the military the same access as *any* other employer, including employers who do not discriminate and whom the schools allow on campus. Interpreting the Solomon Amendment as such, the Court concluded: "Because the First Amendment would not prevent Congress from directly imposing the Solomon Amendment's access requirement, the statute does not place an unconstitutional condition on the receipt of federal funds." The Court added: "The Solomon Amendment neither limits what law schools may say nor requires them to say anything.... It affects what law schools must *do* — afford equal access to military recruiters — not what they may or may not *say*."

The law schools' conduct in barring military recruiters, the Court found, "is not inherently expressive," and, therefore, unlike flag burning, for example, is not "symbolic speech." Applying the *O'Brien* test for restrictions on conduct that have an incidental effect on speech, the Court found that the Solomon Amendment clearly "promotes a substantial government interest that would be achieved less effectively absent the regulation." The Court also found that the Solomon Amendment did not unconstitutionally compel schools to speak, or even to host or accommodate the government's message. As for compelling speech, law schools must "send e-mails and post notices on behalf of the military to comply with the Solomon Amendment...

This sort of recruiting assistance, however, is a far cry from the compelled speech in *Barnette* and *Wooley*.... [It] is plainly incidental to the Solomon Amendment's regulation of conduct." As for forcing one speaker to host or accommodate another, "[t]he compelled speech violation in each of our prior cases... resulted from the fact that the complaining speaker's own message was affected by the speech it was forced to accommodate."

By contrast, the Court wrote, "Nothing about recruiting suggests that law schools agree with any speech by recruiters, and nothing in the Solomon Amendment restricts what the law schools may say about the military's policies." Finally, the Court found that the Solomon Amendment was not analogous to the New Jersey law that had required the Boy Scouts to accept a homosexual scoutmaster, and which the Supreme Court struck down as violating the Boy Scouts' "right of expressive association." Recruiters, unlike the scoutmaster, are "outsiders who come onto campus for the limited purpose of trying to hire students — not to become members of the school's expressive association."

FREE SPEECH RIGHTS OF GOVERNMENT EMPLOYEES AND GOVERNMENT CONTRACTORS

GOVERNMENT EMPLOYEES

In *Pickering v. Board of Education*, the Supreme Court said that "it cannot be gainsaid that the State has interests as an employer in regulating the speech of its employees that differ significantly from those it possesses in connection with the regulation of speech of the citizenry in general." The First Amendment, however, "protects a public employee's right, in certain circumstances, to speak as a citizen addressing matters of public concern." In *Pickering*, the Supreme Court held it unconstitutional for a school board to fire a teacher for writing a letter to a local newspaper criticizing the administration of the school system.

The Court did not, however, hold that the teacher had the same right as a private citizen to write such a letter. Rather, because the teacher had spoken as a citizen on a matter of public concern, the Court balanced "the interests of the teacher, as a citizen, in commenting upon matters of public concern and the interest of the State, as an employer, in promoting the efficiency of the public services it performs through its employees."

In this case, the Court found that the statements in the letter were in no way directed towards any person with whom appellant [the teacher] would normally be in contact in the course of his daily work as a teacher. Thus no question of maintaining either discipline by immediate superiors or harmony among co-workers is presented here. Appellant's employment relationships with the Board... are not the kind of close working relationships for which it can persuasively be claimed that personal loyalty and confidence are necessary to their proper functioning.

In *Arnett v. Kennedy*, the Supreme Court again balanced governmental interests and employee rights, and this time sustained the constitutionality of a federal statute that authorized removal or suspension without pay of an employee "for such cause as will promote the efficiency of the service," where the "cause" cited was an employee's speech. The employee's speech in this case, however, consisted in falsely and publicly accusing the director of his agency of bribery.

The Court interpreted the statute to proscribe only that public speech which improperly damages and impairs the reputation and efficiency of the employing agency, and it thus imposes no greater controls on the behaviour of federal employees as are necessary for the protection of the Government as employer. Indeed, the Act is not directed at speech as such, but at employee behaviour, including speech, which is detrimental to the efficiency of the employing agency.

In *Givhan v. Western Line Consolidated School District*, the Court upheld the First Amendment right of a public school teacher to complain to the school principal about "employment policies and practices at [the] school which [she] conceived to be racially discriminatory in purpose or effect." In *Connick v. Myers*, an assistant district attorney was fired for insubordination after she circulated a questionnaire among her peers soliciting views on matters relating to employee morale.

The Supreme Court upheld the firing, distinguishing *Pickering* on the ground that, in that case, unlike in this one, the fired employee had engaged in speech concerning matters of public concern: When employee expression cannot be fairly considered as relating to any matter of political, social, or other concern to the community, government officials should enjoy a wide latitude in managing their offices, without intrusive oversight by the judiciary in the name of the First Amendment.... We do not suggest, however, that Myers' speech, even if not touching upon a matter of public concern, is totally beyond the protection of the First Amendment. "[T]he First Amendment does not protect speech and assembly only to the extent it can be characterized as political...."... We hold only that when a public employee speaks not as a citizen upon matters of public concern, but as an employee upon matters only of personal interest, absent the most unusual of circumstances, a federal court is not the appropriate forum in which to review the wisdom of a personnel decision taken by a public agency allegedly in reaction to the employee's behaviour.

In *Connick v. Myers*, however, one question in Myers' questionnaire did touch upon a matter of public concern, and, to this extent, Myers' speech was entitled to *Pickering* balancing to determine whether it was protected by the First Amendment. The Court also considered that the questionnaire interfered with working relationships, was prepared and distributed at the office, arose out of an employment dispute, and was not circulated to obtain useful research. The Court repeated something it had said in *Pickering*: it did "not deem it either appropriate or feasible to attempt to lay down a general standard against which all such statements may be judged."

In *Rankin v. McPherson*, the Court upheld the right of an employee to remark, after hearing of an attempt on President Reagan's life, "If they go for him again, I hope they get him." The Court considered the fact that the statement dealt with a matter of public concern, did not amount to a threat to kill the President, did not interfere with the functioning of the workplace, and was made in a private conversation with another employee and therefore did not discredit the office. Furthermore, as the employee's duties were purely clerical and encompassed "no confidential, policymaking, or public contact role," her remark did not indicate that she was "unworthy of employment."

These Supreme Court cases indicate the relevant factors in determining whether a government employee's speech is protected by the First Amendment. It should be emphasized that the Court considers the time, place, and manner of expression. Thus, if an employee made political speeches on work time, such that they interfered with his or others' job performance, he could likely be fired as "unworthy of employment." At the same time, he could not be fired for the particular political views he expressed, unless his holding of those views made him unfit for the job.

Thus, a governmental employer could not allow employees to make speeches in support of one political candidate on work time, but not allow employees to make speeches in support of that candidate's opponent. But a Secret Service agent assigned to guard the President would not have the same right as the clerical worker in *Rankin* to express the hope that the President would be assassinated. In *Waters v. Churchill*, a plurality of justices concluded that, in applying the *Connick* test — "what the speech was, in what tone it was delivered, what the listener's reactions were" — the court should not ask the jury to determine the facts for itself.

Rather, the court should apply the test "to the facts as the employer *reasonably* found them to be." That is, the employer need not "come to its factual conclusions through procedures that substantially mirror the evidentiary rules used in court," but it may not come to them based on no evidence, or on "extremely weak evidence when strong evidence is clearly available." In *United States v. National Treasury Employees Union* (*NTEU*), the Court struck down a law that prohibited federal employees from accepting any compensation for making speeches or writing articles, even if neither the subject of the speech or article nor the person or group paying for it had any connection with the employee's official duties. The prohibition did not apply to books, nor to fiction or poetry.

The Court noted that, "[u]nlike *Pickering* and its progeny, this case does not involve a *post hoc* analysis of one employee's speech and its impact on that employee's public responsibilities.... [T]he Government's burden is greater with respect to this statutory restriction on expression than with respect to an isolated disciplinary action." Doing the balancing it had mandated in *Pickering*, the Court concluded that "[t]he speculative benefits the honoraria ban may provide the Government are not sufficient to justify this crudely crafted burden on respondents' freedom to engage in expressive activities." In *City of San Diego v. Roe*, the Court held that a police department could fire a police officer who sold a video on the adults-only section of eBay that showed him stripping off a police uniform and masturbating.

The Court found that the officer's "expression does not qualify as a matter of public concern... and *Pickering* balancing does not come into play." The Court also noted that the officer's speech, unlike federal employees' speech in *NTEU*, "was linked to his official status as a police officer, and designed to exploit his employer's image," and therefore "was detrimental to the mission and functions of his employer." Therefore, the Court had "little difficulty in concluding that the City was not barred from terminating Roe under either line of cases [i.e., *Pickering* or *NTEU*]." This leaves uncertain whether, had the officer's expression not been linked to his official status, the Court would have overruled his firing under *NTEU* or would have upheld it under *Pickering* on the ground that his expression was not a matter of public concern.

In *Garcetti v. Ceballos*, the Court cut back on First Amendment protection for government employees by holding that there is no protection — *Pickering* balancing is not to be applied — "when public employees make statements pursuant to their official duties," even if those statements are about matters of public concern. In this case, a deputy district attorney had presented his supervisor with a memo expressing his concern that an affidavit that the office had used to obtain a search warrant contained serious misrepresentations. The deputy district attorney claimed that he was subjected to retaliatory employment actions, and sued.

The Supreme Court held "that when public employees make statements pursuant to their official duties, the employees are not speaking as citizens for First Amendment purposes, and the Constitution does not insulate their communications from employer discipline." The fact that the employee's speech occurred inside his office, and the fact that the speech concerned the subject matter of his employment, were not sufficient to foreclose First Amendment protection.

Rather, the "controlling factor" was "that his expressions were made pursuant to his duties." Therefore, another employee in the office, with different duties, might have had a First Amendment right to utter the speech in question, and the deputy district attorney himself might have had a First

Amendment right to communicate the information that he had in a letter to the editor of a newspaper. In these two instances, a court would apply *Pickering* balancing.

GOVERNMENT CONTRACTORS

In *Board of County Commissioners v. Umbehr*, the Court held that "the First Amendment protects independent contractors from the termination of at-will government contracts in retaliation for their exercise of the freedom of speech." The Court held that, in determining whether a particular termination violates the First Amendment, "the *Pickering* balancing test, adjusted to weigh the government's interests as contractor rather than as employer," should be used. The Court did "not address the possibility of suits by bidders or applicants for new government contracts...."

In *Elrod v. Burns* and *Branti v. Finkel*, the Supreme Court held that "[g]overnment officials may not discharge public employees for refusing to support a political party or its candidates, unless political affiliation is a reasonably appropriate requirement for the job in question." In *O'Hare Truck Service, Inc. v. Northlake*, the Court held "that the protections of *Elrod* and *Branti* extend to... [a situation] where the government retaliates against a contractor, or a regular provider of services, for the exercise of rights of political association or the expression of political allegiance."

6

Right of Access to the News Media

The news media refers to the section of the mass media that focuses on presenting current news to the public. These include print media (newspapers, magazines); broadcast media (radio stations, television stations, television networks), and increasingly Internet-based media (World Wide Web pages, weblogs). The term news trade refers to the concept of the news media as a business separate from, but integrally connected to, the profession of journalism.

The newspaper and consumer magazine industry is set for continued challenges in 2009, with developed country markets likely to be most affected.

A medium (plural media) is a carrier of something. Common things carried by media include information, art, or physical objects. A medium may provide transmission or storage of information or both. The industries which produce news and entertainment content for the mass media are often called "the media" (in much the same way the newspaper industry is called "the press"). In the late 20th century it became commonplace for this usage to be construed as singular ("The media is...") rather than as the traditional plural.

BROADCASTING

Broadcasting is the distribution of audio and video signals (programs) to a number of recipients ("listeners" or "viewers") that belong to a large group. This group may be the public in general, or a relatively large audience within the public. Thus, an Internet channel may distribute text or music worldwide, while a public address system in (for example) a workplace may broadcast very limited *ad hoc* soundbites to a small population within its range. The sequencing of content in a broadcast is called a schedule.

Television and radio programs are distributed through radio broadcasting or cable, often both simultaneously. By coding signals and having decoding equipment in homes, the latter also enables subscription-based channels and pay-per-view services. A broadcasting organization may broadcast several programs at the same time, through several channels (frequencies), for example BBC One and Two. On the other hand, two or more organizations may share a channel and each use it during a fixed part of the day. Digital radio and digital television may also transmit multiplexed programming, with several channels compressed into one ensemble:

- When broadcasting is done via the Internet the term webcasting is often used.
- Broadcasting forms a very large segment of the mass media.
- Broadcasting to a very narrow range of audience is called narrowcasting.

NEWSMAGAZINES

A newsmagazine, sometimes called news magazine, is a usually weekly magazine featuring articles on current events. News magazines generally go a little more in-depth into stories than newspapers, trying to give the reader an understanding of the context surrounding important events, rather than just the facts.

NEWSPAPERS

A newspaper is a lightweight and disposable publication (more specifically, a periodical), usually printed on low-cost paper called newsprint. It may be general or special interest, and may be published daily, weekly, biweekly, monthly, bimonthly, or quarterly.

General-interest newspapers are usually journals of current news on a variety of topics. Those can include political events, crime, business, sports, and opinions (either editorials, columns, or political cartoons). Many also include weather news and forecasts. Newspapers increasingly use photographs to illustrate stories; they also often include comic strips and other entertainment, such as crosswords.

NEWSREELS

A newsreel is a documentary film that is regularly released in a public presentation place containing filmed news stories. Created by Pathé Frères of France in 1908, this form of film was a staple of the typical North American, British, and Commonwealth countries (especially Canada, Australia and New Zealand), and throughout European cinema programming schedule from the silent era until the 1960s when television news broadcasting completely supplanted its role. Pathé would eventually merge with RKO...

An example of a newsreel story is in the film *Citizen Kane* (which was prepared by RKO's actual newsreel staff), which includes a fictional newsreel that summarizes the life of the title character.

ONLINE JOURNALISM

Online journalism is reporting and other journalism produced or distributed via the Internet. An early leader was *The News & Observer* in Raleigh, North Carolina, USA. Many news organizations based in other media also distribute news online. How much they take advantage of the medium varies. Some news organizations, such as the Gongwer News Service, use the Web only or primarily. The Internet challenges traditional news organizations in several ways. They may be losing classified ads to Web sites, which are often targeted by interest instead of geography.

The advertising on news Web sites is sometimes insufficient to support the investment. Even before the Internet, technology and perhaps other factors were dividing people's attention, leading to more but narrower media outlets. Online journalism also leads to the spread of independent online media such as open Democracy and the UK, Wikinews as well as allowing smaller news organizations to publish to a broad audience, such as media-strike.

NEWS COVERAGE AND NEW MEDIA

By covering news, politics, weather, sports, entertainment, and vital events, the daily media shape the dominant cultural, social and political picture of society. Beyond the media networks, independent news sources have evolved to report on events which escape attention or underlie the major stories. In recent years, the blogosphere has taken reporting a step further, mining down to the experiences and perceptions of individual citizens.

An exponentially growing phenomenon, the blogosphere can be abuzz with news that is overlooked by the press and TV networks. Apropos of this was Robert F. Kennedy Jr.'s 11,000-word *Rolling Stone* article apropos of the 2004 United States presidential election, published June 1, 2006. By June 8, there had been no mainstream coverage of the documented allegations by President John F. Kennedy's nephew. On June 9, this sub-story was covered by a *Seattle Post-Intelligencer* article.

Media coverage during the 2008 Mumbai attacks highlighted the use of new media and Internet social networking tools, including Twitter and Flickr, in spreading information about the attacks, observing that Internet coverage was often ahead of more traditional media sources. In response, traditional media outlets including such coverage in their coverage. However, several outlets were criticised as they did not check for the reliability and verfiability of the information.

News is shifting from being a product — today's newspaper, Web site or newscast — to becoming a service — how can you help me, even empower me? There is no single or *finished* news product anymore. As news consumption becomes continual, more new effort is put into producing incremental updates, as brief as 40-character e-mails sent from reporters directly to consumers without editing. (The afternoon newspaper is also being reborn online.) Service also broadens the definition of what journalists must supply. Story telling and agenda setting — still important — are now insufficient. Journalism also must help citizens find what they are looking for, react to it, sort it, shape news coverage, and — probably most important and least developed — give them tools to make sense of and use the information for themselves. News people are uncertain how the core values of accuracy and verification will hold up. Some of the experiments, even the experimenters think, are questionable. And people are being stretched thinner, posing hard questions about how to manage time and where to concentrate. But the hope is that service, more than storytelling, could prove a key to unlocking new economics.

A news organization and a news Web site are no longer final destinations. Now they must move toward also being stops along the way, gateways to other places, and a means to drill deeper, all ideas that connect to service rather than product. "The walled garden is over," the editor of one of the most popular news sites in the country told us. A site restricted to its own content takes on the character of a *cul de sac* street with yellow "No Outlet" sign, reducing its value to the user. "Search has become the predominant ... paradigm," an influential market research report circulating throughout the industry reads.

That means every page of a Web site — even one containing a single story — is its own front page. And each piece of content competes on its own with all other information on that topic linked to by blogs, "digged" by user news sites, sent in e-mails, or appearing in searches. As much as half of every Web page, designers advise, should be devoted to helping people find what they want on the rest of the site or the Web. That change is already occurring. A year ago, our study of news Web sites found that only three of 24 major Web sites from traditional news organizations offered links to outside content. Eleven of those sites now offer them. Some of this may simply be automated, which may be a service of limited value.

The prospects for user-created content, once thought possibly central to the next era of journalism, for now appear more limited, even among "citizen" sites and blogs. News people report the most promising parts of citizen input currently are new ideas, sources, comments and to some extent pictures and video. But citizens posting news content has proven less valuable, with too little that is new or verifiable. (It may thrive at smaller outlets with fewer resources.) And the skepticism is not restricted to the traditional mainstream media or "MSM." The array of citizen-produced news and blog sites is reaching a meaningful level. But a study of citizen media contained in this report finds most of these sites do not let outsiders do more than comment on the site's own material, the same as most traditional news sites. Few allow the posting of news, information, community events or even letters to the editors. And blog sites are even more restricted. In short, rather than rejecting the "gatekeeper" role of traditional journalism, for now citizen journalists and bloggers appear to be recreating it in other places.

Increasingly, the newsroom is perceived as the more innovative and experimental part of the news industry. This appears truer in newspapers and Web sites than elsewhere. But still it represents a significant shift in the conversation. A decade ago, the newsroom was often regarded as the root of journalism's disconnection from the public and its sagging reputation. "I think we may need to just blow up the culture of the newsroom," one of the country's more respected editors told a private gathering of industry leaders in 1997. Now the business side has begun to be identified as the problem area, the place where people are having the most difficulty changing. "My middle management in advertising and distribution is where I see the deer-in-the-headlights look," one publisher recently told us.

"Advertising doesn't know how to start to cope," said a major industry trade association leader. A survey of journalists from different media (being released with this year's report) reinforces this sense. Majorities think such things as journalists writing blogs, the ranking of stories on their Web sites, citizens posting comments or ranking stories, even citizen news sites, are making journalism better — a perspective hard to imagine even a few years ago. These new technologies are seen as less a threat to values or a demand on time than a way to reconnect with audiences. News people also are less anxious about credibility, the focus of concern a few years ago. Their worries now are about money.

The agenda of the American news media continues to narrow, not broaden. A firm grip on this is difficult but the trends seem inescapable. A comprehensive audit of coverage shows that in 2007, two overriding stories — the war in Iraq and the 2008 presidential campaign — filled more than a quarter of the newshole and seemed to consume much of the media's energy and resources. And what wasn't covered was in many ways as notable as what was. Other than Iraq — and to a lesser degree Pakistan and Iran — there was minimal coverage of events overseas, some of which directly involved U.S. interests, blood and treasure. At the same time, consider the list of the domestic issues that each filled less than a single per cent of the newshole: education, race, religion, transportation, the legal system, housing, drug trafficking, gun control, welfare, Social Security, aging, labour, abortion and more.

A related trait is a tendency to move on from stories quickly. On breaking news events — the Virginia Tech massacre or the Minneapolis bridge collapse were among the biggest — the media flooded the zone but then quickly dropped underlying story lines about school safety and infrastructure. And newer media seem to have an even narrower peripheral vision than older media. Cable news, talk radio (and also blogs) tend to seize on top stories (often polarizing ones) and amplify them. The Internet offers the promise of aggregating ever more sources, but its value still depends on what those originating sources are providing. Even as the media world has fragmented into more outlets and options, reporting resources have shrunk.

Madison Avenue, rather than pushing change, appears to be having trouble keeping up with it. Like legacy media, advertising agencies have their own history, mores and cultures that keep them from adapting to new technology and new consumer behaviour. The people who run these agencies know the old-media methods and have old-media contacts. New media offer the promise of more detailed knowledge of consumer behaviour, but the metrics are still evolving and empirical data have not yet delivered a clear path. Advertising executives, in other words, do not have answers any more than the news professionals. In the short run, this may be helping traditional media hold onto share of advertising revenue. For now, the future seems to point to more confusion and fragmentation before new models emerge. But the losses could begin to accelerate when answers come. The question of whether, and how, advertising and news will remain partners is unresolved.

These trends add to those we have discussed in earlier years of this report. In the inaugural State of the News Media report in 2004, we outlined the broad contours of the revolution in news. Journalism is not disappearing, we concluded, but it is changing. Consumers trust and rely on journalists less, and expect more of them, because they have alternative sources of information. In subsequent years we have tracked the splintering of journalism into new norms, including the rise of a new commercially driven Journalism of Affirmation, the shift at many traditional news outlets toward becoming niche products, the emergence of what we call the new Answer Culture in news, and growing doubts about the ultimate potential of advertising online. We have also outlined ways in which newsrooms of the future probably need to change.

The study, which we believe is unique in depth and scope, breaks the news industry into eight sectors (newspapers, magazines, network, cable and local television, the Internet, radio and ethnic media) and builds off many of the findings from a year ago. The world is currently facing serious challenges in advancing democratic governance and human development. Progress is threatened by the deep recession in the global economy, the looming challenge of climate change, and the persistence of deep-rooted conflict and terrorism. Within this environment, what ideal roles should the mass media play as watchdogs, agenda-setters, and gatekeepers to strengthen democratic governance and human development? Under what conditions do media systems succeed or fail to meet these objectives? And, strategically, what reforms would close the gap between the promise and performance of media systems?

Working within the notion of the democratic public sphere, the report emphasizes the institutional or collective roles of the news media as *watchdogs* over the powerful, as *agenda-setters* calling attention to social needs in natural and manmade disasters and humanitarian crisis, and as *gatekeepers* incorporating a diverse and balanced range of political perspectives and social actors. Each, we argue, is vital to making democratic governance work in an effective, transparent, inclusive, and accountable manner. The capacity of media systems (and thus individual reporters embedded within these institutions) to fulfill these roles is constrained by the broader context of the journalistic profession, the market, and ultimately the state.

Media systems are compared in places as diverse as Kenya and Mexico, Iraq and Ethiopia, Burma and North Korea, Egypt and Qatar. The evidence suggests that, in reality, the performance of media systems often fall far short of lofty aspirations, with important consequences for the workings of the public sphere. The report identifies the most effective strategic interventions designed to overcome these constraints. These include policies directed at strengthening the journalistic profession, notably institutional capacity building, such as press councils, press freedom advocacy NGOs, and organizations concerned with journalistic training and accreditation. Other important reforms seek to overcome market failures, including developing a regulatory legal framework for media systems to ensure pluralism of ownership and diversity of contents. Lastly, policies also address the role of the state, including deregulation shifting state-run to public service broadcasting, overseen by independent broadcasting regulatory bodies, and the protection of constitutional principles of freedom of the press, speech, and expression.

This study brought together a wide range of international experts under the auspices of the Communication for Governance and Accountability programme (CommGAP) at the World Bank and the Joan Shorenstein Centre on the Press, Politics and Public Policy at Harvard University. It provides a fresh perspective on all these issues, covering in a wider range of countries and regions than ever before. The report is designed for policymakers and media professionals working within the international development community, national governments, and grassroots organizations, and for journalists, democratic activists, and scholars engaged in understanding mass communications, democratic governance, and development.

News organizations need to do more to think through the implications of this new era of shrinking ambitions. The move toward building audience around "franchise" areas of coverage or other traits is a logical response to fragmentation and can, managed creatively, have journalistic value. To a degree, journalism's problems are oversupply, too many news organizations doing the same thing. But something gained means something lost, especially as newsrooms get smaller. There is already evidence that basic monitoring of local government has suffered. Regional concerns, as opposed to local, are likely to get less coverage.

Matters with widespread impact but little audience appeal, always a challenge, seem more at risk of being unmonitored. What do concepts like localism and branding really mean? Should only national newspapers maintain foreign bureaus? Does localism mean provincialism? Should news organizations, so as not to abandon more high-level coverage, enlist citizen sentinels to monitor community news? To what extent do journalists still have a role in creating a broad agenda of common knowledge? Those issues, debated in theory before, are becoming real. And the wrong answers could hasten, not stave off, the decline of news organizations.

The evidence is mounting that the news industry must become more aggressive about developing a new economic model. The signs are clearer that advertising works differently online than in older media. Finding out about goods and services on the Web is an activity unto itself, like using the yellow pages, and less a byproduct of getting news, such as seeing a car ad during a newscast. The consequence is that advertisers may not need journalism as they once did, particularly online. Already the predictions of advertising growth on the Web are being scaled back. That has major implications, (which some initiatives such as "Newspaper Next" are beginning to grapple with).

Among them, news organizations can broaden what they consider journalistic function to include activities such as online search and citizen media, and perhaps even liken their journalism to anchor stores at a mall, a major reason for coming but not the only one. Perhaps most important, the math suggests they almost certainly must find a way to get consumers to pay for digital content. The increasingly logical scenario is not to charge the consumer directly. Instead, news providers would charge Internet providers and aggregators licensing fees for content. News organizations may have to create consortiums to make this happen. And those fees would likely add to the bills consumers pay for Internet access. But the notion that the Internet is free is already false. Those who report the news just aren't sharing in the fees.

The key question is whether the investment community sees the news business as a declining industry or an emerging one in transition. If one believes that news will continue to be the primary public square where people gather — with the central newsrooms in a community delivering that audience across different platforms — then it seems reasonable that the economics in time will sort themselves out. In that scenario, people with things to sell still need to reach consumers, and the news will be a primary means of finding them. If one believes, however, that the economics of news are now broken, with further declines ahead, then it seems inevitable that the investment in newsrooms will continue to shrink and the quality of journalism in America will decline. One thing seems clear, however: If news companies do not assert their own vision here, including making a case and taking risks, their future will be defined by those less invested in and passionate about news.

There are growing questions about whether the dominant ownership model of the last generation, the public corporation, is suited to the transition newsrooms must now make. Private markets now appear to value media properties more highly than Wall Street does. More executives are openly expressing doubt, too, whether public ownership's required focus on stock price and quarterly returns will allow media companies the time and freedom and risk taking they feel they need to make the transition to the new age. The radio giant Clear Channel made that point when it went private. So have a host of private suitors emerging in the newspaper field.

What is unknown is whether these potential new private owners are motivated by public interest, a vision of growth online, having a high-profile hobby (like a sports team), or as an investment to be flipped for profit after aggressive cost-cutting. Public ownership tends to make companies play by the same rules. Private ownership has few leveling influences. And the new crop of potential private owners is unlike the press barons of the past, people trying to create their legacy in news. Most of them are people who made their fortunes in other enterprises.

The Argument Culture is giving way to something new, the Answer Culture. Critics used to bemoan what author Michael Crichton once called the "Crossfire Syndrome," the tendency of journalists to stage mock debates about issues on TV and in print. Such debates, critics lamented, tended to polarize, oversimplify and flatten issues to the point that Americans in the middle of the spectrum felt left out. That era of argument —R.W. Apple Jr. the gifted New York Times Reporter who died in 2006, called it "pie throwing" — appears to be evolving. The programme "Crossfire" has been canceled. A growing pattern has news outlets, programs and journalists offering up solutions, crusades, certainty and the impression of putting all the blur of information in clear order for people.

The tone may be just as extreme as before, but now the other side is not given equal play. In a sense, the debate in many venues is settled — at least for the host. This is something that was once more confined to talk radio, but it is spreading as it draws an audience elsewhere and in more nuanced ways. The most popular show in cable has shifted from the questions of Larry King to the answers of Bill O'Reilly. On CNN his rival Anderson Cooper becomes personally involved in stories. Lou Dobbs, also on CNN, rails against job exportation. Dateline goes after child predators.

Even less controversial figures have causes: ABC weatherman Sam Campion champions green consumerism. The Answer Culture in journalism, which is part of the new branding, represents an appeal more idiosyncratic and less ideological than pure partisan journalism. Blogging is on the brink of a new phase that will probably include scandal, profitability for some, and a splintering into elites and non-elites over standards and ethics.

The use of blogs by political campaigns in the mid-term elections of 2006 is already intensifying in the approach to the presidential election of 2008.

Corporate public-relations efforts are beginning to use blogs as well, often covertly. What gives blogging its authenticity and momentum — its open access — also makes it vulnerable to being used and manipulated. At the same time, some of the most popular bloggers are already becoming businesses or being assimilated by establishment media. All this is likely to cause blogging to lose some of its patina as citizen media. To protect themselves, some of the best-known bloggers are already forming associations, with ethics codes, standards of conduct and more. The paradox of professionalizing the medium to preserve its integrity as an independent citizen platform is the start of a complicated new era in the evolution of the blogosphere. While journalists are becoming more serious about the Web, no clear models of how to do journalism online really exist yet, and some qualities are still only marginally explored.

Our content study this year was a close examination of some three dozen Web sites from a range of media. Our goal was to assess the state of journalism online at the beginning of 2007. What we found was that the root media no longer strictly define a site's character.

The Web sites of the Washington Post and the New York Times, for instance, are more dissimilar than the papers are in print. The Post, by our count, was beginning to have more in common with some sites from other media. The field is still highly experimental, with an array of options, but it can be hard to discern what one site offers, in contrast to another. And some of the Web's potential abilities seem less developed than others. Sites have done more, for instance, to exploit immediacy, but they have done less to exploit the potential for depth.

7

Right of Access to Information from Government

Freedom of information legislation represents the foundational right-to-know legal process by which requesters may ask for government held information and receive it freely or at minimal cost, barring standardized exceptions. Also variously referred to as open records or (especially in the United States) sunshine laws, governments are also typically bound by a duty to publish and promote openness. In many countries there are constitutional guarantees for the right of access to information, but usually these are unused if specific legislation to support them does not exist. Over 85 countries around the world have implemented some form of such legislation. Sweden's Freedom of the Press Act of 1766 is thought to be the oldest.

Other countries are working towards introducing such laws, and many regions of countries with national legislation have local laws.

For example, all states of the United States have laws governing access to public documents of state and local taxing entities, in addition to that country's Freedom of Information Act which governs records management of documents in the possession of the federal government. A related concept is open meetings legislation, which allows access to government meetings, not just to the records of them. In many countries, privacy or data protection laws may be part of the freedom of information legislation; the concepts are often closely tied together in political discourse.

A basic principle behind most freedom of information legislation is that the burden of proof falls on the body *asked* for information, not the person *asking* for it. The requester does not usually have to give an explanation for their request, but if the information is not disclosed a valid reason has to be given.

SOME COUNTRIES WITH EXISTING LEGISLATION

Albania

In Albania, the constitution of 1998 guarantees the right of access to information; the legislation supporting this is the Ligji nr. 8503, date 30.6.1999, Per të drejten e informimit per dokumentat zyrtare (*Law no. 8503, dated June 30 1999, On the right to information over the official documents*). This requires public authorities to grant any request for an official document.

Armenia

The Law on Freedom of Information was unanimously approved by the Parliament on 23 September 2003 and went into force in November 2003.

Australia

In Australia, the Freedom of Information Act 1982 was passed at the federal level in 1982, applying to all "ministers, departments and public authorities" of the Commonwealth.

There is similar legislation in all states and territories:

- Australian Capital Territory, the Freedom of Information Act 1989
- New South Wales, the Freedom of Information Act 1989
- Northern Territory, the Information Act 2003
- Queensland, the Freedom of Information Act 1992
- South Australia, the Freedom of Information Act 1991
- Tasmania, the Freedom of Information Act 1991
- Victoria, the Freedom of Information Act 1982
- Western Australia, the Freedom of Information Act 1992

Azerbaijan

In Azerbaijan, a freedom of information law was approved in 2005. It has gone into effect.

Bangladesh

On October 21, 2008, the Caretaker Government of Bangladesh issued in the Bangladesh Gazette the Right to Information Ordinance (No. 50 of 2008), based loosely on the Indian Right to Information Act, 2005. The Ordinance is in effect until approved or withdrawn by the next elected Parliament.

Belgium

Article 32 of the Constitution was amended in 1993 to include a right of access to documents held by the government.

Belize

In Belize, the Freedom of Information Act was passed in 2000 and is currently in force, though a governmental commission noted that "not much use has been made of the Act".

Bosnia and Herzegovina

In Bosnia and Herzegovina, Freedom of Access to Information Act was adopted by the Parliament Assembly of Bosnia and Herzegovina on 17 November 2000. Both federal entities - the Republika Srpska and the Federation of Bosnia and Herzegovina - passed freedom of information laws in 2001, the Freedom of Access to Information Act for the Republika Srpska and Freedom of Access to Information Act for the Federation of Bosnia and Herzegovina respectively.

Brazil

In Brazil, the Article 5, XXXIII, of the Constitution sets that "everyone shall have the right to receive information of his own interest or of public interest from public entities, which shall be given within the time prescribed by law". Also, article 22 of the Federal law nº 8.159/1991 grants the right to "full access to public documents". There is not, however, any law specifying the manner and the timetable for the information to be given by the State.

Bulgaria

In Bulgaria, the Access to Public Information Act was passed in 2000, following a 1996 recommendation from the Constitutional Court to implement such a law.

Canada

In Canada, the Access to Information Act allows citizens to demand records from federal bodies. This is enforced by the Information Commissioner of Canada. There is also a complementary Privacy Act, introduced in 1983. The purpose of the Privacy Act is to extend the present laws of Canada that protect the privacy of individuals with respect to personal information about themselves held by a federal government institution and that provide individuals with a right of access to that information. It is a Crown copyright. Complaints for possible violations of the Act may be reported to the Privacy Commissioner of Canada.

Canadian access to information laws distinguish between access to records generally and access to records that contain personal information about the person making the request. Subject to exceptions, individuals have a right of access to records that contain their own personal information under the Privacy Act but the general public does not have a right of access to records that contain personal information about others under the Access to Information Act.

Each province and territory in Canada has its own access to information legislation. in many cases, this is also the provincial public sector privacy legislation. For example:

- Freedom of Information and Protection of Privacy Act (Alberta)
- Freedom of Information and Protection of Privacy Act (Manitoba)
- Freedom of Information and Protection of Privacy Act (Nova Scotia)

- Freedom of Information and Protection of Privacy Act (Ontario)
- Freedom of Information and Protection of Privacy Act (Saskatchewan)
- Act respecting access to documents held by public bodies and the protection of personal information (Quebec)

From 1989 to 2008, requests made to the federal government were catalogued in the Coordination of Access to Information Requests System. A 393 page report released in September 2008, sponsored by several Canadian newspaper groups, compares Canada's Access to Information Act to the FOI laws of the provinces and of 68 other nations: "Fallen Behind: Canada's Access to Information Act in the World Context," at www3.telus.net/index100/foi Cayman - The Freedom of Information Law was passed in 2007 and will be brought into force in January 2009.

Chile

In Chile, article 8 of the Constitution provides for the freedom of information. A law titled Law on Access to Public Information (*Ley de Acceso a la Información Pública*) took effect on April 20, 2009.

China

In April 2007, the State Council of the People's Republic of China promulgated the "Regulations of the People's Republic of China on Open Government Information", which came into effect on May 1st, 2008. However, the law has done very little to provide information on many of the Chinese government's practices.

Colombia

Colombian constitution grants the right of access to public information through *Law 57 of 1985* which thereby mandates the publishing of acts and official documents. This is implemented and applies to documents that belong to official facilities (offices or the like). Additionally there is the anti corruption statement of *Law 190 of 1955* also known as *anticorruption act* which in its 51st article mandates public offices to list in visible area all the contracts and purchases made by month. The latter taking place slowly.

Croatia

In Croatia, the Zakon O Pravu Na Pristup Informacijama (*Act on the Right of Access to Information*) of 2003 extends to all public authorities.

Czech Republic

In the Czech Republic, the Zákon è. 106/1999 Sb., o svobodném pøístupu k informacím (*Act No. 106/1999 Coll. on Free Access to Information*) covers the "state agencies, territorial self-administration authorities and public institutions managing public funds" as well as any body authorised by the law to reach legal decisions relating to the public sector, to the extend of such authorisation.

Denmark

In Denmark, the Access to Public Administration Files Act of 1985 applies to most public agencies, and an unusual clause extends coverage to most private or public energy suppliers.

Dominican Republic

Hipólito Mejía approved Ley No.200-04 - Ley General de Libre Acceso a la Información Pública (*Law number 200-04 - Law on Access to Information*) on 28 July 2004, which allows public access to information from the government and private organizations that receive public money to conduct state business. Rough drafts and projects that are not part of an administrative procedure are not included.

Ecuador

In Ecuador, the Transparency and Access to Information Law of 2004 declares that the right of access to information is guaranteed by the state.

Estonia

In Estonia, the Public Information Act of 2000 extends to all "holders of information", which is clarified as being all government and local government bodies, legal persons in public law and legal persons in private law if they are performing public duties (providing health, education etc).

Europe

In matters concerning the local, national and transboundary environment, the Aarhus convention grants the public rights regarding access to information, public participation and access to justice in governmental decision-making processes. It focuses on interactions between the public and public authorities.

European Union

Regulation 1049/2001 of the European Parliament and the Council of 30 May 2001 regarding public access to European Parliament, Council and Commission documents grants a right of access to documents of the three institutions to any Union citizen and to any natural or legal person residing, or having its registered office, in a Member State. "Document" is defined broadly and it is assumed that all documents, even if classified, may be subject to right of access unless it falls under one of the exceptions. If access is refused, the applicant is allowed a confirmatory request. A complaint against a refusal can be made with the European Ombudsman and/or an appeal can be brought before the Court of First Instance. In addition, the Directive 2003/98/EC of the European Parliament and the Council of 17 November 2003 on the re-use of public sector information sets out the rules and practices for accessing public sector information resources for further exploitation.

Finland

In Finland, the Laki yleisten asiakirjain julkisuudesta 9.2.1951/83 (*Act on the Openness of Public Documents* of 1951) established the openness of all records and documents in the possession of officials of the state, municipalities, and registered religious communities. Exceptions to the basic principle could only be made by law, or by an executive order for specific enumerated reasons such as national security.

The openness of unsigned draft documents was not mandated, but up to the consideration of the public official. This weakness of the law was removed when the law was revised in the 1990s. The revised law, the Laki viranomaisten toiminnan julkisuudesta 21.5.1999/621 (*Act on the Openness of Government Activities* of 1999), also extended the principle of openness to corporations that perform legally mandated public duties, such as pension funds and public utilities, and to computer documents.

France

In France, the accountability of public servants is a constitutional right, according to the *Declaration of the Rights of Man and of the Citizen*. The implementing legislation is the Loi n°78-753 du 17 juillet 1978 portant diverses mesures d'amélioration des relations entre l'administration et le public et diverses dispositions d'ordre administratif, social et fiscal (*Act No. 78-753 of 17 July 1978. On various measures for improved relations between the Civil Service and the public and on various arrangements of administrative, social and fiscal nature*). It sets as a general rule that citizens can demand a copy of any administrative document (in paper, digitized or other form), and establishes the *Commission d'Accès aux Documents Administratifs*, an independent administrative authority, to oversee the process.

Georgia

In Georgia, the General Administrative Code contains a Law on Freedom of Information.

Germany

In Germany, the federal government passed a freedom of information law on September 5, 2005. The law grants each person an unconditional right to access official federal information. No legal, commercial, or any other kind of justification is necessary. Nine of the sixteen Bundesländer — Berlin, Brandenburg, Nordrhein-Westfalen, Schleswig-Holstein, Hamburg, Bremen, Mecklenburg-Vorpommern, Saarland and Thüringen — have approved individual "Informationsfreiheitsgesetze" (Freedom of Information laws).

Greece

In Greece, article 16 of Law 1599/1986 introduced the right of all citizens to read most administrative documents. This right is now codified as article 5 of the Administrative Procedural Code, Law 2690/1999. Under this article, citizens have a right to know the content of administrative documents. Administrative documents are defined as those produced by public sector entities, such as reports, studies, minutes, statistical data, circulars, instructions, responses, consultatory responses, and decisions. In addition, citizens with a legitimate interest may also access *private* documents stored by public services.

The right cannot be exercised if the document concerns the private or family lives of others, or if the document's confidentiality is safeguarded by specific legal provisions. Furthermore, the public body can refuse access if the document refers to discussions in the Cabinet, or if accessing the document can seriously hamper criminal or administrative violation investigations carried out by judicial, police, or military authorities. Citizens may study the documents at the place where they are archived, or they may obtain a copy at their own cost. Access to one's own medical data is provided with the help of a doctor. Access to documents should take into account whether they be covered by copyright, patent, or trade secret regulations.

In addition, Law 3448/2006, on the reuse of public sector information, harmonizes the national laws with the requirements on the European Union Directive 2003/98/EC.

Hong Kong

In Hong Kong there are no laws specifically enacted to guarantee the freedom of information. Since March 1995, the Government of Hong Kong has promulgated a "Code on Access to Information" to serve a similar purpose. This code, like other internal regulations of the Government, was not legislated by the Legislative Council and a has minimal legal status. It requires government agencies to appoint Access to Information Officers to answer citizens' requests for governmental records. A fee maybe charged prior to the release of information.

Hungary

In Hungary, the Act on the Protection of Personal Data and Public Access to Data of Public Interest extends a right of access to all data of public interest, defined as any information processed by a body performing a governmental function. Complaints and contested applications may be appealed to the Data Protection Commissioner or to the court. In 2005 the Parliament adopted the Act on the Freedom of Information by Electronic Means (Act XC of 2005). The Act has three basic parts: 1. electronic disclousure of certain data by public sector bodies, 2. publicity of legislation and 3. openness of Court decisions.

Iceland

In Iceland the Information Act (Upplysingalög) Act no. 50/1996 gives access to public information.

India

The Indian Right to Information Act (RTI Act) was passed by the Indian Parliament on 15 June 2005. It came into effect on 12 October 2005. Supreme Court of India had, in several Judgments prior to enactment of the RTI Act, interpreted Indian Constitution to read Right to Information as the Fundamental Right as embodied in Right to Freedom of Speech and Expression and also in Right to Life. RTI Act laid down a procedure to guarantee this right. Under this law all Government Bodies or Government funded agencies have to designate a Public Information Officer (PIO). The PIO's responsibility is to ensure that information requested is disclosed to the petitioner within 30 days or within 48 hours in case of information concerning the life or liberty of a person. The law was inspired by previous legislation from select states (among them Maharastra, Goa, Karnataka, Delhi etc) that allowed the right to information (to different degrees) to citizens about activities of any State Government body.

A number of high profile disclosures revealed corruption in various government schemes such scams in Public Distribution Systems (ration stores), disaster relief, construction of highways etc. The law itself has been hailed as a landmark in India's drive towards more openness and accountability.

However the RTI India has certain weaknesses that hamper implementation. There have been questions on the lack of speedy appeal to non-compliance to requests. The lack of a central PIO makes it difficult to pin-point the correct PIO to approach for requests. The PIO, being an officer of the relevant Government institution, may have a vested interest in not disclosing damaging information on activities of his/her Institution, This therefore creates a conflict of interest. In the state of Maharastra it was estimated that only 30% of the requests are actually realized under the Maharashtra Right to Information act. The law does not allow disclosure of information that affects national security, defence, and other matters that are deemed of national interest.

Ireland

In Ireland the Freedom of Information Act 1997 came into effect in April, 1998. The 1997 Act was subsequently amended by the Freedom of Information (Amendment) Act 2003. The Act has led to a sea-change in the relationship between the citizen, journalists, government departments and public bodies. There are very few restrictions on the information that can be made public. A notable feature is the presumption that anything not restricted by the Act is accessible. In this regard it is a much more liberal Act than the UK Act.

Decisions of public bodies in relation to requests for information may be reviewed by the Information Commissioner.

One particular controversy which has caused concern to journalists and historians is that traditionally government ministers would annotate and sign any major policy or report documents which they had seen. However this practice has fallen out of favour because of the new openness. This annotation and signing of documents has often given a paper trail and unique insight as to "what the minister knew" about a controversy or how he or she formed an opinion on a matter. Also civil and public servants have become more informal, in keeping written records of potentially controversial meeting and avoiding writing memos as a result. While this information would not often be released, and sometimes only under the thirty year rule, the fact that government ministers now do not annotate and sign documents creates the concerns that while government is open it is not accountable as to who did or saw what or how decision making process works.

The Freedom of Information (Amendment) Act 2003 brought in fees for making requests for information and requests for review of decisions taken by Government bodies. As a result, one can incur a fee of up to €240 before even being granted access to information.

Israel

In Israel, the Freedom of Information Law, 5758-1998, supported by the Freedom of Information Regulations, 5759-1999, controls freedom of information. It defines the bodies subject to the legislation by a set of listed categories - essentially, most public bodies - and provides for the government to publish a list of all affected bodies. However, this list does not seem to have been made publicly available, if indeed it was ever compiled. Many public bodies are not obliged to follow the law, which limits the potential for use by the public. The Israeli Freedom of Information Law has actually achieved the opposite intended result. Government agencies now take the position that a citizen may only request information via FOIL, ie an official letter designated as such and including the (approx.) $22 fee. Thus an Israeli citizen in many cases cannot simply write a letter asking a question, and can be asked to file a FOIL application with a fee and wait the minimum statutory 30 days for a reply, which the agency can easily extend to 60 days. In many cases FOIL letters are simply ignored, or some laconic response is sent stating the request is either unclear, unspecific, too vague or some other legalese, anything in order to keep the information away from the public. When the 60 days are up, the anticipated result usually yield nothing significant, and the applicant must petition the District Court to compel disclosure, a procedure that requires attorneys to draft pleadings and a payment a (approx.) $420 court fee. A judgement in such FOIL appeals in Israel can take years, and again the agency can easily avoid disclosure by simply not complying. There are no real sanctions for non-compliance. While there are rare successes in Courts compelling Israeli government agencies to disclose information, they are usually in non-controversial areas such as harmless civil matters. The law provides for the expected "security" exemption and an applicant applying for such information can expect not to benefit from FOIL (and also have his or her court appeal rejected). Applicants can be greatly helped by

Italy

Chapter V of Law No. 241 of 7 August 1990 provides for access to administrative documents. However, the right to access is limited. The law states that those requesting information must have a legal interest. The 1992 regulations require "a personal concrete interest to safeguard in legally relevant situations." The courts have ruled that this includes the right of environmental groups and local councilors to demand information on behalf of those they represent. It was amended in 2005. The revision appears to adopt the court rulings and relax the interest somewhat to allow access when an individual can show they represent a more general public interest.

Jamaica

In Jamaica, the relevant legislation is the Access to Information Act, 2002.

Japan

In Japan, "Law Concerning Access to Information Held by Administrative Organs" was promulgated in 1999. The law was enforced in 2001. In many local governments, it establishes the regulations about information disclosure from the latter half of 1980's.

Latvia

The Constitution of Latvia states: "Article 104. Everyone has the right to address submissions to State or local government institutions and to receive a materially responsive reply."

The Law on Freedom of Information was signed into law by the State President in November 1998 and has been amended a number of times recently. Any person can ask for information in "any technically feasible form" without having to show a reason. The request can be oral or written. Bodies must respond in 15 days.

Macedonia

Article 16 of the Constitution of Macedonia guarantees "access to information and the freedom of reception and transmission of information". The Law on Free Access to Information of Public Character was adopted on 25 January 2006. It is scheduled to go into force in September 2006.The law allows any natural or legal person to obtain information from state and municipal bodies and natural and legal persons who are performing public functions. The requests can be oral, written or electronic. Requests must be responded to in 10 days.

Mexico

The Constitution was amended in 1977 to include a right of freedom of information. Article 6 says in part, "the right of information shall be guaranteed by the state." The Supreme Court made a number of decisions further enhancing that right. The Federal Law of Transparency and Access to Public Government Information was unanimously approved by Parliament in April 2002 and signed by President Fox in June 2002. It went into effect in June 2003.

Montenegro

A freedom of information law was passed in Montenegro late in 2005, after a process of several years.

Netherlands

Article 110 of the Constitution states: "In the exercise of their duties government bodies shall observe the principle of transparency in accordance with rules to be prescribed by Act of Parliament." Freedom of information legislation was first adopted in 1978. The Government Information (Public Access) Act (WOB) replaced the original law in 1991. Under the Act, any person can demand information related to an administrative matter if it is contained in documents held by public authorities or companies carrying out work for a public authority. The request can either be written or oral. The authority has two weeks to respond.

New Zealand

In New Zealand, the relevant legislation is the Official Information Act 1982. This implemented a general policy of openness regarding official documents and replaced the Official Secrets Act.

Norway

The Freedom of Information Act of 19 June 1970 is the implementation of freedom of information legislation in Norway on a national level. Article 100 of the Constitution gives access to public documents.

Pakistan

President Pervez Musharraf promulgated the Freedom of Information Ordinance 2002 in October 2002. The law allows any citizen access to public records held by a public body of the federal government including ministries, departments, boards, councils, courts and tribunals. It does not apply to government owned corporations or provincial governments. The bodies must respond within 21 days.

Paraguay

In Paraguay, a law protects *habeas data*, meaning that any citizen can request a copy of publicly or privately held information relating to him, and request that any inaccurate data found be destroyed. This has been primarily used by former dissidents after the fall of the lengthy dictatorship (1954-1989) of Alfredo Stroessner. In 2005, efforts have been made to add transparency to purchases made by the Government, with a system that publishes bids on the Web, as well as the resulting purchases.

Poland

Article 61 of the Constitution provides for the right to information and mandates that Parliament enact a law setting out this right. The Law on Access to Public Information was approved in September 2001 and went into effect in January 2002.(The Act allows anyone to demand access to public information, public data and public assets held by public bodies, private bodies that exercise public tasks, trade unions and political parties. The requests can be oral or written. The bodies must respond within 14 days.

Republic of Moldova

Article 34 of the Constitution provides for a right of access to information. The Law of the Republic of Moldova on Access to Information was approved by Parliament in May 2000 and went into force in August 2000. Under the law, citizens and residents of Moldova can demand information from state institutions, organizations financed by the public budget and individuals and legal entities that provide public services and hold official information.

Romania

Since 2001 there is one law on Freedom of Information and one on transparent decision making processes in public administration (a sunshine law).

Serbia

In Serbia, the Access to Public Information Act gives access to documents of public authorities.

Slovakia

Slovakia passed the Freedom of Information Act in May 2000 (Num. law: 211/2000 Z. z.). Under the law, everybody can demand information from state institutions, organizations, from municipalities, individuals and legal entities financed by the public budget.

Slovenia

Slovenia passed the Access to Public Information Act in March 2003. The Act governs the procedure which ensures everyone free access to public information held by state bodies, local government bodies, public agencies, public funds and other entities of public law, public powers holders and public service contractors.

South Africa

South Africa passed the Promotion of Access to Information Act on 2 February 2000. It is intended "To give effect to the constitutional right of access to any information held by the State and any information that is held by another person and that is required for the exercise or protection of any rights"; the right of access to *privately* held information is an interesting feature, as most freedom of information laws only cover governmental bodies.

South Korea

The Constitutional Court ruled in 1989 that there is a constitutional right to information "as an aspect of the right of freedom of expression and specific implementing legislation to define the contours of the right was not a prerequisite to its enforcement."

The Act on Disclosure of Information by Public Agencies was enacted in 1996 and went into effect in January 1998. It allows citizens to demand information held by public agencies.

Sweden

In Sweden, the Freedom of the Press Act of 1766 granted public access to government documents. It thus became an integral part of the Swedish Constitution, and the first ever piece of freedom of information legislation in the modern sense. In Swedish this is known as *Offentlighetsprincipen* (The Principle of Public Access), and has been valid since. The Principle of Public Access means that the general public are to be guaranteed an unimpeded view of activities pursued by the government and local authorities; all documents handled by the authorities are public unless legislation explicitly and specifically states otherwise, and even then each request for potentially sensitive information must be handled individually, and a refusal is subject to appeal. Further, the constitution grants the Right to Inform, meaning that even some (most) types of secret information may be passed on to the press or other media without risk of criminal charges. Instead, investigation of the informer's identity is a criminal offense. However it has been mentioned in the media that non-illegal harassment of a public employee who has informed media is not forbidden. For example, one of the most debated events was when a ship hit ground, the shipping authority blamed the pilot, but a map engineer in the shipping authority informed media that it was the shipping authority's fault. He had his work location changed to a light house.

Taiwan

The "The Freedom of Government Information Law", enacted by the

Legislative Yuan of the Taiwanese government (Republic of China), has been in force since 28 December 2005.

Thailand

In Thailand, the relevant legislation is the Official Information Act of 1997.

Trinidad and Tobago

In Trinidad and Tobago, the relevant legislation is the Freedom of Information Act, 1999.

Turkey

In Turkey, the Turkish Law on the Right to Information (Bilgi Edinme Hakký Kanunu) was signed on October 24, 2003 and it came into effect 6 months later on April 24, 2004.

Uganda

- In Uganda, the Access to Information Act was approved in 2005 and went into effect in 2006.

Ukraine

The 1996 Constitution does not include a specific general right of access to information but contains a general right of freedom of collect and disseminate information and rights of access to personal and environmental information. The 1992 Law on Information is a general information policy framework law that includes a citizen's a right to access information. The law allows citizens and legal entities to request access to official documents. The request can be oral or written. The government body must respond in 10 calendar days and provide the information within a month unless provided by law.

United Kingdom

The Freedom of Information Act 2000 (2000 c. 36) is the implementation of freedom of information legislation in the United Kingdom on a national level, with the exception of Scottish bodies, which are covered by the Freedom of Information (Scotland) Act 2002 (2002 asp. 13).

United States

In the United States the Freedom of Information Act was signed into law by President Lyndon B. Johnson on July 4, 1966 and went into effect the following year. Green Party Presidential Candidate, Ralph Nader, has been credited with the impetus for creating this act, among others. The Electronic Freedom of Information Act Amendments were signed by President Bill Clinton on October 2, 1996. The Act applies only to federal agencies. However, all of the states, as well as the District of Columbia and some territories, have enacted similar statutes to require disclosures by agencies of the state and of local governments, though some are significantly broader than others. Many combine this with Open Meetings legislation, which requires government meetings to be held publicly.

Zimbabwe

In Zimbabwe, the Access to Information and Privacy Act (AIPPA) was signed by President Mugabe in February 2002.

Countries with Pending Legislation

- In Argentina, national freedom of information legislation is pending, though some individual regions have legislation on a local level.
- In Bangladesh, the Caretaker Government that assumed power in January 2007 announced in the summer of 2007 that they would implement an RTI Act modeled after the Indian RTI Act of 2005.
- In Barbados, the Government headed by David Thompson has proposed to put in place a Freedom of Information Bill. The Government has launched various initiatives to vett the proposed bill with the citizens of the country for comment.
- In Botswana, as of 2003, the government was quoted as saying "The Freedom of Information Bill is not a priority for the new ministry, but some activities like information gathering and initial planning will start."
- In the Cayman Islands, the Freedom of Information Regulations Act 2008 is expected to go into effect on January 1, 2009.
- In Fiji, the constitution gives a general right of access, but enabling legislation has not yet been passed. A draft Freedom of Information Bill was circulated in 2000 but derailed by political unrest; the government has not yet begun work on a second bill.
- In Ghana, the Right to Information Bill 2003 was resubmitted to the Cabinet in 2005.
- In Indonesia, the House of Representatives drafted and submitted a freedom of information bill in 2004, but as of 2005 it remained dormant, with the government taking no action.
- In Jordan, there is a draft Law on the Guarantee of Access to Information which was passed onto Parliament at the end of 2005.
- In Kenya, the draft Freedom of Information Act 2007 will soon be tabled into Parliament.
- In Lesotho, the Access and Receipt of Information Bill was before Parliament in 2003-4, but the current status of the legislation is unknown
- In the Maldives, there is currently no freedom of information legislation. In 2004, the government announced that a bill was expected to be passed in that year, but this has not yet transpired.

- In Mozambique, the government produced a draft Freedom of Information Bill in August 2005. It is expected to become law within two years.
- In Nauru, the Freedom of Information Act 2004 was laid before the parliament in that year, but was not passed. Further work on the legislation is currently being held back, pending a review of the country's Constitution.
- In Nigeria, the Freedom of Information Bill was approved by the Senate in November 2006. It must now be reconciled with the version approved by the House and signed by the President.
- Philippines. Article III, Section 7 of the country's Bill of Rights recognizes the people's right to information on matters of public concern. Its Supreme Court has upheld this right in many of its decisions. However, there is no legislation that sets the procedures for access and disclosure of information and provides penalties for officials who fail to release the requested information, without justifiable reasons. In 2008, the Lower House of the Philippine Congress passed House Bill No. 3732 (Freedom of Information Act)that addresses these gaps. A counterpart bill is still pending in the Philippine Senate. Leading the campaign for the bill's passage is the Access to Information Network, co-convened by Action For Economic Reforms and Transparency and Accountability Network.
- In Sri Lanka, the 2004 draft Freedom of Information Act has been endorsed by both major parties, but had not been passed as of January 2005.

(Unless stated otherwise, information is current as of July 2008.

This section of the legal guide outlines the wide-array of information available to you from government sources. These sources range from your local city council all the way up to the largest agencies in the federal government. In fact, you might be quite surprised at how much information is available to you. And the best part is that you generally don't need to hire a lawyer or file any complicated forms — you can access most of this information simply by showing up or filing a relatively simple request.

Moreover, you don't need to be a professional journalist to share what you find with others who are interested in these issues; with nothing more than an Internet connection, you can make the information available to anyone in the world. For an impressive example of how some people are using the power of new information technologies in conjunction with government information, check out Adrian Holovaty's Chicagocrime.org, a browsable database of crimes reported in Chicago.

Regardless of what you publish online, it is likely that at least one (if not many) of the information sources we discuss in this section will be valuable to you. For example, you might want to find out whether the drinking water coming out of your faucet contains pollutants (information that is likely contained in documents held by the Environmental Protection Agency or one of its state counterparts). Perhaps you'd like to know more about how your local school board makes decisions (information that you can get by attending school board meetings). Or perhaps you are concerned that a real estate developer may have been sued for fraud (information that is available by visiting the courthouse in person or accessing the court's electronic docketing system).

Information from these government sources will be especially useful to you if you want to take your publishing activities beyond merely commenting on material posted by others. These sources can help you move into original reporting and enable you to comment in an informed fashion on local and national debates. You might even do a periodic post or column on subjects of particular interest to your website or blog. For example, the Gotham Gazette, an independent news site that covers "New York City News and Policy," has an entire section focusing on city government, which is largely based on meetings of the New York City Council.

We should point out, however, that the information you gather from these government sources doesn't have to be limited to the actions of the government itself. Government bodies collect extensive information on individuals, corporations, and other organizations. Much of this information is available to the public. You just have to know where to look. The first thing you will need to consider is which government entity likely has the information you are seeking. Public access to government information extends to a broad range of government sources, including federal and state agencies, Congress and state legislatures, government boards and committees, and the courts. In fact, it might be the case that the information you are interested in is located in more than one place.

A little advanced research on your part can go a long way when dealing with the government. Because different laws apply to different government entities, you will want to review each section of this guide that might apply to your situation. If you are not sure whether the information you seek is associated with a federal, state, or local government body, refer to the page on Federal, State, and Local Government Bodies for some helpful information. It is also worth bearing in mind that laws granting access to government information are only one of many important fact-finding tools in your information gathering toolbox. These laws can be very powerful, but their scope is limited to records and information available through government sources.

INFORMATION HELD

The federal government is a sprawling and far reaching entity headquartered in Washington, D.C., but with agencies and offices in almost every part of the country. A number of important laws govern your access to information associated with the federal government. The most well known of these laws is the Freedom of Information Act ("FOIA"), which provides access to the public records of most departments, agencies, and offices of the federal government. But several lesser known laws are also important, including the Government in the Sunshine Act which gives you the right to attend the meetings of many federal agencies, the Federal Advisory Committee Act, which allows you to attend the meetings of boards and committees that advise agencies of the federal government, and the Presidential Records Act, which sets out the procedures you must follow to request records from the president and his or her close advisers.

If you are seeking records held by a federal government agency, you should review the section on Access to Records from the Federal Government which describes FOIA and provides some practical advice on how to use the law to acquire government records. Keep in mind, however, that FOIA does not cover the President himself/herself, Congress, or the federal judiciary. For information on accessing information from these sources, Access to Congress, and Access to Courts and Court Records sections of this guide, respectively.

The federal government often acts through boards, committees, and other government "bodies." Examples include the Securities and Exchange Commission, the Federal Communications Commission, and the Federal Housing Finance Board. A common feature of these agencies, boards, commissions, and other government bodies is that they meet as groups to deliberate or take action on public business. If you wish to attend these meetings, you will need to become familiar with a category of laws called open meetings laws. These important laws give anyone, including members of the traditional and non-traditional press, the ability to attend the meetings of many federal government bodies and to receive reasonable notice of those meetings. In many instances, they also entitle you to obtain copies of minutes, transcripts, or recordings at low cost.

There are basically two types of federal government meetings you may wish to attend and each is governed by a different set of legal requirements. Federal agency meetings are governed by the Government in the Sunshine Act which gives you the right to attend the meetings of many federal agencies, such as the Federal Election Commission and the Federal Trade Commission. Federal advisory committee meetings, which are a strange hybrid type of meeting involving outside advisers tasked with giving advice to the federal government, are governed by the Federal Advisory Committee Act. Just as with the federal government, a number of important laws govern your ability to access information associated with state and local governments. Every state has some version of a "Freedom of Information" (FOI) law — sometimes called a "sunshine law" — that governs the public's right to access state government records. These FOI laws help the public keep track of its government's actions, from the expenditures of school boards to the governor's decision to pardon prison inmates. For example, in 2003, a parent of a student in Texas, Dianna Pharr, spurred by the financial crisis in her local school district, began filing requests under the Texas Public Information Act to investigate the district's spending and operations. She and other parent volunteers established an online repository for the documents and made them available on a local community website, Keep Eanes Informed. Pharr's efforts received coverage in the local press, and have enabled her community to make informed decisions when dealing with school board proposals.

If the information you are seeking is contained in records held by your state or local government, you will need to review the section on Access to Records from State Governments in order to understand how to make a request under the relevant state law. For example, the California Public Records Act and the New York Freedom of Information Law govern access to records in California and New York, respectively. In many states, local government records can also be requested under the state open records law. Unfortunately, public officials sometimes deny that they are required to turn over information, deny that the public has any right to information, or fail to provide information in a timely way. To ensure that you get the information you need, you should review the section on Practical Tips for Getting Government Records.

If you are interested in attending the meetings of state or local government bodies, you should review the section on Access to State and Local Government Meetings. The most familiar examples of these kinds of government bodies at the local level include school boards, city councils, boards of county commissioners, zoning and planning commissions, police review boards, and boards of library trustees. At the state level, examples include state environmental commissions, labour boards, housing boards, and tax commissions, to name a few.

COURTS AND COURT INFORMATION

The court system is yet another resource-rich place for you to access information. Your right to access the court system stems from the First Amendment, and has been expanded to give you the ability to attend almost all court proceedings and inspect public court records. The law provides important tools that you can use to help you understand the intricacies of a particular case, or watch how the court system performs. For example, you can use court records to check whether a doctor has previously been sued for malpractice, or to find the outcome of a criminal case.

8

Codes of Journalism Ethics

Why media is always inclined towards either Congress or Communists? I feel like all media firms are financed by Congress otherwise why they are constantly making issues regarding Nitish kumar joining Congress? Media is the one responsible for creating confusion in states where there is good developmental work is going on and delivering development since last three years. Does the Media want to bring down the developing states again to poor condition? Media even made the whole situation of Mumbai terror attacks a mockery, by giving a live telecast. What sort of journalism is these channels are preaching.

Where did the Journalism ethics go? Is NDTV & CNN IBN interested only in destabilizing the BJP ruled states by exposing unwanted topics like Modi's PM aspiration, Nitish joining Congress, while the Bihar CM is constantly refusing to ally with Congress. Is Barka Dutt & Rajdeep Sardesai trying to make confusion in stable Governments or are they trying to make a government of their own interest or are they mocking the ordinary people. Why Channel people are giving so much importance to Left party leaders like Prakash Karat, Sitaram Yechuri & co. and why not Mulayam, Nitish, Mayawathi whose parties are having more number of Lok Sabha seats when compared to Left? Is it because these leaders are not 'Convent educated'?

Left parties which merely has 40 LS seats are given so much importance in live TV shows than BJP which which is having a 140 plus Ls seats. Is media worried about the good performance of BJP ruled states? Or is that your journalists cannot see the poverty in left ruled states like Bengal and Kerala? Media should decide their strategy to reach out to people and help them. This should be media's ethics of Journalism, not to give unwanted importance and images to the left leaders who are destroying their states.

How these channel peoples shut their eyes and try to destabilize good governments of BJP, is it not Barka & Co.'s responsibility to highlight corruption and poor development and poverty in Bengal & Tripura? Please don't try to fool the public, only by highlighting issues of BJP ruled states. In other words these media are much hazardous than a tainted politician. Last but not least, don't believe that by conducting a debate session with some convent educated people on a topic in a centralized AC room and by airing some jargons in English won't become sound journalism. For that media should get down to the grass root level to the common man and understand their issues and find way to resolve it irrespective of party or Governments and that is the right ethics of Journalism.

The political and legal controversy generated by Tehelka has brought into focus the growing power of the Internet media. Unlike other media, Internet provides an opportunity for a journalist to be his own publisher. As a result, an investigating journalist can effectively publish his findings to the world if the topic is of general interest. Tehelka episode has opened a few issues of long term implications for web journalism. The Tehelka team of journalists used what is clearly "Illegal" means to develop a story which they can claim would be in public interest to publish. Violation of individual privacy with secret cameras, using leading questions about the involvement of other persons and bringing up the names of innocent politicians, Offering donations and making a quick request for introduction to influential persons, editing tapes to suit their points of view, selective targetting of some officials and politicians, and implying in the press conferences that they have actually come up with proof of corruption in Politics etc were all acts which can be questioned as "Motivated Journalism".

The fact that atleast one of the investigators was a member of Congress Party in the past which is also the apparent beneficiary of the findings also lends credence to this theory. The past record of Tehelka in the Manoj Prabhakar's secret recordings has also not been very distinguished. If tomorrow a journalist kidnaps a son or daughter of an influential official and coerces him into parting with information that can expose some mis deeds of Politicians, would it be acceptable to the Journalistic society? Is Kidnap in a different leaugue of crimes? If so, where do we draw the line? What if the journalist had been caught in the process and the expose had failed?Are such daring "Journalistic Double Agents" taking a personal risk on themselves? or Are they expecting support from the journalistic community?... naavi.org has already raised this issue of using "Proper Means" to a "Proper End" while discussing "Private Cyber Cops".

We have recommended that the Government should have a "Licensing System" for enterprising "Private Web detectives" who would like to "Patrol" the web in search of "Crimes" or "Attempt to Commit a Crime". Today such attempts could be considered as "Hacking" and the persons indulging in such activities may themselves be punished. Journalists cannot be an exception to this rule. They should record their intention to cross the "Yellow Line" in public interest with a suitable "Non Political" organisation to claim "Journalistic protection" on a later date. Today, Internet does not have atleast in India, a voluntary "Self regulating" set up to either guide web journalists or to act as a "Repository" of such "Investigative Journlism projects".

If web journalists are going to use the freedom of "Publication" offerred by Internet to using "Any Means" to gather "News", there is an urgent need for the community of Web Journailsts and Web Publications to distance themselves from illegal means of News generation and take steps towards setting up a body of "Web Journalists" which would undertake the responsibility to guide budding investigative journalists from taking undue risks and motivated projects that could sully the image of web journalism itself. Can this also be a part of the activities of "Netizens's Forum for Credible Cyber Regulations"?, (a project of naavi.org waiting for larger support from the community)..is a point to ponder. In the mean time there is a need to develop a code of ethics for web journalism that would include among other things, the following clauses.

FAIRNESS

Journalists should respect the rights of people involved in the news, observe the common standards of decency and stand accountable to the public for the fairness and accuracy of their news reports. Persons publicly accused should be given the earliest opportunity to respond. But this should not be misused to force unintended words into the mouths of inexperienced interviewees like what many aggressive journalists such as Karan Thapar regularly adopt. Such follow up interviews should be held under a neutral ground and should be clarificatory in nature and not degenerate to cross examination in a "Trial by the Media".

RESPONSIBILITY

Newspapermen and women who abuse the power of their professional role for selfish motives or unworthy purposes are faithless to the public trust reposede in them. Journalists must avoid impropriety and the appearance of impropriety as well as any conflict of interest or the appearance of conflict. They should neither accept anything nor pursue any activity that might compromise or seem to compromise their integrity. (Reporters should declare their past Political background while putting up a story which can be considered motivated. Similar to the ethics in print journalism when a declaration of hospitality received is a part of the news report).

TRUTH AND ACCURACY

Every effort must be made to assure that the news content is accurate, free from bias and in context, and that all sides are presented fairly. Editorials, analytical articles and commentary should be held to the same standards of accuracy with respect to facts as news reports. Errors of fact, as well as errors of omission, should be corrected promptly and prominently

FREEDOM OF THE PRESS

Freedom of the press belongs to the people. It must be defended against encroachment or assault from any quarter, public or private. However

Journalists must be constantly vigilant against all who would exploit the press for selfish purposes.

IMPARTIALITY

To be impartial does not require the press to be unquestioning or to refrain from editorial expression. Sound practice, however, demands a clear distinction for the reader between news reports and opinion. Articles that contain opinion or personal interpretation should be clearly identified. International and regional organizations of professional journalists, representing altogether 400 000 working journalists in all parts of the World, have held since 1978 consultative meetings under the auspices of UNESCO. The second consultative meeting (Mexico City, 1980) expressed its support to the UNESCO Declaration on Fundamental Principles concerning the Contribution of the Mass Media to Strengthening Peace and International Understanding, to the Promotion of Human Rights and to Countering Racialism, Apartheid and Incitement to War.

Moreover, the meeting adopted the "Mexico Declaration" with a set of principles, which represent common grounds of existing national and regional codes of journalistic ethics as well as relevant provisions contained in various international instruments of a legal nature. The fourth consultative meeting (Prague and Paris, 1983) noted the lasting value of the UNESCO Declaration in which it is stated inter alia that "the exercise of freedom of opinion, expression and information, recognized as an integral part of human rights and fundamental freedoms, is a vital factor in the strengthening of peace and international understanding". Furthermore, the meeting recognized the important role, which information and communication play in the contemporary world, both in national and international spheres, with a growing social responsibility being placed upon the mass media and journalists.

The International Principles of Professional Ethics in Journalism were prepared by several consultative meetings of international and regional organizations of journalists between 19 78 and 1983. The following organizations participated. International Organization of Journalists (IOJ), International Federation of Journalists (IFJ), International Catholic Union of the Press (UCIP), Latin-American Federation of Journalists (FELAP), Latin-American Federation of Press Workers(FELATRAP), Union of African Journalists (UJA), Confederation of ASEAN Journalists (CAJ).

The International Federation of Journalists did not participate in the conclusive meeting of this process in Paris, in November 1983, which agreed the document. On this basis the following principles of professional ethics in journalism were prepared as an international common ground and as a source of inspiration for national and regional codes of ethics. This set of principles is intended to be promoted autonomously by each professional organization through ways and means most adequate to its members.

Principle I: Peoples's Right to True Information

People and individuals have the right to acquire an objective picture of reality by means of accurate and comprehensive information as well as to express themselves freely through the various media of culture and communication.

Principle II: The Journalist's Dedication to Objective Reality

The foremost task of the journalist is to serve the people's right to true and authentic information through an honest dedication to objective reality whereby facts are reported conscientiously in their proper context, pointing out their essential connections and without causing distortions, with due deployment of the creative capacity of the journalist, so that the public is provided with adequate material to facilitate the formation of an accurate and comprehensive picture of the world in which the origin, nature and essence of events, processes and states of affairs are understood as objectively as possible.

Principle III: The Journalist's Social Responsibility

International and regional organizations of professional journalists, representing altogether 400 000 working journalists in all parts of the World, have held since 1978 consultative meetings under the auspices of UNESCO. The second consultative meeting (Mexico City, 1980) expressed its support to the UNESCO Declaration on Fundamental Principles concerning the Contribution of the Mass Media to Strengthening Peace and International Understanding, to the Promotion of Human Rights and to Countering Racialism, Apartheid and Incitement to War. Moreover, the meeting adopted the "Mexico Declaration" with a set of principles, which represent common grounds of existing national and regional codes of journalistic ethics as well as relevant provisions contained in various international instruments of a legal nature.

The fourth consultative meeting noted the lasting value of the UNESCO Declaration in which it is stated inter alia that "the exercise of freedom of opinion, expression and information, recognized as an integral part of human rights and fundamental freedoms, is a vital factor in the strengthening of peace and international understanding". Furthermore, the meeting recognized the important role, which information and communication play in the contemporary world, both in national and international spheres, with a growing social responsibility being placed upon the mass media and journalists.

The International Principles of Professional Ethics in Journalism were prepared by several consultative meetings of international and regional organizations of journalists between 19 78 and 1983. The following organizations participated.

International Organization of Journalists (IOJ), International Federation of Journalists (IFJ), International Catholic Union of the Press (UCIP), Latin-American Federation of Journalists (FELAP), Latin-American Federation of Press Workers(FELATRAP), Union of African Journalists (UJA), Confederation of ASEAN Journalists (CAJ). The International Federation of Journalists did not participate in the conclusive meeting of this process in Paris, in November 1983, which agreed the document. On this basis the following principles of professional ethics in journalism were prepared as an international common ground and as a source of inspiration for national and regional codes of ethics. This set of principles is intended to be promoted autonomously by each professional organization through ways and means most adequate to its members.

HONG KONG

Hong Kong Journalists' Association Code of Ethics:

- A journalist has a duty to maintain the highest professional and ethical standards.
- A journalist shall at all times defend the principle of the freedom of the press and other media in relation to the collection of information and the expression of comment and criticism. He/She shall strive to eliminate distortion, news suppression and censorship.
- A journalist shall strive to ensure that the information he/she disseminates is fair and accurate, avoid the expression of comment and conjecture as established fact and falsification, by distortion, selection or misrepresentation.
- A journalist shall rectify promptly any harmful inaccuracies, ensure that correction and apologies receive due prominence and afford the right of reply to persons criticised when the issue is of sufficient importance.
- A journalist shall obtain information, photographs and illustrations only by straight forward means. The use of other means can be justified only by over-riding considerations of the public interest. The journalist is entitled to exercise a personal conscientious objection to the use of such means.
- Subject to justification by over-riding considerations of the public interest, a journalist shall do nothing which entails intrusion into private grief and distress.
- A journalist shall project confidential sources of information.
- A journalist shall not accept bribes or shall he/she allow other inducements to influence the performance of his/her professional duties.
- A journalist shall not lend himself/herself to the distortion or suppression of the truth because of advertising or other considerations.

- A journalist shall not originate material which encourages discrimination on grounds of race, colour, creed, gender or sexual orientation.
- A journalist shall not take private advantage of information gained in the course of his/her duties, before the information is public knowledge.

INDIA

All India Newspaper Editors' Conference: Code of Ethics for the Press in Reporting and Commenting on Communal Incidents Adopted in 1968:

- A free press can flourish only in a free society. Communalism is a threat to the fabric of our free society and to the nation's solidarity.
- The press has a vital role to play in the consummation of the fundamental objectives enshrined in our Constitution, namely, democracy, secularism, national unity, and integrity and the rule of law. It is the duty of the press to help promote unity and cohesion in the hearts and minds of the people, and refrain from publishing material tending to excite communal passions or inflame communal hatred.
- To this end the press should adhere to the following guidelines in reporting on communal incidents in the country:
- All editorial comments and other expressions of opinion, whether through articles, letters to the Editor, or in any other form should be restrained and free from scurrilous attacks against leaders or communities, and there should be no incitement to violence.
- Generalised allegations casting doubts and aspersions on the Patriotism and loyalty of any community should be eschewed.
- Likewise, generalised charges and allegations against any community of unfair discrimination, amounting to inciting communal hatred and distrust, must also be eschewed.
- Whereas truth should not be suppressed, a deliberate slanting of news of communal incidents should be avoided.
- News of incidents involving loss of life, lawlessness, arson, etc. should be described, reported, and headlined with restraint in strictly objective terms and should not be heavily displayed.
- Items of news calculated to make for peace and harmony and help in the restoration and maintenance of law and order should be given prominence and precdence over other news.
- The greatest caution should be excercised in the selection and publication of pictures, cartoons, poems, etc. so as to avoid arousing communal passions or hatred.
- Names of communities should not be mentioned nor the terms "majority" and "minority" communities be ordinarily used in the course of reports.

- The source from which casualty figures are obtained should always be indicated.
- No facts or figures should be published without fullest possible verification. However, if the publication of the facts or figures is likely to have the effect of arousing communal passions, those facts and figures may not be given.

MALAYSIA

Whereas the Malaysian Press reiterates its belief in the principles of Rukunegara and the national aspirations contained therein;

- It acknowledges its role in contributing to the process of nation-building.
- It recognises its duty to contribute fully to the promotion of racial harmony and national unity.
- It recognises communism, racialism and religious extremism as grave threats to national well-being and security.
- It believes in a liberal, tolerant, democratic society and in the traditional role of a free and responsible Press serving the people by faithfully reporting facts without fear or favour.
- It believes that a credible press is an asset to the nation.
- It believes in upholding standards of social morality.
- It believes that there must be no restrictions on the entry of Malaysians into the profession.
- It believes that the Press has a duty to contribute to the formation of public policy.

Whereas the Malaysian Press does hereby adhere to the following Canons of Journalism:

- The primary responsibility of the Malaysian journalist is to report facts accurately and faithfully and to respect the right of the public to the truth.
- In pursuant of this duty he shall uphold the fundamental freedom in the honest collection of news and the right to fair comment and criticism.
- He shall use only proper methods to obtain news, photographs/films and documents.
- It shall be his duty to rectify and publish information found to be incorrect.
- He shall respect the confidentiality of the source of information.
- He shall uphold standards of morality in the performance of his duties and shall avoid plagiarism, calumny or slander, libel, sedition, unfounded accusations or acceptance of bribe in any form.
- He shall avoid publication of news or reports, communal or extremist in nature, or contrary to the moral value of multiracial Malaysia.

- It shall be incumbent upon him to understand public and national policies pertaining to the profession.

PHILIPPINES

Journalist's Code of Ethics Formulated by Philippine Press Institute and National Press Crub:

- I shall scrupulously report and interpret the news, taking care not to suppress essential facts or to distort the truth by omission or improper emphasis. I recognise the duty to air the other side and the duty to correct substantive errors promptly.
- I shall not violate confidential information or material given me in the exercise of my calling.
- I shall resort only to fair and honest methods in my effort to obtain news, photographs and/or documents, and shall properly identify myself as a representative of the press when obtaining any personal interview intended for publication.
- I shall refrain from writing reports which will adversely affect a private reputation unless the public interest justifies it. At the same time, I shall fight vigorously for public access to information.
- I shall not let personal motives or interests influence me in the performance of my duties; nor shall I accept or offer any present, gift or other consideration of a nature which may cast doubt on my professional integrity.
- I shall not commit any act of plagiarism.
- I shall not in any manner ridicule, cast aspersions on, or degrade any person by reason of sex, creed, religious belief, political conviction, cultural and ethnic origin.
- I shall presume persons accused of crime of being innocent until proven otherwise. I shall exercise caution in publishing names of minors and women involved in criminal cases so that they may not unjustly lose their standing in society.
- I shall not take unfair advantage of fellow journalists.
- I shall accept only such tasks as are compatible with the integrity and dignity of my profession, invoking the 'conscience clause' when duties imposed on me conflict with the voice of my conscience.
- I shall comport myself in public or while performing my duties as journalist in such manner as to maintain the dignity of my profession. When in doubt, decency should be my watch word.

Press Foundation of Asia Reporting Ethnic Tensions the principles below evolved out of a nine-nation journalism conference conducted by the Press Foundation of Asia in Davao City, April 1970:

- Factual accuracy in a single story is no substitute for the total truth. A single story which is factually accurate can nonetheless be misleading.

- Prejudice may sell newspapers but newspapers should resist the temptation to exploit human fears for commercial gains.
- In mixed societies, editors should be aware of the danger of feeding by selective reporting, common prejudicial stereotypes about groups. Generalisations based on the behaviour of an individual or a small number of individuals are invariably unjust.
- When there is potential for communal tension, there should be a constant effort to investigate and expose the underlying causes.
- Statistics can be used to excite passion. It should always be checked and interpreted.
- All stories of communal, racial or religious nature should be scrupulously ascribed to their source. The authority of the source should be properly evaluated.
- Advertisement of an unfair discriminating nature should not be accepted.
- Editors have a responsibility for the tone and truth of the letters' column.
- Harm can be done by distortion in translation, especially in areas where several languages are spoken. Words and phrases may have different connotations among different groups.
- It should be recognised that editorial comment, however benign, does not necessarily compensate for the harm done by a misleading news report.
- Journalists should always use cool and moderate language, especially in headlines and also in display. No concession should be made to rhetoric. Lurid and gory details and emotive reference to past history should be avoided.
- In mixed societies where extra-territorial loyalties are often alleged and are a cause of tension, great care should be taken about stories imputing interference by a foreign power unless it is clearly established.
- The traditional newspaper standards of checking for accuracy should be applied with even greater rigour in any stories involving racial, religious or communal groups. Statements should not be accepted at face value from any source, including official ones, and where necessary, these should be accompanied in the news columns by corroboration and interpretation.
- Unverified runour is not the proper content of news columns especially when there is great danger in speculation about violence.
- When there is violence, particular care should be taken about publication of the first incidents.
- Every effort should be made to portray ethnic groups in other than conflict situations.

- When violence has broken out, the role of government in the supply of information is crucial. There must be a continuous supply of information from this source to prevent rumour, speculation and needless panic. In these circumstances, a close working relationship between the Press and the Government is essential and there should be no division of interest.
- Casualty figures can cause chain reactions, and experience has shown that official figures may be under or over estimated.
- Pictures can distort reality. An unrepresentative picture may lie even more than a news story and add to prejudices.
- Journalists, particularly foreign correspondents, should not report crises without a sufficient understanding of the background of events and trends.
- In newspaper groups publishing in different languages, care should be taken that they speak with the same voice on explosive issues and in times of tension. The cumulative effect of differing coverage and opinion is deadly.
- In mixed societies with underlying causes of tension - social, economic or religious - newspapers and the broadcast media should initiate investigative and interpretative stories with sociological content. These would spread understanding and also help disperse an environment of resentment and suspicion which can turn a minor incident into a riot.

SINGAPORE

Singapore National Union of Journalists' Code of Professional Conduct:

- Every member shall maintain good quality of workmanship and high standard of conduct.
- No member shall do anything that will bring discredit on himself/herself, his/her union, his/her newspaper or other news media or his/her profession.
- Every member shall defend the principles of freedom in the honest collection and dissemination of news and the right of fair comment and criticism.
- Every member shall realise his/her personal responsibility for everything he/she prepares for his/her newspaper or other news media.
- Every member shall report and interpret the news with scrupulous honesty.
- Every member shall use only honest methods to obtain news, pictures and documents.
- No member shall accept any form of bribe whether for publication or suppression nor permit personal interest to influence his/her sense of justice.

- Every member shall respect all necessary confidence regarding sources of information and private documents.
- Every member shall keep in mind the dangers in the laws of libel, contempt of court and copyright.
- Every member shall observe at all times the fraternity of their profession and shall never take unfair advantage of a fellow member.

SOUTH KOREA

Press Ethics Code, 1986:

The social mission of Korean journalists is extremely important, all the more so because the nation is confronted with the task of reconstructing the homeland into a democratic, unified, independent country. Thoroughly aware of this, Korean journalists have organised the Korean Newspaper Editors Association chiefly among the editors of daily newspapers and news agencies across the country and have adopted the Press Ethics Code in order to rectify press ethics and firmly uphold their journalistic integrity.

Journalists have pledged themselves to be faithfully to the Code and to fulfil the people's expectation of good journalism. Not only editors but all engaged with the press shall abide by this Code. Since this Code calls for voluntary implementation, there is no authoritative organisation which enforces it. However, if newspapers and journalists are unfaithful to the Code, they will surely lose public support and thereby endanger their very survival.

- *Freedom.* Freedom of the press, one of the most basic rights of human beings, must be protected so as to satisfy the people's right to know. The press has complete freedom to report and comment. Although any violation of public interest is subject to control under general law, there can be no law restricting or interfering with the freedom of the press. Freedom of the press, of course, includes freedom to criticise and oppose any such law.
- *Responsibility.* The press, being a social instrument, has a special public position, and journalist command a unique social standing. However, this position results only if the press gives the public a true picture of affairs and the public uses this picture as the basis for their judgements. Therefore, the most important responsibility of the press is to faithfully serve the public interest based on the realisation that the public relies upon the press. This responsibility also constitutes the most important reason for preserving the press's special public position. The press displays its special position concretely by being always dauntless in the pursuit of justice, courageous in opposing injustice and in siding with and speaking for the weak.
- *Reporting and Commenting.* The speedy and faithful dissemination of facts is vial to reporting. Therefore, the facts subject to reporting must be limited to those whose value can be verified in terms of their source and content. In commenting, a journalist's independent

beliefs and opinions should be expressed fairly and courageously; in particular, any prejudice that deliberately distorts or evades the truth should be guarded against. Journalists should be sincere towards the public by being as thorough and correct in reporting and commenting as possible.

- *Independence.* The press should stand on the principle that all persons are equal before the law, and should not be swayed by any political, economic or other social prejudices. At the same time, the press cannot be used privately for individual interests running counter to the public interest or for worthless or immoral purposes. Journalists cannot escape responsibility simply because others ordered or requested special treatment.
- *Honour and Freedom.* The press should respect the honour of others and cannot violate individual rights or sentiment out of curiosity or evil intent. In parallel with the demand for the freedom of the press, the press should have the magnanimity to recognise the freedom claimed by others.
- *Dignity.* A high degree of dignity and pride is required of the press because of its public position In particular, vulgar conduct or any activity resulting in vulgarity cannot be tolerated.

Guidelines *for reporting:*

Interpretation of the provisions of Articles 3 and 4, Chapter "Honour and Freedom of Others", Guidelines for Implementation of the Press Ethics Code (October 13, 1961):

- Offenders caught in the very act shall be excepted from he "principle that in reporting criminal cases, the accused shall be treated as not guilty until convicted, " Guidelines for Implementation of the Press Ethics Code'
- The term "minor" mentioned in Article 4, Chapter "Honour and Freedom of Others" Guidelines for Implementation of the Press Ethics Code, means those who are under twenty years of age.
- In the provision that the name and picture of minor suspects and the accused and sexually assaulted women shall not be disclosed. in Article 4, Chapter "Honour and Freedom of Others" Guidelines for Implementation of the Press Ethics Code, no number of home address in the case of Seoul and other cities, nor name of village in other provincial areas, can be disclosed.
- In giving addresses, no number, "doing" and "ban" in Seoul and other cities, nor village "ban" and number in other provincial areas can be disclosed.

Regarding sexually assaulted women, the Commission made the ruling on May 26, 1965, that "in giving address, no number, `doing' and `ban' in Seoul and other cities, nor village `ban' and number in other provincial areas can be given." Again on October 2, 1978, the Commission ruled that even if an address is not given directly, any information leading to the inference of the victim's address, such as a case in which the culprit is identified with the remark, "he assaulted a woman of his village," or in which the location of the victim's office is given or the names of her relatives are identified is also subject to control.

Interpretation of the provisions of Articles 1 and 2, Chapter "Honour and Freedom of Others" Guidelines for Implementation of the Press Ethics Code (February 15, 1963).

- No individual honour shall be damaged unless so doing is for the sake of public interest.
- Even if it is for public interest, no undue personal attacks or low language can be used.
- The same is true for individuals, public officials, offices or organisations, and of juridical persons, non-juridical persons or groups.

Reporting of Suicides (January 8, 1967)

In consideration of the effect the reports of suicide have on society, the Commission makes the following rules as the criteria for such reports:

- The name and amount of the lethal dose of the medicine used in suicide shall not be given. However, such may be reported in incidents related with crime or carrying a special social significance.
- Cruel methods of suicide shall not be described.
- Since the words "group suicide" can be an inaccurate expression in case it involves children and other family members not willing to die, accurate expression shall be used depending on the incident. At no time should such incidents be reported in a way that caters to the public's curiosity, nor should they be beautified.

Notice on Reports about Stimulants. (April 18, 1979)

Since the giving or the names of stimulants such as Sekonal and adhesive glue in reporting the cases of adolescents using stimulants is apt to influence innocent adolescents into making similar mistakes, an instruction was handed out not to make public the names of such medicine or material.

Reports on Kidnapping (August 30, 1967)

- Reports on kidnappings should be made with an emphasis on the safe return of the
- kidnapped victim. Such reports shall in principle be withheld so long as the victim remains in the hands of the abductor. However, reports may be made when such reporting is considered necessary for the rescue of the victim.

- The whole picture of the kidnapping incident may well be made once the incident has come to a solution.

Reports on Suspects (September 6, 1967)

- Excepting those caught in the act or those against whom evidence is salient, the address, name, picture and occupation of suspects shall not be disclosed.
- No reports that prompt the assumption that suspects are guilty shall be made without any express evidence.
- No picture of the brutal scene of an on-the-spot investigation of a criminal case shall be released.

Reports on Protection of Surrendered Agents and Those Informing on Communist Agents (February 14, 1968):

- In reports about those who have reported espionage agents and Communist guerrillas, pseudonyms shall be used and their pictures, workshops and addresses shall not be made public. Addresses, however, down to city, county or ward, can be disclosed.
- The provision of the preceding paragraph shall also be applied to surrendered espionage agents and Communist guerrillas. However, if government authorities make official announcements or if there exists the need to inform the people, they shall be made public.

Reports without credits (July 26, 1964)

The following violates the provisions of in Article 4, Chapter "Dignity" Guidelines for Implementation of the Press Ethics Code:

- Use of distributed articles after replacing its by-line name with that of one's own correspondent.
- Use of the whole of distributed articles without giving any credit.
- Use of distributed articles after altering (plagiarising) leads.
- Use of plagiarised part of wire service articles in one's own article.

Children's newspapers or columns and advertisement on medicine for venereal diseases. (June 1, 1966) On newspapers where advertisements or medicines for venereal disease are carried, no children's columns shall be used.

SRI LANKA

Sri Lanka Press Council Code of Ethics for Journalists:

Part I: Section (I) - General

Government Notifications. RULES made by Sri Lanka Press Council setting out the Code of Ethics for Journalists under Section 30(i) (a) of the Sri Lanka Press Council Law, No.5 of 1973, and approved by Parliament under Section 30 (3) of the said Law.

- These rules may be cited as the Press Council (Code of Ethics for Journalists) Rules, 1981. Every journalist shall —

- Use all reasonable means within his power to ascertain prior to publication the veracity of the contents of any article written by him for publication;
- Refrain from reporting or causing to be printed or published any matter which he knows or has reason to believe to be false or inaccurate;
- Refrain from distorting the truth by any act of commission or willful omission;
- Take all possible steps to correct within the shortest possible space of time any inaccuracy or incorrect information in any report or article for the writing or publication of which he is responsible; and
- Refrain from publishing or causing to be published any matter which may offend public taste or morality or tend to lower the standards of public taste or morality.

• Every journalist shall use all reasonable means at his command in any report or article he writes or causes to be printed or published to draw a clear distinction between any statement of fact on the one hand and any expression of opinion or criticism on the other.
• Every journalist shall observe secrecy regarding any source of information unless the person who gave him such information authorizes the disclosure of his identity.
• Every journalist shall respect the reputation of an individual and refrain from reporting or causing to be printed or published any information or comment regarding an individual's private life unless the publication of said matter is in the public interest as distinguished from public curiosity.
• (1) In reporting or causing to be printed or published accounts of crimes or criminal cases, a journalist shall not –
  - Name victims of sex crimes;
  - Name any young person accused of a criminal offense who to his knowledge is below the age of eighteen and to his knowledge is a person who has no previous convictions; or
  - Name any person as being a relative of a person accused or convicted of a crime for the sole purpose of informing the reader of the relationship between the person so named and the person charged, unless the public interest would be served by the publication of the said matter.
• (2) In reporting or causing to be printed or published accounts of matrimonial causes or actions, a journalist shall refrain from reporting or publishing any offensive details
• A journalist shall not commit plagiarism.

- A journalist shall not present any matter in a manner designed to promote sadism, violence or salacity.
- A journalist shall not report or cause to be printed or published any matter that is obscene unless the public interest is served by the publication thereof.
- A journalist shall not report or cause to be printed or published any matter for the purpose of promoting communal or religious discord or violence.
- Every journalist shall safeguard the dignity of his profession. He shall not accept any bribe in money, kind or service for any matter connected with or incidental to his profession.

The goal of The New York Times is to cover the news as impartially as possible — "without fear or favour," in the words of Adolph Ochs, our patriarch — and to treat readers, news sources, advertisers and others fairly and openly, and to be seen to be doing so. The reputation of The Times rests upon such perceptions, and so do the professional reputations of its staff members. Thus The Times and members of its news department and editorial page staff share an interest in avoiding conflicts of interest or an appearance of a conflict. For more than a century, men and women of The Times have jealously guarded the paper's integrity. Whatever else we contribute, our first duty is to make sure the integrity of The Times is not blemished during our stewardship. Conflicts of interest, real or apparent, may come up in many areas.

They may involve the relationships of staff members with readers, news sources, advocacy groups, advertisers, or competitors; with one another, or with the newspaper or its parent company. And at a time when two-career families are the norm, the civic and professional activities of spouses, family and companions can create conflicts or the appearance of conflicts. In keeping with its solemn responsibilities under the First Amendment, The Times strives to maintain the highest standards of journalistic ethics. It is confident that its staff members share that goal. The Times also recognizes that staff members should be free to do creative, civic and personal work and to earn extra income in ways separate from their work at The Times. Before engaging in such outside activities, though, staff members should exercise mature professional judgment and consider the stake we all have in The Times's irreplaceable good name.

THE SCOPE OF THESE GUIDELINES

These guidelines generally apply to all members of the news and editorial departments whose work directly affects the content of the paper, including those on leaves of absence. They include reporters, editors, editorial writers, photographers, picture editors, art directors, artists, designers, graphics editors and researchers. This group of professional journalists is what this text means by "staff" or "staff members." News clerks, administrative assistants, secretaries and other support staff are generally not bound by these strictures, with two important exceptions: First, no newsroom or editorial page employee may exploit for personal gain any nonpublic information acquired at work, or use his or her association with The Times to gain favour or advantage. And second, no one may do anything that damages The Times's reputation for strict neutrality in reporting on politics and government; in particular, no one may wear campaign buttons or display any other form of political partisanship while on the job. Our contracts with freelance contributors require them to avoid conflicts of interest, real or apparent. The Times believes beyond question that its staff shares the values these guidelines are intended to protect. In the past The Times has resolved differences of view over applying these values amiably through discussion, almost without exception. The paper has every reason to believe that pattern will continue. Nevertheless, The Times views any deliberate violation of these guidelines as a serious offense that may lead to disciplinary action, potentially including dismissal, subject to the terms of any applicable collective bargaining agreement. Our fundamental purpose is to protect the impartiality and neutrality of The Times and the integrity of its report. In many instances, merely applying that purpose with common sense will point to the ethical course. Sometimes the answer is self-evident. Simply asking oneself whether a course of action might damage the paper's reputation is often enough to gauge whether the action is appropriate. Every staff member is expected to read this document carefully and to think about how it might apply to his or her duties.

A lack of familiarity with its provisions cannot excuse a violation; to the contrary, it makes the violation worse. The provisions presented here can offer only broad principles and some examples. Our world changes constantly, sometimes dramatically. No written document could anticipate every possibility. Thus we expect staff members to consult their supervisors and the standards editor or the deputy editorial page editor if they have any doubts about any particular situation or opportunity covered by this document. In most cases an exchange of e-mails should suffice. Thus this handbook is not an exhaustive compilation of all situations that may give rise to an actual or perceived conflict of interest. It does not exclude situations or issues giving rise to such conflicts simply because they are not explicitly covered within this document, nor does the document or any of its particular provisions create an implied or express contract of employment with any individual to whom the guidelines apply.

The Times reserves the right to modify and expand the guidelines from time to time, as appropriate. The authority to interpret and apply these guidelines is vested in department heads and ranking editors, most notably in the standards editor and the deputy editorial page editor. They may delegate that duty to their ranking assistants, but they remain responsible for decisions made in their name. In addition to this handbook, we observe the Newsroom Integrity Statement, promulgated in 1999, which deals with such rudimentary professional practices as the importance of checking facts, the exactness of quotations, the integrity of photographs and our distaste for anonymous sourcing; and the Policy on Confidential Sources, issued in 2004. These documents are available from the office of the associate managing editor for news administration or on the Newsroom home page under Policies. As employees of the Times Company, we observe the Rules of the Road, which are the axiomatic standards of behaviour governing our dealing with colleagues and going about our work.

The Rules are available from the office of the associate managing editor for news administration. The Times treats its readers as fairly and openly as possible. In print and online, we tell our readers the complete, unvarnished truth as best we can learn it. It is our policy to correct our errors, large and small, as soon as we become aware of them. We treat our readers no less fairly in private than in public. Anyone who deals with readers is expected to honour that principle, knowing that ultimately the readers are our employers. Civility applies whether an exchange takes place in person, by telephone, by letter or online. Simple courtesy suggests that we not alienate our readers by ignoring their letters and e-mails that warrant reply. The Times gathers information for the benefit of its readers. Staff members may not use their Times position to make inquiries for any other purpose. As noted in paragraph 6, they may not seek any advantage for themselves or others by acting on or disclosing information acquired in their work but not yet available to readers. Staff members who plagiarize or who knowingly or recklessly provide false information for publication betray our fundamental pact with our readers. We will not tolerate such behaviour. The Times treats news sources just as fairly and openly as it treats readers. We do not inquire pointlessly into someone's personal life. Staff members may not threaten to damage uncooperative sources. They may not promise favorable coverage in return for cooperation. They may not pay for interviews or unpublished documents. Staff members should disclose their identity to people they cover (whether face to face or otherwise), though they need not always announce their status as journalists when seeking information normally available to the public. Staff members may not pose as police officers, lawyers, business people or anyone else when they are working as journalists. (As happens on rare occasions, when seeking to enter countries that bar journalists, correspondents may take cover from vagueness and identify themselves as traveling on business or as tourists.) Theater, music and art critics and other writers who review goods or services offered to the public may conceal their Times connection but may not normally assert a false identity or affiliation.

As an exception, restaurant critics may make reservations in false names to protect their identity. Restaurant critics and travel writers must conceal their Times affiliation to eliminate the possibility of special treatment. Relationships with sources require the utmost in sound judgment and self discipline to prevent the fact or appearance of partiality. Cultivating sources is an essential skill, often practiced most effectively in informal settings outside of normal business hours. Yet staff members, especially those assigned to beats, must be sensitive that personal relationships with news sources can erode into favoritism, in fact or appearance. And conversely staff members must be aware that sources are eager to win our good will for reasons of their own. Even though this topic defies hard and fast rules, it is essential that we preserve a professional detachment, free of any whiff of bias. Staff members may see sources informally over a meal or drinks, but they must keep in mind the difference between legitimate business and personal friendship.

A City Hall reporter who enjoys a weekly round of golf with a City Council member, for example, risks creating an appearance of coziness, even if they sometimes discuss business on the course. So does a reporter who joins a regular card game or is a familiar face in a corporation's box seats or who spends weekends in the company of people he or she covers. Scrupulous practice requires that periodically we step back and take a hard look at whether we have drifted too close to sources we deal with regularly. The acid test of freedom from favoritism is the ability to maintain good working relationships with all parties to a dispute. Clearly, romantic involvement with a news source would foster an appearance of partiality. Therefore staff members who develop close relationships with people who might figure in coverage they provide, edit, package or supervise must disclose those relationships to the standards editor, the associate managing editor for news administration or the deputy editorial page editor. In some cases, no further action may be needed. But in other instances staff members may have to recuse themselves from certain coverage.

And in still other cases, assignments may have to be modified or beats changed. In a few instances, a staff member may have to move to a different department — from business and financial news, say, to the culture desk—to avoid the appearance of conflict. Staff members must obey the law in the pursuit of news. They may not break into buildings, homes, apartments or offices. They may not purloin data, documents or other property, including such electronic property as databases and e-mail or voice mail messages. They may not tap telephones, invade computer files or otherwise eavesdrop electronically on news sources. In short, they may not commit illegal acts of any sort. Staff members may not use the identification cards or special license plates issued by police or other official agencies except in doing their jobs. Staff members who have applied for or hold "NYP" or other special plates should disclose that fact to the associate managing editor for news administration or the deputy editorial page editor. Staff members whose duties do not require special plates must return them. Staff members may not record conversations without the prior consent of all parties to the conversations. Even where the law allows recording with only one party aware of it, the practice is a deception.

Masthead editors may make rare exceptions to this prohibition in places where recordings made secretly are legal. The Times pays the expenses when its representatives entertain news sources (including government officials) or travel to cover them. In some business situations and in some cultures, it may be unavoidable to accept a meal or a drink paid for by a news source. For example, a Times reporter need not decline every invitation to interview an executive over lunch in the corporation's private dining room, where it is all but impossible to pick up the check. Whenever practical, however, the reporter should suggest dining where The Times can pay. A simple buffet of muffins and coffee at a news conference, for example, is harmless, but a staff member should not attend a breakfast or lunch held periodically for the press by a "newsmaker" unless The Times pays for the staff member's meals.

Staff members may not accept free or discounted transportation and lodging except where special circumstances give us little or no choice. Among them are certain military or scientific expeditions and other trips for which alternative arrangements would be impractical — for example, a flight aboard a corporate jet during which an executive is interviewed. Staff members should consult their supervisors and the standards editor or the deputy editorial page editor when special circumstances arise. 30. Staff members who review artistic performances or cover athletic or other events where admission is charged (for example, the New York Auto Show) may accept the press passes or tickets customarily made available. No other staff members, not even editors in the culture and sports departments, may accept free tickets.

Even when paying the box office price, no staff member may use his or her Times position to request choice or hard-to-get seats unless the performance has a clear bearing on his or her job. Staff members compete zealously but deal with competitors openly and honestly. We do not invent obstacles to hamstring their efforts. When we use facts reported by another publication, we attribute them. Staff members may not join teams covering news events for other organizations, and they may not accept payment from competitors for news tips.

They may not be listed on the masthead of any non-Times publication, except for publications serving organizations of the sort described in paragraph 70. Common examples include a church or synagogue newsletter, an alumni magazine or a club bulletin. Staff members may not accept gifts, tickets, discounts, reimbursements or other inducements from any individuals or organizations covered by The Times or likely to be covered by The Times. (Exceptions may be made for trinkets of nominal value, say, $25 or less, such as a mug or a cap with a company logo.) Gifts should be returned with a polite explanation.

Staff members may not accept employment or compensation of any sort from individuals or organizations who figure or are likely to figure in coverage they provide, edit, package or supervise. Staff members may not accept anything that could be construed as a payment for favorable coverage or as an inducement to alter or forgo unfavorable coverage. They may share in reprint fees that other journalistic media pay The Times, according to the terms of our contract with the Newspaper Guild. They may also share in fees paid by non-journalistic parties for permission to reprint Times material in advertisements or promotions, though their share of those fees may not exceed $200 an article. Staff members may accept any gifts or discounts available to the general public. Normally they are also free to take advantage of conventional corporate discounts that the Times Company has offered to share with all employees (for example, corporate car rental rates). And staff members may accept free admission at museums or other benefits extended to all Times employees by virtue of the Times Company Foundation's support of various cultural institutions. Staff members must be mindful, however, that large discounts — even those negotiated by the Times Company — may create the appearance of partiality, especially by those who have a hand in the coverage of the company or industry offering the discount. If General Motors, for instance, offers substantial trade discounts to all Times Company employees, the Detroit correspondent should not accept without discussing the possible appearance of favoritism with the responsible editors. If any such discounts do raise doubts, staff members should bring them to the attention of their department heads and the standards editor or the deputy editorial page editor before accepting.

Unless the special terms are offered by The New York Times Company or a Times subsidiary or affiliate, staff members may not buy stock in initial public offerings through "friends and family shares" where any plausible possibility exists of a real or apparent conflict of interest. Staff members may not accept allocations from brokerage firms. It is an inherent conflict for a Times staff member to perform public relations work, paid or unpaid. Staff members may not advise individuals or organizations how to deal successfully with the news media (though they may of course explain the paper's normal workings and steer outsiders to the appropriate Times person). They may not, for example, advise candidates for public office, write or edit annual reports or contribute to the programs of sports teams. They should not take part in public relations workshops that charge admission or imply privileged access to Times people, or participate in surveys asking their opinion of an organization's press relations or public image.

They are free, however, to offer reasonable help to institutions such as their child's school, a small museum, a community charity or their house of worship. Staff members may not serve as ghost writers or co-authors for individuals who figure or are likely to figure in coverage they provide, edit, package or supervise. They may not undertake such assignments for organizations that espouse a cause. Staff members may not engage in financial counseling. They may not manage money for others, proffer investment advice, or operate or help operate an investment company of any sort, with or without pay. They may not do anything that would require registration as an investment adviser. They may, however, help family members with ordinary financial planning and serve as executors or administrators of estates of relatives and friends and as court-appointed conservators and guardians.

The Times freely acknowledges that outside appearances can enhance the reputation of its bylines and serve the paper's interests. Nevertheless, no staff member may appear before an outside group if the appearance could reasonably create an actual or apparent conflict of interest or undermine public trust in the paper's impartiality. No staff member who takes part in a broadcast, Webcast, public forum or panel discussion may write or edit news articles about that event. Staff members should be especially sensitive to the appearance of partiality when they address groups that might figure in coverage they provide, edit, package or supervise, especially if the setting might suggest a close relationship to the sponsoring group.

Before accepting such an invitation, a staff member must consult with the standards editor or the deputy editorial page editor. Generally, a reporter recently returned from the Middle East might comfortably address a suburban synagogue or mosque but should not appear before a group that lobbies for Israel or the Arab states. A reporter who writes about the environment could appropriately speak to a garden club but not to conservation groups known for their efforts to influence public policy. Staff members may not accept invitations to speak before a single company (for example, the Citigroup executive retreat) or an industry assembly (for example, organized baseball's winter meeting) unless The Times decides the appearance is useful and will not damage the newspaper's reputation for impartiality.

In that case, The Times will pay expenses; no speaker's fee should be accepted. Staff members invited to make such appearances should consult their supervisors and the standards editor or the deputy editorial page editor. 45. Staff members should not accept invitations to speak where their function is to attract customers to an event primarily intended as profit-making. Staff members may accept speaking fees, honorariums, expense reimbursement and free transportation only from educational or other nonprofit groups for which lobbying and political activity are not a major focus. If a speaking fee exceeds $5,000, the staff member must consult the standards editor, the associate managing editor for news administration or the deputy editorial page editor before accepting. Staff members who accept fees, honorariums or expenses for speaking engagements must file with the associate managing editor for news administration or the deputy editorial page editor by January 31 of each year an accounting of the previous year's appearances. If their fees total less than $5,000, no annual accounting is required. Fees earned under Times auspices for promotional or other approved purposes need not be included.

Staff members who write books and want to promote them must give their supervisor a schedule of proposed appearances. They may accept routine expenses and fees in promotional appearances, but they must make every effort to ensure that their appearances conform to the spirit of these guidelines and do not interfere with their responsibilities to the paper. If they have doubts about an appearance, they must consult their supervisor and the standards editor or the deputy editorial page editor. Speeches and other outside endeavors by staff members, paid or unpaid, should not imply that they carry the endorsement of The Times (unless they do). To the contrary, the staff member should gracefully remind the audience that the views expressed are his or her own. Outside commitments should not interfere with the speaker's responsibilities at The Times.

Thus no staff member should agree to an extensive speaking schedule without approval from a supervisor. Staff members may not enter competitions sponsored by individuals or groups who have a direct interest in the tenor of Times coverage. They may not act as judges for these competitions or accept their awards. Common examples are contests sponsored by commercial, political or professional associations to judge coverage of their affairs. The standards editor or the deputy editorial page editor may make exceptions for competitions underwritten by corporate sponsors if broad in scope and independently judged, such as the University of Missouri awards for consumer journalism, long sponsored by J.C. Penney.

Staff members may compete in competitions sponsored by groups whose members are all journalists or whose members demonstrably have no direct interest in the tenor of coverage of the field being judged. Times staff members may act as judges for such competitions and accept their awards. For example, a staff member may enter a university-sponsored competition for coverage of economic or foreign affairs but not accept an advocacy group's prize for outstanding environmental coverage. This prohibition on taking part in sponsored competitions applies to film festivals or awards in which critics are asked to vote and to such competitions as the Tony Awards, the Heisman Trophy, most valuable player and rookie of the year honors and admission to sports halls of fame. Cooperation of this sort puts the paper's independence into question.

A current list of some competitions that The Times has approved is posted on the Newsroom home page under Policies. Staff members who would like to enter others should consult their supervisors and the standards editor or the deputy editorial page editor. A critical factor in approving a competition, whatever its sponsorship, is a record of arm's-length decisions, including a willingness to honour critical reporting. Staff members who win unsought awards from groups that do not meet the criteria established here should decline politely. Normally staff members are free to accept honorary degrees, medals and other awards from colleges, universities and other educational institutions. Those who cover higher education or supervise that coverage should be sensitive to any appearance of coziness or favoritism. Those in doubt should consult the standards editor or the deputy editorial page editor. Staff members who borrow equipment, vehicles or other goods for evaluation or review must return the borrowed items as soon as possible. Similarly, items borrowed to be photographed, such as fashion apparel or home furnishings, should be returned promptly.

Staff members may keep for their own collections — but may not sell or copy — books, recordings, tapes, compact discs and computer programs sent to them for review. Such submissions are considered press releases. Recorded or digital media, such as tapes or disks, must be destroyed or returned to the provider if not retained by the journalist; they may not be copied, given away or left where they could be carried off for illicit copying or reuse. Staff members may not collaborate in ventures involving individuals or organizations that figure or are likely to figure in coverage they provide, edit, package or supervise. Among other things, this prohibition applies to collaborating in writing books, pamphlets, reports, scripts, scores or any other material and in making photographs or creating artwork of any sort. Except in reviews or columns published in The Times or on its Web site or appropriately voiced in authorized public appearances, staff members may not offer endorsements, testimonials or promotional blurbs for books, films, television programs or any other programs, products or ventures.

Masthead editors may authorize rare exceptions (for instance, when a staff member has become expert in a field unrelated to his or her Times duties). This restriction does not apply when permission is given to reprint Times material. Staff members of The Times are family members and responsible citizens as well as journalists. The Times respects their educating their children, exercising their religion, voting in elections and taking active part in community affairs. Nothing in this policy is meant to infringe upon those rights. But even in the best of causes, Times staff members have a duty to avoid the appearance of a conflict. They should never invoke The Times's name in private activities. Certain of these requirements apply to all newsroom and editorial page employees, journalists and support staff alike.

No newsroom or editorial employee may do anything that damages The Times's reputation for strict neutrality in reporting on politics and government. In particular, no one may wear campaign buttons or display any other sign of political partisanship while on the job. Journalists have no place on the playing fields of politics. Staff members are entitled to vote, but they must do nothing that might raise questions about their professional neutrality or that of The Times. In particular, they may not campaign for, demonstrate for, or endorse candidates, ballot causes or efforts to enact legislation. They may not wear campaign buttons or themselves display any other insignia of partisan politics. They should recognize that a bumper sticker on the family car or a campaign sign on the lawn may be misread as theirs, no matter who in their household actually placed the sticker or the sign. Staff members may not themselves give money to, or raise money for, any political candidate or election cause.

Given the ease of Internet access to public records of campaign contributors, any political giving by a Times staff member would carry a great risk of feeding a false impression that the paper is taking sides. No staff member may seek public office anywhere. Seeking or serving in public office plainly violates the professional detachment expected of a journalist. It poses a risk of having the staff member's political views imputed to The Times, and it can sow a suspicion of favoritism in The Times's political coverage when one of its staff is an active participant. Staff members may not march or rally in support of public causes or movements, sign ads taking a position on public issues, or lend their name to campaigns, benefit dinners or similar events if doing so might reasonably raise doubts about their ability or The Times's ability to function as neutral observers in covering the news.

Staff members must keep in mind that neighbors and other observers commonly see them as representatives of The Times. Staff members may appear from time to time on radio and television programs devoted to public affairs, but they should avoid expressing views that go beyond what they would be allowed to say in the paper. Op-Ed columnists and editorial writers enjoy more leeway than others in speaking publicly because their business is expressing opinions. The Times nevertheless expects them to consider carefully the forums in which they appear and to protect the standards and impartiality of the newspaper as a whole. Staff members must be sensitive that perfectly proper political activity by their spouses, family or companions may nevertheless create conflicts of interest or the appearance of conflict. When such a possibility arises, the staff member should advise his or her department head and the standards editor or the deputy editorial page editor.

Depending on circumstances, the staff member may have to recuse himself or herself from certain coverage or even move to a job unrelated to the activities in question. A staff member with any doubts about a proposed political activity should consult the standards editor or the deputy editorial page editor. These restrictions protect the heart of our mission as journalists. Though The Times will consider matters case by case, it will be exceedingly cautious before permitting an exception. Staff members may not serve on government boards or commissions, paid or unpaid. They may not join boards of trustees, advisory committees or similar groups except those serving journalistic organizations or otherwise promoting journalism education.

Those in doubt about such activities should consult their supervisors and the standards editor or the deputy editorial page editor. Depending on circumstances, exceptions may be made to permit staff members to serve their alma mater (or their children's alma mater) as a trustee or visitor at schools that seldom if ever generate news of interest to The Times. The Times has no wish to impede good community citizenship. Normally the restriction on joining trustee boards or advisory committees will not apply to organizations that are highly unlikely to generate news of interest to The Times and that do not generally seek to shape public policy. These typically include houses of worship, community charities, local libraries, fine arts groups, hobby groups, youth athletic leagues, country clubs and alumni groups. Within reason staff members may help such groups with relatively modest fundraising. They should not play a leading role or ever lead a donor to expect a favour in return. They should never solicit anyone with whom they or The Times has professional dealings.

Those in any doubt about what is permissible should consult the standards editor or the deputy editorial page editor. Staff members may not solicit funds for political, social, religious, educational, philanthropic or other causes that reach beyond the sorts of groups described in paragraph 70. Doing so could create an expectation of a favour in return. Staff members should think carefully about their own contributions to various causes, bearing in mind the need for neutrality on divisive issues. Those in doubt about contributions should consult their supervisors and the standards editor or the deputy editorial page editor. The Times treats advertisers as fairly and openly as it treats readers and news sources. The relationship between The Times and advertisers rests on the understanding, long observed in all departments, that news and advertising are strictly separate — that those who deal with either one have distinct obligations and interests and neither group will try to influence the other.

Members of the news department should maintain their disinterest and objectivity by avoiding discussions of advertising needs, goals and problems except where those needs or problems are directly related to the business of the news department. In many instances, for example, the news and advertising departments may properly confer on the layout and configuration of the paper or the timing of special sections. When authorized by the executive editor, members of the news staff may take part in interdepartmental committees on problems that affect several departments, including news. As far as possible they should leave advertising issues to colleagues from the business side. From time to time, when authorized by the executive editor or the editorial page editor, staff members may take part in events organized by The Times for marketing or promotion. But they should stick to their expertise and refrain from saying anything that sounds like a sales pitch.

No one in the news department below the masthead level (except when authorized by the executive editor) may exchange information with the advertising department or with advertisers about the timing or content of advertising, the timing or content of articles or the assignment of staff or freelance writers, editors, artists, designers or photographers. The Times's good name does not belong to any of us. No one has a right to expropriate it for private purposes. Staff members may not use Times identification cards for purposes not connected with Times employment. Cards may not be used to obtain special treatment or advantage from governmental, commercial or other organizations (except when the card is required for a benefit available to all Times Company employees by virtue of its foundation's charitable relationships, such as free admission to the Metropolitan Museum). Staff members may not use Times stationery, business cards, forms or other materials for any purpose except the business of the newspaper. Staff members must not disclose confidential information about the operations, policies or plans of The Times or its corporate affiliates.

Department heads and masthead executives may authorize other staff members to comment publicly on policies or plans within the staff members' areas of responsibility and expertise. If staff members are approached by other media or other outsiders to discuss Times content or policy, they should refer the questioners to a masthead executive or the corporate communications department. Staff members are free to discuss their own activities in public, provided their comments do not create an impression that they lack journalistic impartiality or speak for The Times. None of these restrictions should be interpreted as barring a staff member from responding openly and honestly to any reasonable inquiry from a reader about that staff member's work. If a reader asks for a correction, that request should be passed promptly to a supervisor. If the request threatens legal action or appears to be from a lawyer, the complaint should be promptly referred to the legal department through a department head.

Any staff member intending to write or assemble a nonfiction book based on material that derives from his or her assignment or beat must notify The Times in advance, so The Times can decide whether to make a competitive bid to publish the work. In this regard, staff members cannot accept or entertain any sort of preemptory bid from an outside publisher before allowing The Times to consider the project. Staff members are required to inform The Times of any such project or proposal, in writing, by sending a letter or e-mail to their department head, as well as to the standards editor or the deputy editorial page editor. The notification should include any information about the anticipated time frame of the project, including (if applicable) the time frame that an outside publisher has set for bidding on the project. Within a reasonable period, taking into account the time frame for the project, The Times will inform the staff member in writing whether it wants to compete for the project. If it does, The Times will provide the staff member with a competitive bid. In the end, the staff member and his or her agent have no obligation to accept The Times's offer.

This process is intended to assure The Times a seat at the table in any negotiations, including auctions, involving books based on materials derived from a Times assignment or beat. These guidelines do not apply to book proposals or projects that involve the reproduction of articles, columns, photographs, artwork or other material created by staff members and published in The Times or on nytimes. The Times owns such material outright, and no such material may be reproduced elsewhere without the prior written permission of The Times, nor may it be rewritten, updated or otherwise altered and then republished without The Times's prior written permission. Staff members are often approached by agents, producers, studios or others seeking rights to Times material. Such inquiries must be forwarded immediately to the standards editor or to the deputy editorial page editor and to the legal department.

If a staff member represented by the Newspaper Guild has questions about rights to payment for reprints of articles that the staff member has written, he or she should refer to The Times's collective bargaining agreement with the Guild. In general, this agreement calls for a 50/50 split of the fees involved. In contemplating book projects — or other outside endeavors — staff members must never give an impression they might benefit financially from the outcome of news events. Staff members may not negotiate with any outside person or entity for any rights to an article or story idea before the article has run in The Times. Staff members involved in covering a running story may not negotiate over books, articles, films, programs or media projects of any sort based on that coverage until that news has played out, unless they have written permission in advance from the standards editor or the deputy editorial page editor.

No staff member may serve as a ghost writer or co-author for individuals who figure or are likely to figure in coverage they provide, edit, package or supervise. No staff member will be given a leave of absence, paid or unpaid, to write a book without the explicit permission of the executive editor or the editorial page editor. Ideally, a staff member who feels he or she will need to leave to complete a book project should inform The Times of the intention to seek a leave at the same time he or she first makes the book project available for consideration by The Times. A decision to grant or deny a request for a book leave — like requests for most other leaves of absence — will be based on many factors, including previous book leaves or accommodations the newspaper has granted to the staff member; the impact the leave will have on departmental staffing needs, and the degree to which The Times believes the book project will accrue to the newspaper's interests.

If a staff member represented by the Newspaper Guild has a question about a leave of absence, he or she should refer to The Times's collective bargaining agreement with the Guild. At no time may a staff member turn over notes, interviews, documents or other working materials to any third party, including agents, producers, studios or outside production agencies, or share those materials with them unless legally compelled to do so. Staff members are advised that in such circumstances, The Times's legal department will provide assistance. (Those represented by the Guild should refer to their collective bargaining agreement for the parameters of that assistance.) As a matter of policy, The Times will not give commercial producers or publishers access to working materials any more than it would turn them over to government prosecutors for use in court. This paragraph applies only to television and film: Staff members offered "consulting" agreements by agents, producers, studios or others must consult the standards editor or the deputy editorial page editor before accepting. No staff member may serve as a consultant to a film or programme that he or she knows in advance is tendentious or clearly distorts the underlying facts. In no case should a consulting role be described in a way that invokes The Times or implies its endorsement or participation. Staff members are generally entitled to accept freelance assignments that do not directly compete with The Times's own offerings. Normally, work for competitors will not be permitted. When allowed in rare instances, permission will be limited to cases in which The Times is not interested in assigning the staff member a similar piece or project.

The Times competes in a far larger arena today than in the past. The printed paper remains our flagship, as does The International Herald Tribune internationally, but we reach an audience of millions through The New York Times on the Web. We are learning to translate our journalism into outstanding television. We publish numerous books, both original and drawn from past articles; we offer archival photos of museum quality. We deliver The New York Times in its complete form via the Web. Our bedrock mission is to serve a high-quality audience that values Times journalism, relying on any appropriate medium. Competitors include any newspaper, magazine or other media of publication, regardless of form, with an editorial focus on either New York City or general-interest news and information. If the competitive status of a publication, Web site or TV production is unclear, a staff member should consult with the standards editor or the deputy editorial page editor. Staff members are encouraged (but not required) to offer their freelance work to The Times or, in the case of a Web site, to The New York Times on the Web before trying to sell it elsewhere.

The Times offers a number of outlets for work for which a staff member is paid extra, including the Times Magazine, the Week in Review, the Book Review and special sections. (As paragraph 84 requires of book proposals, any freelance material that derives from a Times assignment or beat must first be offered to The Times before a staff member offers it elsewhere.) Staff members must ensure that their freelance work does not interfere with their responsibilities to The Times and that it is consistent with these policies and guidelines. If any doubt exists, they must consult their supervisors and the standards editor or the deputy editorial page editor before accepting outside assignments. Before accepting a freelance assignment, a staff member should make sure that the tone and content of the publication, Web site or programme are in keeping with the standards of The Times.

In general, a staff member should write nothing elsewhere that could not fit comfortably under his or her byline in The Times or that implies The Times's sponsorship or endorsement. An outside publication, programme or Web site may identify staff members by their Times positions but only in a routine way. Because their primary identification is with The Times, staff members who accept freelance assignments should adhere to these guidelines in carrying out those assignments. For example, a staff member on freelance assignment may not accept compensation, expenses, discounts, gifts or other inducements from a news source. Similarly, staff members who establish their own sites on the World Wide Web must insure that their online conduct conforms to these guidelines. Frequency matters. Freelance work might create a conflict of interest if it is pursued with such regularity that it interferes with Times assignments or compromises the integrity or independence of The Times.

Freelancing might also create a conflict if it identifies a staff member as closely with another publication or Web site as with The Times. A business reporter who wrote a column in every issue of a trade magazine might soon become more identified with that magazine than with The Times. A critic writing regularly for an arts magazine might foster the impression that The Times was not his or her prime responsibility. The use of a pseudonym does not alter the obligation to comply with this provision. A regular contribution to an outside enterprise is permissible if it does not interfere with or flow from Times responsibilities or involve intellectual matter owed to The Times and its readers. Examples of acceptable affiliations might be a foreign desk copy editor who writes a monthly column on stamp-collecting or a mapmaker working as a freelance illustrator. Staff members considering such continuing ventures should confer with their supervisors and with the standards editor or the deputy editorial page editor.

Staff members may participate in radio, television or Internet interviews or discussions, paid or unpaid, that deal with articles they have written or subjects that figure in the coverage they provide, edit, package or supervise. Such occasional appearances must not imply that they carry the sponsorship or endorsement of The Times (unless they do). Staff members should be careful about the use of their names and that of the newspaper in materials promoting the appearances. As a courtesy, they should let their department head know about their plans to appear. In deciding whether to make a radio, television or Internet appearance, a staff member should consider its probable tone and content to make sure they are consistent with Times standards. Staff members should avoid strident, theatrical forums that emphasize punditry and reckless opinion-mongering. Instead, we should offer thoughtful and retrospective analysis.

Generally a staff member should not say anything on radio, television or the Internet that could not appear under his or her byline in The Times. New York Times Television draws on the paper's staff in producing programs for broadcast on its partly owned channel, DiscoveryTimes, and on networks and channels owned by outside parties, such as Public Television and the Discovery Channel. Staff members may not appear on broadcasts that compete directly with The Times's own offerings on television or the Internet. They may not accept assignments from the Times's TV clients or potential clients without its approval. As the paper moves further into these new fields, its direct competitors and clients or potential clients will undoubtedly grow in number. A staff member who has any doubt about the status of a particular programme should consult the standards editor or the deputy editorial page editor. Appearances might create a conflict of interest if they come so regularly that they interfere with Times assignments or compromise the integrity or independence of The Times. They might also create a conflict if they identify a staff member as closely with a radio or television programme or a Web site as with The Times.

A Washington reporter who appeared weekly on a television programme might soon become more known for that programme than for work done for The Times. Occasional appearances on the same programme would not run that risk. Staff members who want to promote their books through broadcast appearances must conform to the requirements set out in paragraph 48. In a day when most families balance two careers, the legitimate activities of companions, spouses and other relatives can sometimes create journalistic conflicts of interest or the appearance of conflicts. They can crop up in civic or political life, professional pursuits and financial activity. A spouse or companion who runs for public office would obviously create the appearance of conflict for a political reporter or an editor involved in election coverage.

A brother or a daughter in a high-profile job on Wall Street might produce the appearance of conflict for a business reporter or editor. To avoid such conflicts, staff members may not write about people to whom they are related by blood or marriage or with whom they have close personal relationships, or edit material about such people or make news judgments about them. For similar reasons, staff members should not recruit or directly supervise family members or close friends. Some exceptions are permissible — in a foreign bureau, for instance, where a married couple form a team, or in the case of an article by a food writer profiling her brother the Yankee star, where the kinship is of genuine news interest.

DISCLOSURE OF POSSIBLE CONFLICTS

Staff members must be sensitive to these possibilities. Any staff member who sees a potential for conflict or a threat to the paper's reputation in the activities of spouse, friends or relatives must discuss the situation with his or her supervising editor and the standards editor or the deputy editorial page editor. In some cases, disclosure is enough. But if The Times considers the problem serious, the staff member may have to withdraw from certain coverage. Sometimes an assignment may have to be modified or a beat changed. In a few instances, a staff member may have to move to a different department — from business and financial news, say, to the culture desk — to avoid the appearance of conflict. Although this policy necessarily imposes restraints, The Times has no wish to intrude upon the private lives of its staff members and their families. Nothing in this document seeks to prohibit a companion, spouse or other relative of a Times staff member from taking part in any political, financial, commercial, religious or civic activity.

The Times understands that friends and relatives of its staff have every right to pursue full and active lives, personally and professionally. If restrictions are necessary, they fall on the Times employee. But any attempt to disguise a staff member's participation in prohibited activity by using a relative's name or any other alias (or by acting anonymously) violates this guideline. In all cases The Times depends on staff members to disclose potential problems in a timely fashion so that we can work together to prevent embarrassment for staff members and Every member of the Times staff must be constantly vigilant against any appearance that he or she is abusing nonpublic information for financial gain. That imperative applies to all departments. Though staff members must necessarily accept certain limits on their freedom to invest, this policy leaves a broad range of investments open to them. Any staff member, regardless of assignment, is free to own diversified mutual funds, money market funds and other diversified investments that the reporter or editor cannot control.

Any member also may own treasury bills, investment-grade municipal bonds, debt securities other than speculative bonds, and securities issued by the New York Times Company. And staff members are of course free to own stocks entirely unrelated to their Times assignment. No staff member may own stock or have any other financial interest in a company, enterprise or industry that figures or is likely to figure in coverage that he or she provides, edits, packages or supervises regularly. A book editor, for example, may not invest in a publishing house, a health writer in a pharmaceutical company or a Pentagon reporter in a mutual fund specializing in defence stocks. For this purpose an industry is defined broadly; for example, a reporter responsible for any segment of media coverage may not own any media stock. "Stock" should be read to include futures, options, rights, and speculative debt, as well as "sector" mutual funds (those focused on one industry).

Staff members may not buy or sell securities or make other investments in anticipation of forthcoming articles that originate with The Times. In general, staff members must refrain from acting on such information before noon Eastern time the day of print publication. This restriction does not apply to spot news that first appears on wire services or that originates elsewhere. That information is public. Staff members in any department will be asked when hired to affirm that they have no investments that would violate paragraph 114 with respect to the assignment they are being given. If a new staff member is unable to make this affirmation, the staff member may choose to sell the conflicting holding.

If not, he or she must be given a different assignment where no such conflict exists. Staff members should be acutely sensitive that the investments and business interests of their spouse, family and companions may create real or apparent conflicts of interest by raising questions of favoritism. Staff members will be asked when hired to affirm that to the best of their knowledge no spouse, family member or companion has financial holdings that might reasonably raise doubts about the impartiality of the staff member's reporting or editing in his or her proposed assignment.

Depending on circumstances, the new staff member may have to recuse himself or herself from certain coverage or accept an alternative assignment unrelated to the holdings in question. The associate managing editor for news administration or the deputy editorial page editor may from time to time ask staff members in any department to affirm that they have no investments in violation of paragraph 114. Such a request might be expected, for example, when a staff member is about to begin a new assignment or work on a particularly sensitive article. Similarly, staff members may be asked on occasion to affirm that to the best of their knowledge no spouse, family member or companion has financial holdings that might reasonably raise doubts about the impartiality of the staff member's reporting or editing.

If and when such conditions come up, the staff member must alert his or her department head and the standards editor. Depending on circumstances, the staff member may have to recuse himself or herself from certain coverage or even to move to a job unrelated to the holdings. If a reporter who owns stock in a company outside his or her regular beat is assigned to write an article about that company or its industry, the reporter must discuss the investment with the assigning editor before beginning the work.

Similarly, editors assigned to major articles or a series about companies or industries in which they have investments must advise their supervisors of potential conflicts before beginning the editing. In many instances it will be perfectly permissible for the work to proceed, but the reporter or editor who works on such an article or series may not buy or sell stock in the company or industry until two weeks after publication.

BUSINESS-FINANCIAL, TECHNOLOGY AND MEDIA NEWS

Staff members in business-financial news regularly work with sensitive information that affects financial prices. Because of that sensitivity, they are subject to additional and stricter requirements. Staff members in technology news and media news are subject to the same rules as those in business-financial news, for the same reason. Members of these three departments may not play the market. That is, they may not conduct in-and-out trading (buying and selling the same security within three months). They may not buy or sell options or futures or sell securities short. Any of these actions could create the appearance that a staff member was speculating by exploiting information not available to the public. In special circumstances — a family financial crisis, for example — the associate managing editor for news administration may waive the three-month holding period.

Supervising editors in business-financial, technology or media news should be especially cautious in investing because they may reasonably expect to become involved in the coverage of virtually any company at any time. Their counterparts in other departments should be equally sensitive to possible conflicts in supervising coverage of companies in their domain. Because of the sensitivity of their assignments, some business- financial staff members may not own stock in any company (other than the New York Times Company).

These include the Market Place writer, other market columnists, the regular writer of the daily stock market column, reporters regularly assigned to mergers and acquisitions, the daily markets editor, the Sunday investing editor, the Sunday Business editor, the business and financial editor and his or her deputies. Masthead editors and other editors who play a principal part in deciding the display of business and financial news, including its display on Page 1, may not own stock in any company (other than the New York Times Company). The editorial page editor, the deputy editorial page editor and the Op-Ed editor may not own stock in any company (other than the New York Times Company). Nor may editorial writers and Op-Ed columnists regularly assigned to write about business, finance or economics. A staff member who owns stock and moves into an assignment where such holdings are not permitted must sell the stock.

Those who are newly barred from owning stock of any sort (for example, on being promoted to deputy business and financial editor) may dispose of their shares in phases, following a reasonable plan worked out with the associate managing editor for news administration. But the phase-out does not apply to reporters or editors who own shares in specific industries they are newly assigned to cover. For instance, it is manifestly untenable for a new Automobiles editor to own stock in an auto company, so divestiture must be prompt. Whenever this document requires the sale of stock holdings, a staff member can satisfy the requirement by putting the shares into a blind trust (or into an equivalent financial arrangement that meets the same goal: preventing an individual from knowing at any given time the specific holdings in the account and blocking the individual from controlling the timing of transactions in such holdings). If The Times assigns a staff member to a new job where mandatory divestiture would impose an undue hardship, The Times will reimburse the staff member for the reasonable costs of setting up a blind trust.

ANNUAL FILING BY RANKING EDITORS

To avoid an appearance of conflict, certain editors must annually affirm to the chief financial officer of The Times Company that they have no financial holdings in violation of paragraphs 125-127 or any other provision of these guidelines. They include the executive editor, the managing editor, deputy and assistant managing editors, associate managing editors, the business and financial editor, his or her deputies and the Sunday Business editor. They also include the editorial page editor, the deputy editorial page editor and the Op-Ed editor.

To avoid an appearance of bias, no member of the sports department may gamble on any sports event, except for occasional recreational wagering on horse racing (or dog racing or jai alai). This exception does not apply to staff members who cover such racing or regularly edit that coverage. Except as provided in paragraph 30, members of the sports department may not accept tickets, travel expenses, meals, gifts or any other benefit from teams or promoters. Sports reporters assigned to cover games may not serve as scorers. Members of the sports department may not take part in voting for the Heisman Trophy, most valuable player and rookie of the year awards, entry into the Baseball Hall of Fame or similar honors.

CULTURE, STYLES, DINING

The Times has exceptional influence in such fields as theater, music, art, dance, publishing, fashion and the restaurant industry. We are constantly scrutinized for the slightest whiff of favoritism. Therefore staff members working in those areas have a special duty to guard against conflicts of interest or the appearance of conflict. Reporters, reviewers, critics and their editors in the Book Review, the Times Magazine and the cultural news, media news and styles departments, beyond abiding by the other provisions of this document, may not help others develop, market or promote artistic, literary or other creative endeavors. They may not suggest agents, publishers, producers or galleries to aspiring authors, playwrights, composers or artists. They may not suggest chefs to restaurant owners or designers to clothing manufacturers. They may not recommend authors, playwrights, composers or other artists to agents, publishers, producers or galleries.

RULES FOR SPECIALIZED DEPARTMENTS

They may not offer suggestions or ideas to people who figure or are likely to figure in coverage they provide, edit, package or supervise. They may not invest in productions that figure or are likely to figure in their coverage. (Food writers and editors may not invest in restaurants.) They may not comment, even informally, on works in progress before those works are reviewed. They may not serve on advisory boards, awards juries, study committees or other panels organized by the people they cover or whose coverage they supervise. They may not accept awards from such people. And they may not request extra copies of books, tapes or other materials that are routinely submitted for review.

An arts writer or editor who owns art of exhibition quality (and thus has a financial stake in the reputation of the artist) may inspire questions about the impartiality of his or her critical judgments or editing decisions. Thus members of the culture staff who collect valuable objects in the visual arts (paintings, photographs, sculpture, crafts and the like) must annually submit a list of their acquisitions and sales to the associate managing editor for news administration. The Times recognizes that members of its talented staff write books, operas and plays; create sculpture, and give recitals. It further recognizes that such projects require commercial arrangements to come to fruition. A writer requires a publisher, a playwright a production company.

Nevertheless those commercial ties can be a breeding ground for favoritism, actual or perceived. Staff members who enter into such arrangements must disclose them to their supervisors, who may require them to withdraw from coverage of the parties involved. Staff members who have a publisher or a movie contract, for example, must be exceedingly sensitive to any appearance of bias in covering other publishers or studios. Those with any doubts about a proposed arrangement should consult the standards editor or the deputy editorial page editor. Certain positions, such as those of the Book Review editor and the culture editor, have such potential for conflicts that those editors may not enter into any commercial arrangements with publishers, studios, or other arts producers without the executive editor's written approval.

Art, Pictures, Technology

Beyond honoring all the other provisions of this document, Times photographers, picture editors, art directors, lab personnel and technology editors and reporters may not accept gifts of equipment, programs or materials from manufacturers or vendors. They may not endorse equipment, programs or materials, or offer advice on product design. This guideline is not meant to restrict The Times from working with vendors to improve its systems or equipment. With the approval of the picture editor, the design director, the technology editor or the Circuits editor, staff members may test equipment or materials on loan from manufacturers or vendors, provided such tests are properly monitored. The equipment or materials should be returned promptly after testing unless purchased by The Times.

Automobiles

It is our policy that no one may test drive or review a vehicle for The

Times unless the paper is paying the vehicle's owner the normal market rental or its equivalent. Rare exceptions may occur when an equivalent rent is largely hypothetical, as with military vehicles, vintage autos or race cars.

Reviewers should carry out their testing expeditiously and return the vehicle promptly. A reasonable amount of personal use is permissible provided that the use contributes to the review. No writer or editor for the Travel section, whether on assignment or not, may accept free or discounted services of any sort from any element of the travel industry.

This includes hotels, resorts, restaurants, tour operators, airlines, railways, cruise lines, rental car companies and tourist attractions. This prohibition applies to the free trips commonly awarded in raffles at travel industry events. It does not apply, however, to routinely accumulated frequent-flyer points.

Travel editors who deal with non-staff contributors have a special obligation to guard against conflicts of interest or the appearance of conflict.

They must bear in mind that it is our policy not to give Travel assignments to freelance writers who have previously accepted free services. Depending on circumstances, the Travel editor may make rare exceptions, for example, for a writer who ceased the practice years ago or who has reimbursed his or her host for services previously accepted. It is also our policy not to give Travel assignments to anyone who represents travel suppliers or who works for a government tourist office or as a publicist of any sort.

The Travel editor may make rare exceptions, for example, for a writer widely recognized as an expert in a particular culture. Writers on assignment for Travel must conceal their Times affiliation. The validity of their work depends on their experiencing the same conditions as an ordinary tourist or consumer. If the Times affiliation becomes known, the writer must discuss with an editor whether the reporting to that point can be salvaged. On rare occasions, the affiliation may be disclosed, for example, when a special permit is required to enter a closed area.

9

Constructing Alternative Press Theories

Both Eastern and Western media researchers have tried to redress the deficiencies of the four-theory model by creating their own models. Three more theoretical concepts-development journalism, democratic-participant media, and the revolutionary media-were developed to accommodate the progress and changes in press systems and to supplement the dominant paradigm's four press categories.

Of the new theoretical concepts, development journalism has caused more controversies because the degree of press freedom varies greatly from society to society, and the very concept may imply a role for the government. The controversy also seems to stem from the fact that the deciding factor in creating the four press theories was the presence or absence of press freedom, which was defined mainly in terms of government control.

Based on such a criterion, how can one type of press system allow vastly different degrees of press freedom in different societies? When a new concept cannot be fit into the established paradigm, it becomes" controversial." Progressive, insightful, and creative as these new theories are, they are mostly supplementary to the established four press theories.

More ambitious efforts were made by Ralph Lowenstein, J. Henry Altschull, John C. Merrill, and Shelton A. Gunaratne, who constructed alternative models reclassifying press systems. Ralph Lowenstein developed a" progressive typology," according to which," press systems evolved from authoritarian to libertarian, to social libertarian or social centralist, and then to a big futuristic question mark".

This typology seems to have the same tendency as the established four theories of basing its discussions mainly on the development paths of Western press systems, which makes it less relevant to the evolution of press systems elsewhere in the world. J. Henry Altschull proposed three basic media models - market, Marxist, and developing. To make the concepts value free, Altschull described them as market, communitarian, and advancing. In trying to reclassify media systems, Altschull brought in the element of culture and belief systems. He explained that the market system emphasized the" individual" while the communitarian system focused on the" communal life" or the" collective." Altschull also analysed the role of the media - preserving status quo under both market and communitarian models and advocating change under the advancing model.

He explained that there were variations within each model, giving the classification much flexibility. With the exception of the advancing model describing press systems in the South, Altschull's models were also based mainly on the analysis of Western media systems even though he classified his models also as East, West, and South, where East refers to Marxism and the former Soviet communist bloc in Eastern Europe rather than to Asia.

The only Eastern society mentioned in the analysis was Japan. Altschull explained that despite the variations within the market model, the basic belief systems - hostility to a communitarian belief system - remain intact." Discord notwithstanding, the broad sweep of the first movement of the symphony is heard throughout the industrialized capitalist world, in Japan as in Denmark and Canada".

Despite Western influence, the Japanese society, steeped in Asian culture and Confucian traditions, has no such hostility. As discussed earlier in this chapter, the press club system in Japan dictates communal behaviour within the industry by discouraging competition and scoops and encouraging collective reporting. A mixture of the East and the West, Japan proves to be a difficult case to be classified. John C. Merrill's circular model shows that individualistic press systems gravitate toward libertarianism and more collectivistic systems are at the authoritarian end. Merrill said,"... the basic model is a simple spectrum, with authoritarianism at one end and libertarianism at the other. All press systems fall somewhere along this continuum".

Merrill's model resembles Altschull's models without the" advancing" or" South" element. Men-ill's model has the merit of built-in flexibility. The classification of a press system depends on in which direction the system gravitates. But it is still difficult to place Japan on Merrill's model. The Japanese press is mostly free from government control, but it is not individualistic. The press club system emphasizes collective action, but it cannot be described as authoritarian. The models proposed by Altschull and Merrill represented major improvements over the four-theory model - AltschulPs model moved away from the exclusive emphasis on government control, and Men-ill's model had the merit of built-in flexibility to accommodate different types of press systems and changes within those systems.

Despite Men-ill's inclusion of the communitarian factor, the two models still seem to largely rely on Western philosophies, scholarship, and examples of Western media performances. Jiafei Yin called for the construction of a new model, which would be based on a broader foundation of both Western and Eastern philosophies and cultural influences, but did not produce an actual model. Shelton A. Gunaratne brought in both Eastern and Western philosophical, religious, and cultural traditions in building his model-The Dao of the Press. There are two parts to Gunaratne's model: one part is the libertarian-authoritarian (L-A) continuum with varying shades of social responsibility across the continuum, and the other part is a centre-semiperiphery-periphery world system with individuals and groups, nation-states, and the world system at different levels. And all the three levels" autopoietically adjust the degree of free expression" along the L-A continuum. Gunaratne's model emphasizes both Eastern and Western cultural values in the definitions and interpretations of the term" social responsibility," giving the model much needed flexibility in accommodating different shades of social responsibility found in world cultures.

Merrill also addressed the relativity of the concept of responsibility among societies and even within a society. Similar to many of the previous press theories and models, Gunaratne's L-A continuum also focuses on the libertarian-authoritarian dichotomy, reflecting Western emphasis on freedom and liberty.

With the rich heritage of Asian philosophies and cultures, can a new model reflect diverse global cultural values and describe and explain press systems around the world without bias either from the West or the East?

After all, different cultures prioritize values differently. Therefore, press theories that are supposed to address global press systems should have a wider base to reflect a broader, more balanced global view. With adequate attention to factors such as world history, global cultures, and economic pressure, the problems inherent in the four established theories because of the authors'Western bias and their sole focus on governmental influences can be addressed.

For a new paradigm of press theories, the optimal balance between specificity and universality should also be considered. The four theories of the press have the beauty and elegance of a very simple but clear structure - four categories under a dichotomy, which aimed to describe and explain press systems in the whole world.

Conveniently general as they are, the four or five theories have difficulties in providing a reliable guide to the global press systems. The universality of the theories is limited. However, if categories are too specific and accurate in describing particular press systems, there may be too many categories for the model to be an effective guide. One other important factor that needs to be paid attention to in building a more reliable press model is that the model should be dynamic so that it can accommodate the changes in the press systems around the world. Obviously, press systems in the new democracies in Eastern Europe are very different from the press systems in the West even though they all operate under democratic systems now.

The press systems in the new democracies in Asia, such as Indonesia, Cambodia, the Philippines, Taiwan, and South Korea, vary from those in Eastern Europe despite the fact that they are all new democracies and share some similarities. And the press system in China today cannot be compared with the Chinese press system two decades ago, or the press system in North Korea. It would defeat the purpose of having models if every time any changes occur, new models have to be created.

A DICHOTOMY OF VALUES, EAST AND WEST

A new paradigm of press theories requires new ways of thinking in order to broaden the foundation. In this section, an examination is conducted of the dominant Eastern and Western cultural values, which are by no means exclusive to either the East or the West but rather reflect the quintessence of each.

To summarize Asian, or more particularly the Confucian, culture, leading Confucian scholar Tu Wei-ming said: "Industrial East Asia, under the influence of Confucian culture, seems to have developed a different kind of modern civilization, less adversarial, less individualistic, and less self-interested. One sees there the coexistence of market economy and government leadership, democratic parity with meritocracy and individual initiatives with group orientation."

THE INDIVIDUAL VERSUS THE STATE AND FAMILY (THE GROUP)

Western libertarian philosophy values the independence and rights of each individual. John Stuart Mill's On Liberty spelled out classic liberal individualism-it "set out the limits to the legitimate interference of collective opinion with individual independence". Mill wrote that the only warranted interference with the liberty of an individual is for mankind's self-protection, that is, to prevent harm to others, and that no power should be exercised over an individual for his own good. "Over himself, over his own body and mind, the individual is sovereign."

The Confucian thought, however, focuses on the state and the family. Confucius believed that only when the state and families are strong can the well-being of individuals be guaranteed. In the equation of the state, family, and individuals in Confucian societies, individuals are often encouraged and expected to sacrifice their own rights and interests for the sake of the state and family if contradictions should arise, which is in sharp contrast to Mill's belief that the individual is sovereign.

In Confucian societies, the state is sovereign. In Western culture, individualism is extolled, but in Eastern culture, people are taught to think about "us." In the West, ideal societies are composed of free individuals while in Confucian societies the individual "is not viewed as an isolated individual but as a centre of relationships".

The Chinese tradition has largely been influenced by a Confucian-based relational and social definition of person instead of by any concept of discrete individuality. "Under the sway of this relational understanding of human being, the mutuality and interdependence of personal, familial, societal, and political realization in the classical Chinese model can and has been generally conceded."

FREEDOM AND RIGHTS VERSUS RESPONSIBILITY

John Locke, an early libertarian, believes that freedom is essential to the full development of a human being. Merrill summarized Locke's philosophy as "Each person has a natural right to be free and not to be subjected to the will of another." Freedom, for Locke, is a "natural" right.

"Besides being bound by natural law, humans possess natural rights, in particular the right to life, self-defence, and freedom. They have also duties; in particular, the duty not to give away their rights".

The Enlightenment in eighteenth century Europe led to the rise of classical liberalism and capitalism. It also led to the French and American revolutions, which uprooted the power of religion and the aristocracy in France and heavily influenced the most distinguished leaders of the American Revolution-Jefferson, Washington, Franklin, and Paine.

"The language of natural law, of inherent freedoms, of self-determination, which seeped so deeply into the American grain, was the language of the Enlightenment..". "Give me liberty or give me death." Patrick Henry's rallying call meant that there was no compromise over liberty-to be free is the precondition to live.

In the East, the emphasis is on being responsible and loyal rather than on being free. Western libertarian philosophers' focus of attention falls on the welfare of the individual, so it is only logical that these philosophers advocate that these individuals should be equal and free to pursue what they want.

Confucian thought lays emphasis on the group; hence, there is the concern of being responsible and loyal to the group. In his research, Tu pointed out the Asian focus on the ethic of service and obligation.

INDIVIDUAL FREEDOM AND HAPPINESS VERSUS PUBLIC GOOD AND RESPONSIBILITY

Mill, a defender of personal and political liberty, said in his On Liberty: "The only freedom which deserves the name, is that of pursuing our own good in our own way, so long as we do not attempt to deprive others of theirs, or impede their efforts to obtain it". Mill's "sovereign self" echoed the U.S. Bill of Rights and the Declaration of Independence in upholding individual freedom and rights and the pursuit of happiness, not individual or collective responsibility.

So when President Kennedy demanded, "Ask not what your country can do for you; ask what you can do for your country," it was refreshing to the American youth as their civic education focused mostly on the value of equality, freedom, and rights embedded in the Constitution when they grew up. Confucius teachings emphasize a strong commitment to the world and encourage sacrifice of self-interest to be ethical. The Confucian concept of the ethical links up directly with the public good. And Confucius believes "self-realization is fundamentally a social undertaking, therefore, 'selfish' concerns are to be rejected as an impediment to one's own growth and self-realization".

LEGAL VERSUS MORAL

In Western democratic societies, the legal system is very well developed as the law embodies the ideal that everyone is equal before the law. And citizens have a strong sense of the law, which sets the boundary of people's behaviour, including what parents legally can or cannot do in disciplining their children. In Asian societies, especially more traditional and less developed societies such as China, the legal system is much less well developed.

With the opening up of the country's economy, China's legislative body, the National People's Congress, has been busy making laws as conflicts in the past were resolved mostly through mediation based on judgments of who was right and who was wrong.

And a major part of Confucius's teachings comprises moral guidelines, which is why he was also considered a moralist. Confucius firmly believes that children are the responsibility of their parents and that aging parents are the responsibility of their grown-up children whether it is legally required or not. As a result, Chinese press occasionally exposes cases of mistreating aging parents by their grown-up children even though it is a private matter.

Likewise, Confucius believes that it is parents' fault if a child goes astray. Even today some immigrant Asian parents are surprised by the child abuse laws of the United States, where children are encouraged to call the police if they are spanked by their parents.

Such laws would shock Confucius. Confucius's teachings also place emphasis on being just and public minded. It would be unimaginable to Confucius that one country could have billionaires the same time it had a trillion dollars of national debt.

According to the moral teachings of Confucius, those who pursue only personal interests (Ii) are the "little men" (xiaoren), people of no character; only those who think about what is appropriate and beneficial to all concerned (yi) are the "gentlemen" (junzi), people of noble character.

TO BE FREE TO EXPLORE VERSUS TO KNOW RIGHT FROM WRONG

Western libertarians advocate for a free marketplace of ideas, where the public should be left free to explore and discover the truth on their own. In his pamphlet, Areopagitica, John Milton argues that truth would emerge victorious over falsehood should the two be locked in a grapple. John Milton also wrote about the importance of diversity of opinions and perspectives. In Asian societies influenced by Confucian thinking, especially in the case of China after almost 5,000 years of civilization, truth seems to be self-evident.

In such cases, the focus is on teaching the people what is right and what is wrong rather than the freedom to explore what is right and what is wrong.

The real challenge becomes the task of convincing the people, or in an ideal Confucian way, for people to convince themselves, to always make the right choice. Confucian scholar Tu Wei-ming phrased the contrast as "the right to think" versus "right thinking." In Western democracies, the emphasis is on the process-if decisions are made with public input. In Confucian societies, the emphasis is on the result-if the right decision is made. The process often is deemed less relevant.

DEMOCRACY VERSUS MERITOCRACY

The U.S. Declaration of Independence states unequi-vocally at the very beginning, "all men are created equal." The conviction in the equality among men forms the basis of Western democratic governments-government of the people, by the people, and for the people. Such libertarian thinking has deep roots in the history of Western philosophy. In Two Treatises of Civil Government, Locke maintains that before there were any states to make statutes, men were aware of a natural law, which taught that all men were equal and independent.

"These men, with no earthly superior above them, are in a state of liberty, but not a state of licence."In his book, A Theory of Justice, John Rawls promotes the adoption of a "veil of ignorance," which would ideally eliminate all the personal identifiers of each individual-male or female, black or white, rich or poor, intelligent or not-and return everyone to his or her original position of being equal with everyone else. "Rawls believes that justice will come forth from a discussion by rational and equal people concerned with their own interests but without anyone being advantaged or disadvantaged". Western societies are democratic and horizontal, emphasizing public participation in the government, while Confucian societies are hierarchical and vertical, believing in meritocracy instead of democracy.

For more than a thousand years in the history of China, only top scholars after rigorous national exams became government officials. In Singapore today, the brightest young people are selected for education in world's top universities supported with government funding so they will become the next generation of worthy leaders. "Statecraft is an integral part of Confucian learning". The ideal Confucian officials are people with "inner sagehood and outer kingliness." Equality in human relations is a foreign concept in Confucian thinking as he decreed three sets of subservient relationships: subjects should obey their kings, sons should obey their fathers, and wives should obey their husbands. Confucius was not a democrat as some Confucian scholars tend to believe.

CIVIL LIBERTIES VERSUS SOCIAL ORDER AND STABILITY

The concept of human rights was developed during the Enlightenment.

The Bill of Rights as amendments to the U.S. Constitution marked a milestone in mankind's fight for civil liberties. Western democratic societies keep a watchful eye on the government to prevent it from encroaching upon those rights. The most recent example was the heated U.S. Congressional debate on the Bush administration's domestic spying programme.

In contrast, a salient feature of Confucian thinking in government is the primacy of political order. In China, the traditional assumption has been that personal order and the order of a society entail each other. Thus, in Confucian societies, governments expect respect and obedience to keep social order.

Social stability often takes precedence over civil liberties and is regarded as vital to the strength of a country and the welfare of its people. The Confucian order was built on traditional values and norms. Confucius's unwavering focus on social order and stability might have been the result of the endless wars China was embroiled in during his lifetime.

Thousands of years later, some Asian leaders could not agree more with the ancient Chinese philosopher. Fighting back criticism about too much control in his country, Lee Kuan Yew, first and former prime minister of Singapore who led the city-state for thirty-one years, said, "Without order and stability, nothing can be achieved". Lee was responsible for turning Singapore from a fishing village at the end of the Second World War into one of the cleanest and richest countries in the world today.

COMPETITION VERSUS HARMONY

Capitalism thrives on free competition on the market, which is supposed to drive economic growth even though such growth may be achieved at a social cost. Competition presupposes freedom and equality, but competition spawns conflicts as well-disputes between management and labour, hostile business takeovers, smearing political campaigns, fights in sports arenas, and even the constant race to be the most popular teen in high school.

As a result of competition, people are labeled as winners and losers. And the rule of competition decides that there are often more losers than winners, resulting in many unhappy people.

In some Asian societies such as China and Singapore, and even in some European countries such as Germany, comparative advertising is banned. In Japan and South Korea, state-guided capitalism softens real competition. "Harmony is at the core of the Chinese culture". Preferred methods of resolving conflicts are building consensus and making compromise rather than many voices competing.

"A pertinent contrast can be developed between the western liberal commitment to many voices and the traditional Chinese concern for a communitarian consensus as a social good". One values pluralism; the other harmony. The "promotion of harmony and goodwill among individuals and their families and community in the context of the five constants: ran, yi, li, zhi, and xin (humanity, righteousness, decorum, wisdom, and trust) is a social responsibility from the Confucian point of view". However, the ancient Chinese sage would be flabbergasted to witness the transformations China is going through today. Since China ushered in the market economy and private enterprise, competition is becoming a new way of life, bringing relentless assault on traditional values and leaving the conservatives lamenting the decline in moral standards.

ADVERSARIAL WATCHDOG

Press in the West takes pride in being a watchdog of the government. The uncovering of the Watergate scandal has inspired young journalists to follow the footsteps of Bob Woodward and Carl Bernstein. Dan Rather's dogged pursuit of the truth in Bush's service in the National Guard cost his career. To deal with an inquiring press, government officials hide behind press secretaries.

In traditional societies, people tend to be in deference to their governments. In Confucian societies, the government is supposed to take care of the people, and the people are expected to respect the government. "Confucianism holds that man is born for uprightness, and that people's goodwill is essential for good government in the context of an intellectual democracy headed by a benevolent ruler". Chinese "benevolent despotism" fascinated Western thinkers. In Confucian societies, the press becomes a tool for nation building. Even in Japan and South Korea, both democratic societies, press tends to keep cozy relationships with the government and is, thus, reduced to a lapdog.

The dichotomy of dominant Western and Eastern values does not imply that there are no overlapping areas between Western and Eastern cultures. There are Western philosophers such as Plato and Rousseau who put emphasis on the state and the collective rather than the individual and preferred rule by the elite, which is very close to the Confucian ideal of government.

In The Social Contract, Rousseau promotes public good and common interest instead of interests of individuals. In the East, there are also philosophical schools such as Taoism that focuses on individuality and extols the virtue of being free, free from the constraints of governments and institutions for the full and free development of the potential of each individual.

But these philosophical schools in the East or the West have not become the dominant influence in their respective cultures. By and large, contemporary Western societies extol freedom and individuality, while Asian societies emphasize interests of the collective and the concept of responsibility regardless of political systems. Some critics may contend that few Asian societies today including China can be described as Confucian societies because of the influence from the West. Indeed, modernization has inevitably had an impact on Asian societies, especially the young, who are much more accepting of what is Western.

Tu Wei-ming said: "The Westernization of Confucian Asia, including Japan, the two Koreas, mainland China, Hong Kong, Taiwan, Singapore, and Vietnam, may have forever altered its spiritual landscape. But its indigenous resources, including Mahayana Buddhism, Daoism, Shintoism, Shamanism, and other folk traditions, have the resiliency to resurface and make their presence known in the new syntheses."

Confucianism is neither a political system nor a religion; it is a way of thinking and a way of life. It is deep-rooted in the cultures of Confucian societies, and it is reflected in the decisions people make in their everyday lives, including the value of family ties, education, and hard work. A recent media farce in China provides a glimpse of the undisputable respect Confucius still enjoys in China today.

A Peking University professor was quoted in the media as saying that Zhang Ziyi, an internationally known Chinese actress, who was featured on the cover of an issue of Newsweek in 2005 and at the Oscar award ceremony in 2006, was greater than Confucius.

The statement, perceived as an insult to the Chinese culture, sparked a public outcry on the Internet condemning the professor. Bombarded with interview requests from the media, the professor had to post an article on his blog, claiming that he was misquoted by the media for sensationalism.

He explained that Confucius represented China's elite culture, while Zhang Ziyi represented its pop culture. The professor hoped that with the actress's international appeal, she could attract more worldwide interest in Confucianism.

An examination of dominant Eastern and Western values helps provide a more balanced foundation for building a new press model. A New Model: The Two-Dimensional Freedom Responsibility Coordinate System

THE SYSTEM

Based on earlier press models and on an analysis of the salient values of the Western and Eastern cultures, a new press model is proposed here, which is a two-dimensional coordinate grid with the horizontal axis denoting the degree of freedom in a press system and the vertical axis indicating how responsible a press system is. The system illustrates that a free press can be responsible or irresponsible, and that a press that is not free can also be responsible or irresponsible. Merrill also believes in the possible existence of responsible authoritarian systems and responsible libertarian systems.

THE TWO-DIMENSIONAL MODEL

The major difference between what is proposed here and most of the theories and models before it is that this proposed model has departed from the traditional one-dimensional models, which focus mainly on the degree of freedom in a press system, reflecting Western philosophical emphasis on the concept of freedom.

The proposed two-dimensional model, instead, has broadened the foundation of theory building to include a key Asian cultural emphasis on the concept of responsibility. The Asian emphasis on the concept of responsibility is not only a result of Confucian moral influence, but also a result of the socio-economic realities of Asia, where development journalism originated and is still being pursued and where guerrilla warfare or religious and ethnic rivalries can flare up as a result of provocative news articles.

And even in Hong Kong, where dominant discussions tend to focus on the survival of press freedom, Chief Executive Donald Tsang encouraged journalists to think about what was important to society rather than what was popular to readers at the 2005 News Awards ceremony.

Confucius's teachings mesh well with the aspirations of development journalists in Asia, who see the role of the press as agents for social change. Through their work, they want to improve the quality of life of their people. Pakistani media researcher Owais Aslam AIi (undated) analysed the major differences between Western news values and Asian news values, which he summarized as elitist press versus press for national development.

He pointed out the futility of Western news values in "thc monumental uphill struggle" of the Third World toward economic progress. Given the diverse economic and social realities of the countries of the world, it is not difficult to see why different philosophies of journalism and news values exist around the world. Some Western libertarian thinkers also addressed the issue of responsibility, rationality, or limits in exercising freedom. Locke gave impetus to the concept of "responsible individualism," predicated on a love of reason and the importance of natural law. According to Locke, individuals live in a social context and need order, not anarchy, for their own well-being.

"Therefore, reason serves as an automatic limitation on freedom. In order to guide themselves in living an orderly and moral life, which is the essence of humanity, rational people voluntarily give up much freedom". Even though well known for his libertarian ideas in his pamphlet On Liberty, Mill held an elitist view on entitlement to freedom. "Mill felt that his freedom principle was appropriate only in societies of relatively high educational standards in which people could rationally exercise freedom".

In the field of journalism, debates on press responsibility and accountability have never stopped, such as the work of the Hutchins' Commission, which gave rise to the social responsibility press theory, and the ongoing experimentation with civic or public journalism in the United States. If there is public concern over press responsibility, the concern should be addressed in building a new theoretical model. The newly added dimension of press responsibility adds balance to existing press models by bringing in cultural values important not only to the West but also to the East, presents a fuller description of a press system, and helps address an important public concern over press responsibility and accountability.

DEFINING AND MEASURING PRESS RESPONSIBILITY

The immediate question that arises is the definition of responsibility as what is considered responsible in one culture may be viewed as irresponsible in another culture. The notion of responsibility is always culture-specific. Similar to the argument that all concepts of responsibility are relative, the concept of "a free press" is also relative, as there is no absolute freedom of the press in this world, not even in the United States. Addressing press freedom worldwide, Merrill said, "... in fact, there are no free-press nations".

Because of the challenges in setting the standards of a responsible press that can be universally accepted and in deciding who should have the authority in setting the standards, and because of media's aversion to the concept of "a responsible press" imposed from the outside as illustrated by the fate of the Hutchins' report and by the "survey methodology" section of the 2005 Freedom House report that practically equates press responsibility with government control, discussions about press responsibility often hit a dead end.

They do not have to be. Ali (undated) emphasized the watchdog role of the media in development journalism, warned against the discussions on Asian values in journalism being hijacked by government officials as justification for the control of the media, and urged Asian journalists, "who have been struggling to reduce government involvement in the media," to create a form of journalism relevant to the needs of their societies. Only then will the concept of Asian values have credibility, Ali wrote.

UNIVERSAL VALUES IN JOURNALISM

A starting point in exploring the standards of a responsible press can be the search for universal values in journalism, and the Hutchins' report can serve as a helpful reference, such as being accurate and providing balance and diversity of opinion in news coverage, acting as a watchdog of the government, businesses and all other powerful social institutions, addressing issues of public concern, covering all sectors of the society instead of just the prominent, and avoiding invasion of privacy and sensationalism.

If the list continues to include the elimination of hate speech, which is banned in Germany, and pornography, which is banned in the Muslim world, most of the Asian countries, and perhaps some African and South American countries as well, the exploration for universal standards of a responsible press will soon become controversial. And questions such as what is balanced to one may not seem to be balanced to another remain.

CURRENT COMMUNITY STANDARDS

To deal with such tricky issues in setting the standards of a responsible press, the standards used for deciding what is obscene can be borrowed-current community standards. If the majority of readers believe their press is responsible, then they have a responsible press. Vice versa, if the majority of readers believe their press is irresponsible, then they have an irresponsible press. As the concept of responsibility is highly cultural-specific, the best solution is to let the local population decide instead of imposing standards from the outside.

INDEX OF PRESS RESPONSIBILITY-A COMBINATION OF UNIVERSAL VALUES AND LOCAL STANDARDS

Based on accepted universal values in journalism, which may include truth, accuracy, and balance, and results of public opinion surveys on press responsibility, an index of press responsibility can be compiled for each country to help media researchers and students better analyse the characteristics of a particular press system. If survey results distort reality such as in a controlled society, where a survey of honest public opinion is not feasible, universal values in journalism can serve as primary checkpoints.

In the meantime, despite the fact that they sometimes serve as a helpful reference, the criteria of the Freedom House in determining the ratings of press freedom in each country should be revised to add balance to the current standards, which do not take into account media content. The current methodology examines the legal, political, and economic environment of the media, but not the results of those environments-media content.

The survey questions are predominantly negative. Data are not collected through systematic or scientific method but through arbitrary answers by a small group of hand-picked interviewees, including "correspondents overseas, staff and consultant travel, international visitors," and "specialists in geographic and geopolitical areas." Such data collection methods raise serious questions about both the reliability and validity of the results.

THE FOUR CORNERS ANDFOUR QUADRANTS

If a pair of dotted diagonal lines are superimposed on the coordinate grid, four corners of the grid will appear, representing four extreme types of press systems-free and responsible, free but not responsible, not free but responsible, and not free and not responsible. As the four corners indicate maximum or minimum degrees of freedom and responsibility, very few press systems fall exactly on those four corners; most of the press systems will fall somewhere within the four quadrants.

FREE AND RESPONSIBLE

While it may be hard to find a perfect example of a free and socially responsible press, some media endeavors are definitely directed toward that goal, such as public broadcasting in Britain and the United States, the civic and public journalism in the United States, and community and development journalism in India and Pakistan. Even though these types of journalism do not represent the mainstream media in their respective societies, they are the free press's attempts to be responsible and relevant to its readers.

The press in this group is mostly free and chooses to avoid sensationalism and play a positive role in society on its own. With or without public funding, it provides mostly quality information and often a public servicefighting crime in neighborhoods, boosting voter turnout, and educating and empowering the poor rural population.

Depending on events of the day, its content can be a mixture of negative and positive stories. In well-developed and free media markets, the press can afford to choose to be responsible because such a press would be assured of market support if there is public demand for a free and responsible press. Even in underdeveloped societies such as those in South Asia, press responsibility in the form of development journalism can exist because of support from the vast rural audience. For the press to be free and responsible, the market has to demand it and has to be well developed enough to finance it.

FREE AND NOT RESPONSIBLE

It is not very difficult to find free but irresponsible press around the world, press that chases profits or power under the name of press freedom.

Under such press systems, the press is free to pursue whatever story sells on the market with little concern for the consequences of such reporting. In the race to be the first on the market, accuracy in reporting and ethical standards are often compromised. If criticized for their low professional standards and lack of accountability, journalists in such media environment often invoke the defence of freedom of the press. Such press systems tend to exist in intensely competitive media markets, such as new democracies in Taiwan, Indonesia, the Philippines, and some East European countries, where media outlets mushroom and bring immense pressure on the media market and where new regulations are still taking shape.

Even in China where the press is becoming increasingly commercialized, tabloids, sensationalized news, or even made-up news stories are not hard to find. Such press systems may also exist in well-developed, saturated and consolidated media markets where it is very challenging to expand market share such as Hong Kong and Thailand. Because of the profit-oriented nature of such press systems, media companies are regarded as moneymakers, regulated by market demand only. Circulations and ratings become the only measure of success. Whatever sells is repeated in the media, resulting in over-coverage of some topics and events, such as celebrity journalism and press conferences, and the undercoverage of other less glamorous topics and events, such as poverty. Under such systems, the media spend far too much time covering and far too little time uncovering.

As they become pure businesses, such media are financed mostly with advertising dollars and subscriptions. Another form of press irresponsibility is the partisan press or political patronage of the press, in which case some press allows itself to be used as political tools especially when the democratic system is still young.

With a political power vacuum as a result of the dismantling of control mechanisms, political families, parties, or organizations often rush to take control of the media and use the media to advance their particular agendas, often employing such tactics as personal attacks or smear campaigns. Such a press tends to exist in free but less developed media markets as political patronage provides much needed financial support for the media.

Under such press systems, media content is often negative, full of political attacks in partisan press, or sex and violence in tabloids instead of stories about progress, which is often a long and less dramatic process. Tabloids and partisan press are typical products of such a press system.

RESPONSIBLE BUT NOT FREE

The very term seems to be an oxymoron. Critics may ask how a press can be classified as responsible if it is not free. The answer can depend on the definition of responsibility according to local community standards.

Such press systems tend to exist in more traditional societies where the emphasis is on the group rather than the individual and where cultural traditions or religions have a major impact on public life. Press in this group tends to stress the importance and interests of the country, society, community, and families rather than freedom and rights of individuals.

It tends to follow moral or religious principles and societal goals in news coverage rather than follow market demand because to publish what is perceived to be responsible is more important than to publish what sells.

The emphasis is on publishing what is right versus the right to publish, which is the difference between what is ethical and what is legal. The goals of such a press may vary from country to country, including social order and stability, economic development, or reinforcement of religious values. The press in this category tends to support these societal goals under government or public pressure, or both. For example, in Saudi Arabia and much of the Islamic world, newspapers devote sections to the teachings or discussions of Islam while criticism of Islam is forbidden. And in most of the Islamic press, the content is very clean, free of pornography.

Elsewhere in the world, many of the developing countries in Asia, Africa, and South America see national development as the top priority and expect the media to serve as a tool for nation building. In Singapore, because of the fear of ethnic and religious riots and the importance of its relations with its neighbors, the press cannot report on issues concerning race, religion, or its neighbors to maintain order and stability.

If the majority of the people in these societies support those goals, then the press is responsible. However, in some cases, especially when a country is involved in a war, current community standards may prove unreliable when the public is caught up in a patriotic frenzy. When that happens, it would depart from the universal values in journalism, such as accuracy and balance.

Because it has special roles to play in society, press in this group may obtain financial support from the government, public or social institutions, or the church even though a major part of its income may still come from the market.

NOT FREE AND NOT RESPONSIBLE

The press in this group does not enjoy much freedom of operation, and the controls applied unilaterally by the government are most likely not supported by the people. The most typical examples are perhaps the press in North Korea and Turkmenistan, where there is very little information but plenty of glorifications of the state leaders in the press. Hardships endured by the people can hardly be found in the news media.

The press in this group is also prohibited from criticizing the government or exposing corruption. The press in this group does not have the freedom to make its own editorial decisions, and public opinion is suppressed. After a review of the different types of press systems, where should the Japanese press be plotted on the coordinate grid?

It should perhaps be placed somewhere close to the origin of the coordinate grid as being partly free and partly responsible. It is free from government control but not free from industry control. And if the press refrains from uncovering high-level scandals in the government or big corporations, it cannot be described as socially responsible.

But until the Japanese people start to reject their press, which is opposite to the fact that Japanese newspapers enjoy the highest circulations in the world, the press in Japan cannot be described as irresponsible either. A responsibility index as discussed earlier plus a more accurate press freedom rating can help determine the position of the Japanese press on the grid and the positions of the press in other countries.

A Dynamic Model

The proposed two-dimensional Freedom-Responsibility coordinate system attempts to provide a more balanced press model in explaining press systems around the world, measuring not only the degree of press freedom but also the level of press responsibility. The validity of the new model will be determined by how many press systems in the world it can satisfactorily describe and explain. But societies are constantly changing, and so are their press systems. One of the advantages of the new model is that it can accommodate such changes in the system.

For example, the American press seems to be trying to be more responsible and relevant to its readers while having some of its freedom curtailed because of the War on Terror. Comparing with the press elsewhere in the world, the American press is best known for being free but not necessarily for being responsible. The low credibility of the news media in repeated public opinion polls shows public dissatisfaction with media performance. Civic and public journalism seems to be pushing the American press toward more press responsibility when the press tries to be more relevant to its readers and more conscious of the role it can play in society, such as helping crime-fighting and boosting voter turnout.

And in the age of war on terror, the Bush administration is tightening up press access to information, citing national security concerns. It also launched an investigation into the leaking of the National security Agency's domestic spying programme to discourage such disclosure of information.

During the war in Iraq, the government controlled reporters' access on the battlefield with a system of embedded reporters. And the concentration of ownership also reduces the independence and freedom the press once had.

The press in China seems to be moving slowly in the opposite direction-freer but messier even though sometimes more relevant to its readers. The press in China used to follow only Party lines. Now it also has to follow market demand by addressing public concerns. Some local papers target rural poverty by providing tips on how to grow better crops or how to generate cash by engaging in non-farming businesses. Competition, unheard of before the economic reforms, has given rise to diversity in the media. The Internet has provided a channel for news stories turned down by the traditional media. These changes are clearly pushing the Chinese press toward more freedom and responsibility.

However, competition also drives down the quality of news coverage and the ethical standards of journalists as sensationalism and bribery are prevalent. The Chinese press is in a state of flux as different factors are pulling it in different directions with deepening economic reforms. The most important factor, however, is still government policies. The press in Russia presents perhaps the most intriguing case for study as the degree of press freedom and responsibility shifted dramatically with the changing political climate of the country. Described as the prototype communist media, the press in the former Soviet Union was a political tool, following Lenin's ideal of press's functioning as collective agitator, propagandist, and organizer.

After the fall of communism, the press in Russia changed overnight from not free to completely free. Then under the presidency of Putin, press freedom in Russia was once again being curtailed. With a new president coming into the Kremlin, the status of press freedom in Russia is yet to be determined. The proposed new Freedom-Responsibility model is dynamic not only because it can accommodate the changes within particular press systems, but also because it can reflect changes in the structure of the model. In the debate on press freedom and press responsibility in the West, the concept of press freedom often trumps the concept of press responsibility.

The same is true on the global scene as free news media in the West dominate the global information flow. The call for the New World Information and Communication Order from developing countries was drowned out in the West's battle cry for the free flow of information.

And the Freedom House measures press freedom, not press responsibility. Given the dominant position of press freedom in the coordinate system, the press freedom axis represents the yang arm of the coordinate system while the press responsibility axis stands for the yin arm of the system. The yang and yin axes complement each other, forming a balanced system.

However, the pendulum of history never stops swinging. Laozi, an ancient Chinese philosopher, sees reversal as the way the natural order operates: "everything that has gone far in one direction will move in the opposite direction, and to be in a low or weak position is to be in a state in which one will thrive". That is the law of the dialectics. If the abuse of press freedom becomes a global issue and the world's press is forced to be more responsible because of public pressure, there can be a paradigm change within the coordinate system with the concept of press responsibility becoming the dominant feature of the model and thus, the yang axis of the system, and the concept of press freedom becoming the yin axis of the system.

But that may take a long time to occur even though such changes will never stop. Confucius advocated the "middle path" and Aristotle promoted the "golden mean," each avoiding the extremes at either end. The same principle applies to press performance-there is neither absolute press freedom nor absolute press responsibility. The desirable middle path would be the optimal combination of press freedom with press responsibility, a blend of the West and the East.

The two-dimensional system proposed in this chapter is an attempt at exploring a more balanced model in studying press systems around the world. The major challenge in the application of the model would be the measurement of press responsibility in a press system. So far no effort is ever made in that regard, given the expected controversies it is bound to draw.

If media observers and researchers can agree that development journalism and press responsibility do not automatically translate into government control of the press, measuring press responsibility does not have to be a forbidden task. The compilation of a global press responsibility index can provide a helpful guide in studying the characteristics of a press system. A good starting point can be the identification of universal values in journalism as discussed earlier. The more universal values societies can agree upon, the more reliable the index can be. "Current community standards" in the form of public opinion surveys offer a way of accommodating values specific to local culture.

Debates on universal values in journalism can be messy, but the results can be crystallizing and enlightening. With more research, media researchers from the East and the West may find more common ground than they expect. One weakness of the model is perhaps that Western and Confucian philosophies and values tend to dominate the discussions even though there are so many other religious and philosophical influences in the world. Therefore, this study is only exploratory in nature. It can be enriched and improved with perspectives from more cultures or serve as a starting point for future research.

In future research, alternative concepts or dichotomies can be explored in building new models, such as an observer-interventionist/activist dichotomy, or commercial-ideological dichotomy. The point of departure will depend on the angle of analysis and on the perspectives and approaches of researchers.

10

Interaction of Reader and Reporter

The hypothesis that public journalism designs would visually convey interactivity between readers and the media more than non-public journalism (H2) was also significant. Seventy-five per cent of the public journalism issues in this sample used visual elements to encourage readers to contact the media, while 46 per cent of non-public journalism issues sampled did so.

In addition, the number of different ways public journalism provided for readers to contact them (address, phone, e-mail, web site, fax) was highly significant. Small circulation mean = 2.1, large circulation mean =.5). There were no significant differences between small and large circulation issues on this variable, as would be expected if all size papers were practicing public journalism the same way.

PHOTO OPS AND PHOTOS OF 'REAL PEOPLE'

The two public journalism characteristics that were not significant when public and non-public journalism issues were compared but whose means were in the direction hypothesized both dealt with photographs; whether public journalism relied on managed photo opportunities less often than non-public journalism (H3), and whether public journalism photos featured citizens and real people more often than candidates or experts (H4). The non-significant findings may be due to the low number of cases sampled (N = 41), but it is important that for both hypotheses the mean ratios of non-managed photos and photos of real people to total photos showed that the public journalism issues sampled used fewer photographs from managed photo opportunities and also used more photos of citizens and real people than candidates or experts.

Comparisons within public journalism showed no significant differences between small and large papers' photos in this sample regarding photo opportunities or the use of citizens and real people in photos versus candidates or experts. Textual analysis revealed both small public journalism papers, Binghamton and Wisconsin, used all photos of real people from non-managed photo sources. In the large public journalism category, San Francisco used all non-managed photos featuring citizens in its series on transportation. Since

Binghamton's series was on the local economy and primarily covered the citizen's forums, and San Francisco's series was on commuter woes, it is perhaps not surprising that they were able to find photo subjects that did not involve officials and experts.

It is more unusual for election coverage to avoid photos of candidates, yet that is just what the Wisconsin paper did. It achieved this goal mainly by running only one photo (citizens at a forum) over all seven issues; six issues had no photos at all. In the large non-public journalism genre, Omaha used all photos of candidates, as would be expected for traditional journalism.

The variation is mainly explained by the non-public journalism Philadelphia paper's use of all non-managed photos of real people, and the public journalism Charlotte paper's heavy use of managed photo ops of candidates – findings that are counter to what would be expected in ideal public journalism. The story subjects provide partial explanation.

In its series on a typical suburban neighborhood, Philadelphia used five to eight pictures every day in its non-public journalism series, all were of real people and none were from photo opportunities. In its election coverage, the public journalism Charlotte paper used mug shots or photo collages of candidates on nearly every cover, plus cutout photos of candidates in its full-page graphic of candidates' answers to voters' questions. In addition, Charlotte used four conventional campaign trail photos over the course of the series, in traditional political photojournalism style.

The only real-people photos Charlotte used were approximately three to five photos daily of the citizens who asked questions of the candidates or whose opinions were quoted. The Charlotte design director indicated in a telephone interview that the amount of campaign-trail photographs shot were "not nearly as many as five years ago... An effort was made to take photos of real people, but that makes things harder." The convention of candidate photographs for election coverage apparently remains strong, even at papers that have embraced public journalism principles.

The design director's acknowledgment that finding photos of real people is harder than attending photo opportunities is a candid admission that goes to the root of the difficulty of altering established conventions.

Comments by designers at the public journalism papers in Binghamton, Madison, and San Francisco, all indicated their photographers tried to avoid photo opportunities in favour of real people; however, photo ops could not be entirely eliminated. The former graphics editor at the Madison paper provided some background on the thinking: The photo staff hates dull pictures, first of all. There is nothing worse than a talking head (politician) or a grip-and-grin. They do try and look for action or images from the issue they are addressing. It is a combination of public journalism and aesthetics. He also attributed the lack of photos (one photo over seven issues) to aesthetics: With 'We the People,' the premiere events are these town meetings. They don't make particularly good photos. They are often held in the capitol, which has miserable lighting, and it's a sea of people sitting around. The marching orders are we will shoot that, but we would probably try to limit that to one. Otherwise, we would have photos and stories about journalists from different media getting together to organize 'We the People'."

The idea of using photos of real people that are not the result of photo ops orchestrated by people seeking to manipulate publicity goes to the heart of public journalism philosophy and reflects a conscious effort to avoid agenda-setting effects. The use of this type of photo would be a sign that public journalism's goals are beginning to be translated into practice. Helping citizens participate in civic life

Of the two remaining hypotheses, neither showed any significant differences between public and non-public journalism. One was the hypothesis that public journalism would visually convey more mobilizing information to help citizens participate in their communities than non-public journalism (H1). There were no significant differences between the sampled public and non-public journalism issues' use of mobilizing information.

However, when comparisons were made within public journalism between large and small papers' issues, there was a highly significant difference in the visual communication of mobilizing information, with small papers scoring better. Only 14 per cent of large papers' stories used visual elements to convey mobilizing information, whereas 71 per cent of small papers' stories used one visual element, and 7 per cent used two. In the public journalism genre, issues from both large papers sampled (Charlotte, San Francisco) used no mobilizing information in visual format. However, both small public journalism papers sampled visually conveyed mobilizing information. The topics—the Charlotte Observer's election coverage — cannot be the reason, however, since the two other papers which carried election coverage, including one non-public journalism paper (Omaha), listed mobilizing information.

The other large public journalism paper, San Francisco, gave almost no mobilizing information on its transportation series. Both small public journalism papers listed mobilizing information frequently; Wisconsin had the most and most regular mobilizing information with its boxes for forum broadcasts, call-in lines and registration information for upcoming town meetings. Wisconsin even developed regular graphic devices its designers called democracy boxes.

Perhaps the convention of having these boxes to fill kept mobilizing information in the forefront for Wisconsin designers. Binghamton usually publicized an upcoming priority setting conference or results of the economic teams' reports. One reason for these results could be that mobilizing information is not new or unique to public journalism the way other variables can be. For this study, mobilizing information consisted of news citizens could use to participate in community life. However, the importance of information which allows people to take action has been discussed in scholarly and trade publications since at least the 1970s. Well before the advent of public journalism, traditional journalism has offered dates of neighborhood watch meetings, names and addresses of redevelopment agencies that offer grant money, etc. Because of the length of time over which journalists have been aware of the importance of mobilizing information, and the ubiquitous nature of such information, it may not be surprising that there are no significant differences in the amount of mobilizing information conveyed visually in public and non-public journalism.

The greater resources at larger papers cannot help explain why small papers used more visual devices for mobilizing information than large papers. Mobilizing information should be quite familiar and top-of-mind to designers at both small and large papers, public journalism and non-public journalism.

Perhaps another explanation for the highly significant difference between small circulation and large circulation public journalism designs that visually convey mobilizing information can be found in James Lemert and colleague's findings. Because small papers may better reflect their small communities, there is more awareness of readers' desire for visual display of mobilizing information. If large public journalism papers are not providing mobilizing information, this supports Lemert's theory that mobilizing information is regularly missing when issues are located outside of town, where audiences ordinarily can't look up addresses and phone numbers. This may be the case for large newspapers that cover many different communities.

VIEWS OF REAL PEOPLE

The other hypothesis that was not significant was that public journalism would use more visual devices to convey views of real people (H5). This non-significant finding between the public and non-public journalism issues sampled is interesting because views of real people rather than experts or politicians are one of the central tenets of public journalism. Although all designers interviewed said they tried to include views of real people, two said it was a copy desk decision and would be done mainly through pullquotes. However, textual analysis revealed that not all public journalism papers visually displayed views of real people. Both Wisconsin and San Francisco used no graphics or design elements for views of real people, although these views were carried within the text.

A lack of significant difference between public and non-public journalism's use of views of real people may signify that visual journalists do not fully understand or embrace this idea. If a significant difference were found to exist in the written communication of views of real people, but not in the visual communication, this would have implications for the integration of the designers and copy editors with the reporters and editors. It may indicate that designers have not been included in sessions devoted to explaining the philosophies of public journalism and do not understand its principles fully, or, they are aware of the importance of views of real people but are leaving it to reporters to include in stories rather than employing content-driven design to convey this visually. There was also no difference in the sampled issues between small and large public journalism's use of visual devices to convey views of real people, but this would be expected if all papers practiced public journalism the same way.

THE IMPORTANCE OF UNDERSTANDING

Two final points of interest were revealed in the interviews when designers were asked whether they designed differently for public journalism than for non-public journalism. Designers at two papers said yes, public journalism design was different from non-public journalism design, and designers at the other two papers replied no, there was no difference.

Interestingly, the no difference responses came from designers whose papers did not have training sessions on the concepts and techniques of public journalism, or who did not include visual journalists in those sessions. Both affirmative responses came from newspapers whose designers did participate in public journalism education sessions. Understanding of public journalism principles was one of the explanations offered for some of the findings in this study, and the perception of designers regarding the difference in designing for public journalism reinforces such an explanation.

Visual journalists who did not attend sessions aimed at explaining public journalism's goal and principles may not understand it as well as those who did and, therefore, may not consider ways to visually communicate those goals and principles. Also, one of the designers interviewed complained that too many journalists at the paper felt like they had been ordered to do public journalism with no opportunity for discussion or input. This chapter did not offer training sessions in public journalism. "If they're really going to get people on board to do this and do this well, there has to be that discussion," said the designer, who asked to remain anonymous. "There are numerous ethical challenges in doing this, and they need to at least be explored, as do the possible pitfalls." Both these insights have implications for managing editors contemplating introducing public journalism into their newsrooms.

Table. Large Public Vs. Large Non-Public Journalism: Percentages and Fisher's Exact Test of Public Journalism Characteristics by Size of Paper

Variables (per cent with yes values)	Large PJ stories	Small PJ stories	Exact Probabilities
Common ground and solutions	36%	0%	.025
Interactivity with media	71%	46%	.13
Mobilizing information	25%	63%	.42
Views of real people	50%	39%	.25
N=27			

This study has used the emerging theory of public journalism, which claims a significantly different content than non-public journalism, and the theory of content-driven design, which says that visual meaning must reflect the written content, to examine the question prompted by these theories: If the content of stories generated through public journalism methods is different, and design is driven by content, shouldn't design for public journalism be different than design for non-public journalism?

The results from this study are mixed. Of six hypotheses that speak to the question of whether public journalism is visually different from non-public journalism, two showed significant differences among the newspaper issues sampled. Public journalism stories in this study used more visual devices to convey common ground and solutions, and ways to contact the media than did non-public journalism stories.. Four hypotheses showed no significant differences between public journalism and non-public journalism, but two had means in the direction hypothesized. The public journalism issues sampled were more likely than non-public journalism to use fewer managed photo opportunities and more photos of real people than candidates or experts, but the differences were not significant

These are signs that some of public journalism's goals may be beginning to be translated into practice by visual journalists, but that there are other goals that are not being addressed visually, at least in these newspapers. The fact that the public journalism issues sampled were not significantly different from the non-public journalism issues in how they visually conveyed views of real people — one of the central tenets of public journalism — should be of concern. That the public journalism issues sampled visually communicated no more mobilizing information than the non-public journalism issues is less cause for worry because mobilizing information is not unique to public journalism the way the other characteristics can be.

This study has also found that, in some cases, public journalism papers that have established new conventions in place of the old have found it easier to adhere consistently to public journalism principles; for instance, the development of standing graphics such as democracy boxes for mobilizing information. One problem in the consistent communication of public journalism characteristics seems to be with journalists' fundamental understanding of public journalism. Confusion over and even unawareness of public journalism principles seems to be a basic, underlying reason why the practice of public journalism is not significantly different from non-public journalism in terms of visual communication. In addition, it appears that not all designers are practicing content-driven design. For instance, this research found stories which included views of real people in the text but not in the design. In conclusion, there appear to be some significant differences in this sample in the way public journalism is visually communicated compared with non-public journalism. However, there is not enough significance to say that it represents a radical departure from non-public journalism, at least in the issues studied here. It appears another researcher's conclusion regarding the content of public journalism may be correct for the visual display as well: "there is no overriding, core philosophy of public journalism at some of the papers practicing it; instead it has become a label used to name a variety of special projects."

The news industry has been undergoing a fundamental paradigm shift since the end of last century. An increasing number of media companies around the United States, such as the Washington Post in Washington, DC, Media General in Virginia, the Tribune Company in Chicago, and New England Cable News, have taken solid steps to merge different media such as newspapers, television stations, radio stations, and online journalism companies to disseminate news content on multiple media platforms.

As a result, in a metropolitan area, one company would own print, TV, and online venues. Media call this industrial trend "media convergence," though the concept means much more than media mergers. Media convergence muddies the lines among broadcast journalism, print journalism, and online journalism, leaving college journalism educators to wonder whether traditional journalism programs have become dinosaurs.

After surveying 200 newspaper publishers worldwide, the World Association of Newspapers (WAN) found, "Despite a somewhat gloomy outlook for wholesale convergence in media companies worldwide in the near term, convergence is already being implemented with varying degrees of enthusiasm and speed among the world's media companies". The Innovation International Media Consulting Group estimates that at least 100 of the world's multiple media companies are planning and implementing integration strategies. South and Nicholson (2002) drew a sketch of a converged media company: Daily journalists need to embrace the 24-hour news cycle, with continuous deadlines. And the story needs to be reported and produced for a multi-platform audience. That may mean delivering content first to the Web and cell phones, a streaming video broadcast later in the day, a TV talk-back interview still later, and a "second day" interpretive story for the next morning's newspaper.

Dominic Gates pointed out, "Convergence with broadcast and online media is the shape of things to come for newspapers." The trend remains controversial. Critics complain that such cross-ownership of both a television station and a newspaper in the same market is a threat to democracy because it limits the number of voices.

Delegates of the Communication Workers of America, a 60,000-member guild, passed a resolution in June of 2002 at the group's annual convention in Las Vegas, pledging to increase public awareness about the risks of ongoing media convergence. The delegates complained that shrinking media markets are a threat to editorial diversity and job security. In 1975, the Federal Communications Commission (FCC) ruled that no new broadcast licenses would be granted to companies that own a major daily newspaper and a local television station in the same city. Fairness & Accuracy In Reporting (FAIR) calls on the FCC to roll back limits on media consolidation.

The Newspaper Association of America (NAA), on the other hand, has asked the FCC to appeal the rule. On June 2, 2003, the FCC voted 3 to 2 to relax or eliminate some ownership restrictions, such as a rule barring media companies from owning television stations in markets where they publish daily newspapers. Although some lawmakers and advocacy groups are still fighting in the courts and on Capitol Hill to overturn the FCC's new media ownership rules, these rules will be likely to encourage cross-media ownership in the years to come.

The mergers have raised questions about whether they are good for the craft of journalism itself. Critics complain that by requiring journalists to be jacks of both trades, print and broadcast, the journalists will be masters of none. Robert J. Haiman, president emeritus of The Poynter Institute, compared the media convergence trend to an Amphicar, a cross between a boat and a car.

The Amphicar, hawked in Florida during the 1950s, flopped. "It flopped because people quickly discovered that while it really was an ingenious combination of a car and a boat, it was a lousy car (because it also had to be a boat), and it was a lousy boat (because it also had to be a car)".

Willingly or unwillingly, many news practitioners' functions are gradually changing or are expected to change as media convergence rolls on. For a reporter in a converged media environment, knowing how to write is probably no longer enough. S/he could be expected to write the same story for different media in a timely manner. Ideally, s/he can readily talk in front of a video camera. As a photographer, knowing how to tell a story both in video and in still images is more and more in demand.

A designer should know how to prepare still graphics for print, moving graphics for television and dynamic graphics for the Web. At the online version of the Chicago Tribune, for instance, staffers are supposed to cover stories, take pictures, operate video cameras, and create digital pages. The editors, too, need a wider variety of skills than the traditional paper editors. Along with infrastructure changes and the attempt to create synergy among the various media outlets, a new breed of journalists-digital or multimedia journalists-is expected.

As media jobs become more demanding, some news practitioners are beginning to team up to complete projects. At the same time, fear, confusion, and frustration from news practitioners are creeping into newsrooms. Carr wrote: "Convergence frightens many people who wonder whether their current skill sets have prepared them for-or will even be needed in-that great undiscovered country, the future. This is probably the primary reason why I still find such great hostility to convergence among certain journalists." Killebrew, a mass communications professor from the University of South Florida, suggested that "journalists must be prepared to either crosstrain themselves or seek training from other sources while management must be prepared to give them the opportunities and time to do so." The 1999-2000 president of the Association for Schools of Journalism and Mass Communication (ASJMC), Shirley Staples Carter, questioned whether, in the midst of the "Internet revolution," programs are prepared to educate journalists of the future. When specifically talking about writing, Keith Hartenberger, manager of news and programming for Tribune Regional Programming, said that journalism schools should make their students aware of the many ways to present the news. "It's a multimedia world out there," he said. "If you're just being prepared to write newspaper stories, you won't be prepared". "At some point, this [cross-media training] is something we're going to expect from everyone".

Media convergence, as a trend that is gradually shaping the landscape of the media industry in the new century, has called into question the conventional journalism school practice of having separate tracks-print, broadcast, etc.

Journalism educators around the country also are trying to figure out what they should do, if anything, to better prepare students for the converged media. For instance, should journalism educators consider merging different sequences such as magazine, newspaper, broadcast, and photojournalism, or still teach all such courses as if they were unrelated media? "Traditionally defined segments of the communications industry are less and less distinguishable for technological and market convergence," observed Moon. Are college journalism educators themselves both theoretically equipped and technologically prepared to teach their students for converged media? What do media companies expect from future news practitioners? What do current news practitioners in converged media feel is lacking? For both news practitioners and professors, the two most urgent questions cry for answers: Should journalism schools train specialists or fit for-all generalists?

And how should college journalism education balance the teaching of critical thinking and technical skills? Apart from all these education-related questions, we are also interested in finding out what are the driving forces behind the media mergers, who are regarded as the beneficiaries of this trend, and how people's political beliefs are related to their attitude toward teaching media convergence in colleges? These questions pertain closely to college journalism education, which has been the subject of debate and criticism for two decades.

A national survey was conducted among colleges, daily newspapers, and commercial television stations to explore the issue of how journalism schools should prepare students for the trend of media convergence from the perspectives of news editors, news professionals, and journalism professors. The study measured the level of general support for convergence education and determined if a new model of journalism education was called for.

If so, it examined whether consensus existed among the three groups on the direction educators should take when revisiting programme designs. Where consensus was not apparent, divisions among the sample of educators, editors, and reporters were defined. The goal of the study is to provide evidence that will help journalism educators make informed decisions about how to respond to media convergence in their curricula and courses and lay an empirical foundation for further discussions and conversations about media convergence.

The search results show that media convergence is a comparatively new topic in media research, though articles about it have inundated the Internet, magazines, and newspapers. Most research writings appeared no earlier than 1998. Articles about the relationship between media convergence and higher education are rare and have shown up more recently in trade magazines such as Presstime, Quill, and Journalism Education Today and in Web sites. A few research writings were found in academic conference (i.e., AEJMC) proceedings. Many writings have addressed one of the toughest questions: What is media convergence? How to define "media convergence" had a direct bearing on how we conducted this study. Out of these writings, we identified four categories of media convergence that directly affect how journalism will be taught in colleges.

CONTENT CONVERGENCE

As Tremayne noted, decades ago, the term media convergence referred to the content convergence between competing newspapers and even among newspapers, magazines, and television. Today, pure content convergence continues on the Internet. For instance, the St. Petersburg Times has incorporated local Channel 10's TV news into its online newspaper though they are independent business entities. In other words, media convergence may not necessarily be tied to media merger. Form convergence (or technological convergence). Around the mid-1990s, as Tremayne and Wurtz noted, computer technology and Internet technology made possible the convergence of all forms of mediated communications including video, audio, data, text, still photo, and graphic art for "on-demand" audiences.

Using these different forms to tell news stories on the World Wide Web has been widely regarded as the future of mass communication regardless of the fact that most online news sites have had a hard time making ends meet, let alone making a profit. Form convergence, often called technological convergence, has been a fundamental force to guide and lead convergence in the market, industry, and regulation.

CORPORATE CONVERGENCE

Since the late 1990s, media convergence has been escalated to the level of media mergers. The News Centre located in Tampa, Florida, owned by Media General, and the Tribune Interactive, owned by the Tribune Company, for instance, are the products of media mergers. In The News Centre, WFLA-TV, The Tampa Tribune, and Tampa Bay Online operate out of the same building. They share daily tips and information, spot news, photography, enterprise reporting, franchises, events, and public service. Each of the three entities in The News Centre has its own independent newsroom, but they issued a joint statement of coverage principles, titled "News Centre Pledge".

The Tribune Interactive has brought together the interactive functions of the company's four newspapers and more than a score of television stations including WGN-TV and CLTV. The individual media outlets have their own newsgathering staff, but their coverage is enhanced by their multimedia desks in the Chicago Tribune newsroom and the Tribune Media Centre in Washington. "A synergy-team of print editors and TV news veterans at the Chicago Tribune work together to manage resource sharing and the relationship". Media merger has made both content convergence and form convergence handy. Corporate convergence via vertical and horizontal integration, mergers, alliances, and acquisitions will make traditionally defined segments of the communications industry less and less distinguishable.

11

Role Convergence of Press and Media

Russial identified several examples of role convergence in newsrooms. For instance, the roles of reporter and librarian, the roles of copyeditor and compositor, the roles of graphic artist and Web designer, and the roles of photo editor, darkroom technician, and photographer are all converging in different media. In more recent years, content convergence, form convergence, and especially corporate convergence have sparked more in-depth role convergence among news practitioners.

For instance, Victoria Lim from The News Centre in Tampa revealed at a February 2002 conference on media convergence at the University of Florida that she primarily works as a television reporter for WFLA-TV, but she also has to write for the company's newspaper, The Tampa Tribune, as a senior consumer investigative reporter and for the Web company TBO.com on a daily basis; at the time of the conference, she was working on 31 stories.

A newspaper reporter may also produce a newspaper in QuarkXPress or serve as a TV news anchor, while a newspaper photographer may shoot video stories or produce interactive online stories in Flash. Role convergence requires that both reporters and editors re-equip themselves both journalistically and technologically.

Of the four types of convergence, role convergence has the most direct effect on future journalism education. Within the media industry, there are serious doubts about whether training cross-media journalists are possible or desirable. When asked whether reporters of the future must be equally skilled in print, TV, and online, Forrest Carr, news director of WFLA-TV at The News Centre in Tampa, said no.

He said he believed that there would always be areas of specialization and students may still choose specialties, but said that it no longer makes any sense to pretend print journalists and electronic journalists are in different professions. On the other hand, he said that journalists who have skills in TV, print, and online media certainly will be more valuable to their employers; and he emphasized that prospective employees must be willing to work in an environment where reporters cooperate across platforms. In most cases currently, he said, cooperating across platforms simply comes down to the sharing of tips and information. Charles Kravetz, the vice president for news and station manager of New England Cable News (NECN), the largest regional news network in America, concurs with Forrest Carr. When asked "Do you see a time when all journalists will have to be able to file stories on all platforms (print, TV, radio, online)?" Kravetz said: "I am not sure that is the way it is going to work out.

This notion we had that one-journalist-fits-all-media is perhaps not that realistic.... There are very few people we will talk about in the future that are TV/newspaper/internet reporters". Gates agreed, "The 'backpack journalist'-a superhack master of multimedia who can do it all and who routinely packs a laptop and a video camera along with the tape recorder and steno notebook-may be the subject of avant-garde j-school courses, but it's not likely to become the norm."

Some other media executives have tried to define the extent to which role convergence is expected. Gil Thelen, executive editor and senior vice president of The Tampa Tribune, for instance, gave suggestions to journalism educators based on his two years of experience in The News Centre.

"The fully formed, all-purpose, multiplatform, gadget-laden journalism grad is NOT what we're looking to hire.... Journalism schools must continue to produce graduates who are competent in one craft area: reporting, design, producing, directing, editing." However, Thelen encouraged journalism schools to train writers to write for print, online, and broadcast and train print photographers to learn how to shoot and produce TV packages. Thelen said that cultural resistance is the biggest hurdle for converging newsrooms, and that employees or current journalism students need to learn to cooperate and collaborate across newsrooms.

What is unclear is whether these media administrators' predictions are limited by the status quo of the current generation of news practitioners who might not be very well prepared for convergence or who might even resist the notion of media convergence. At Brigham Young University, students with multiple skills are more valued and feel more comfortable in the converged media environment.

In addition, sharing tips and information does not entail convergence. Reporters have been doing this for decades. It seems that keeping convergence only on the level of sharing tips and information can hardly justify the high cost of rebuilding infrastructures like The News Centre. We are interested in finding out what expectations media companies have for future journalists. From news professionals' self-evaluations of their preparedness for media convergence, we should also be able to infer what is most desirable in the media industry nowadays. In the face of increasing demand for technically skilled journalists-conversant with QuarkXPress, Photoshop, Avid, and Dreamweaver and able to crunch statistics using spreadsheets and other statistical methods in order to uncover the hidden story-should longstanding staples such as ethics, law, and theory remain at the heart of journalism curricula? Or should such materials, commonly grouped together as "critical thinking", share equal hilling with technology or "skills" training? In other words, how should journalism schools balance the teaching of professional skills and that of critical thinking in an era when technology penetrates every facet of news gathering, preparation, editing, production, and delivery? Convergence further complicates this age-old battle in journalism education. Abraham noticed that the goal of most restructuring in journalism institutions is to provide an integrated skills environment where students would get the chance to practice the skills of multimedia production. Abraham argued: "The role of journalism academy should be very different from that of the industry. Its role should not simply be to inculcate skills that will help students to flag down jobs. They should aim to provide a scholarly background for a deeper intellectual understanding of our lives, media forms and of communication in general".

The dean of the University of Nevada at Reno thinks the ability to use multiple media skills is essential. Brigham Young University, which has built a working converged newsroom into its curriculum, expects students to graduate with multiple skills. University News Director, Dean Paynter, said, "We expect our students to more than anchor, more than report, and more than produce. The best ones can do it all, including write for the newspaper".

Mitchell Stephens, professor of journalism and mass communications at New York University, holds up the other end. "In a world where corporate pressures on 'content providers' seem to be increasing and civic affairs decreasing, the argument for emphasizing the basics does have much to recommend it."

Thomas Kunkel, dean of the Philip Merrill College of Journalism at the University of Maryland, sums it up: "Today's journalists, first and foremost, must be strong critical thinkers who know enough about geography, history and the human condition to understand why events play out as they do. They must be intellectually curious. They should speak a second language. They should read something other than Jim Romenesko's MediaNews site. They ought to have a world view."

A controversy in late 2002 at Columbia University demonstrates how volatile the argument is currently. The debate arose when the graduate school of journalism at Columbia University halted its search for a dean. The new university president, Lee Bollinger, wanted to re-evaluate the school's mix of craft versus theory, and the move created a flurry of opinion about the journalism school's existing curriculum. This critical curriculum question is often reflected in the questions of whether and how new technology classes should be included in the existing curriculum and how they should be taught. Some journalism schools are preparing to embrace the wave of media convergence in their new curricula by converging print and electronic media sequences to adapt to the industrial trends and the new technological environment. Blanchard and Christ warn that universities with limited resources will no longer tolerate duplicating specializations with separate courses such as writing for television, writing for newspapers, writing for public relations, and writing for advertising. Blanchard and Christ add that the communications revolution (the media's convergence and related trends) is making journalism and mass communication's traditional sequences obsolete.

Actually, Blanchard and Christ's opinion is not something new. Early in 1972, the University of Iowa School of Journalism already eliminated its sequences but at the expense of being denied reaccreditation by ACEJMC. About thirty years later, their decision seemed to be finding more sympathy.

Many schools are still exploring where to go. In October 2001, seventeen professors and leaders of new media from thirteen journalism programs across the country gathered in Berkeley, California, and had a discussion about new media in journalism education. The University of Nevada, Reno, offered several different elective courses in new media, but it did not have a special sequence.

It was struggling with how to incorporate them in other classes. The University of Florida had a concentration in online media, which was equivalent to other concen-trations such as reporting and editing and photojournalism. Students who were not in that concentration couldn't always squeeze in the online media courses because they did not have any leftover électives they could take in the school. American University had three divisions, journalism, public communication, and visual media, but they did not work together very well most of the time.

The University of South Carolina was restructuring its graduate masters programme in newspaper leadership and was focusing it on convergence. The University of Maryland had an online curriculum, but it was not formally structured as such. Northwestern University had an introductory New Media course at the undergraduate and graduate level, which was offered as an elective.

It was packed with everything from new skills training to wrestling with the business issues of new media to actual production. After three admission cycles, enrollment declined. The University of Minnesota established the Institute for New Media Studies, which merged broadcast journalism and print journalism programs to make them a concentration with the idea that future journalists would work in a multi-channel environment and should know how to operate within all those channels.

Although editors and academics sometimes agree on the qualifications a journalism student needs, an ideal curriculum doesn't always include convergence preparedness courses. In a 2000 poll, editors and educators agreed "on the same five of 14 types of knowledge considered most necessary for journalism graduates and listed them in the same order of importance". Technical skills were not mentioned in the top five, surpassed instead by "understanding of a journalist's responsibility to the public, understanding of the ethics of journalism, knowledge of current events, broad general knowledge, and knowledge of government".

With so much variance across universities, we are interested in finding out how many journalism schools have revamped their curricula to prepare students for the trend of media convergence, what professors' attitudes are toward teaching critical thinking vs. teaching technical skills and training generalists vs. training specialists, and what editors' and news professionals' attitudes are toward the same issues. In this regard, several scholars and news practitioners have tried to give advice to journalism professors and students in the context of media convergence.

In 2002, David Bulla from the University of Florida presented his "Media convergence: Industry practices and implications for education" to the AEJMC annual conference in Miami. This is the first research writing of its kind. The theme of the paper is the closest to that of this study. Bulla's study looked at the changing nature of contemporary mass communications practices, focusing on multimedia or converged journalism.

It described what scholastic journalism scholars are doing to prepare their students for these changes and provided recommendations to educators about how to update curricula to account for convergence.

The research questions for that study were:

- What are journalism educators currently doing to incorporate convergence into their curricula;
- What abilities, skills, and attitudes do professional journalists expect from their newest employees?

Media convergence in Bulla's study was defined as multimedia journalism, which means reporting, writing, and disseminating content in two or more media platforms.

Because of the controversy about media mergers, Bulla tried to find answers to some hot issues concerning democracy including: Does corporate media merging reduce public discourse and hinder democracy? Will it ultimately mean the need for fewer and fewer reporters, as the development of other technology has meant a decline in the number of employees in other areas of the production process? All these questions pertain to our study.

Bulla obtained a sample of 114 news practitioners working at newspapers, television stations, wire services, magazines, radio stations, and online publications in the United States. The sample was randomly selected from Editor & Publisher and Yahoo lists of media companies in the U.S. Media Web sites. With a response rate of 36 per cent, Bulla interviewed 41 news practitioners. Bulla also interviewed college educators, but he did not state how he sampled them.

What is unclear is the extent to which the Yahoo list and Editor & Publisher list overlap each other and if a sample from two potentially overlapping lists is any longer a random sample. In addition, since Bulla's questions were almost all unstructured, that is, he conducted interviews, he did not really need a random sample. Researchers strive for depth rather than breadth and don't mean to claim external validity in the statistical sense by conducting interviews. Finally, if he did need a random sample, a sample of 114 people with a 36 per cent response rate could be statistically defective because of big statistical errors. Bulla needed a better research design to make his study valid and reliable.

Some scholars doubt whether journalism school professors are theoretically and especially technologically prepared to teach media convergence. In an article written for Journalism Education magazine, John Irby, a professor from Washington State University and a veteran newspaper editor and publisher, for instance, was concerned about the disconnection between the newsroom and the classroom. Irby asked: Are universities and educators effectively preparing students for the work force? Do educators understand what newspapers are looking for in future reporters and editors? Does the newspaper industry have a responsibility in the division between educators and professionals? Are journalism educators "discounted" by professionals who believe those who teach couldn't succeed in newspapers?

Irby said older generations of newspaper reporters also appeared on radio and television periodically though they had no training; they never even felt like it was part of their job and thus did not take it very seriously.

But now, he continued, print journalists do need to take it seriously; journalism educators need to re-evaluate, and probably modify, the separatetrack approach in training print and broadcast journalists. Irby believed that there is still a need for specialization, but he told students to take both broadcast and print courses and told them that computer literacy is as crucial as the old-fashioned kind.

A study about the impact of media convergence on journalism education without consulting Robert J. Haiman's article "Can convergence float?" should be considered incomplete.

Haiman's fervent talk against media convergence raised some challenging questions that educators must face. Haiman, president emeritus of The Poynter Institute, argued that the converged media world is one from which good journalism, and good journalists, are going to be in great need of defence.

He stuck to his notion of the mission of good journalism he stated 40 years ago: "To inform the public about the public's business, creating a society that is equipped with the knowledge it needs to make the right civic decisions more often than it makes the wrong civic decisions, and thus helping to perpetuate self-government and democracy."

Expressing his deep concern for journalism, Haiman said: "I think that convergence may end up being good, maybe even very good, for media companies. I fear, however, that it is going to be bad, and maybe even very bad, for journalism." He continued to explain:

I think it is going to be bad for journalism because, even if it goes as well as it possibly can, I believe that it is going to distract journalists, journalism teachers, and journalism students away from that single most important imperative of the craft - to create an informed society capable of intelligently governing itself.

And if it does not go well, I fear it is going to subject journalists to time, resource, craft, and ethical pressures, all of which will be bad for journalists, bad for journalism, and bad for the country. In his talk, Haiman mentioned a top education reporter who had done a" superb job" for more than 18 years. Now, he had to do short reports for the TV station with which that newspaper was converged.

However," he's not exactly ready for prime time." After this reporter retires, Haiman is afraid that that he will be replaced by" someone who may not report like a buzz saw and write like a dream, but who probably will report and write education okay and who will also look good and sound good on television." " When that happens," he continued," the journalism quality of all of the education reporting coming out of that converged news operation is going to go down." We believe that few people would disagree with Haiman's point that quality content is the king, to use his own words, but Haiman's above comment could be limited, again, by the performance of the current generation of reporters who are not prepared for media convergence.

Haiman was suggesting that a future reporter who has been trained to work for different media platforms and who has learned more about reporting would produce reporting of less quality.

In our study, we would like to find out to what extent Haiman's concern is shared by editors, news professionals, and professors. While convergence is still in its infancy, Haiman suggested that journalists, journalism students, and journalism teachers do three" terribly important things":

- For journalists who want to keep good journalism alive in the converged world to take a blood oath to fight, scrap, kick and scream whenever any attempt is made to dilute good journalism values.
- For journalism schools and journalism teachers to offer students the right curriculum to function best in that converged world, and this does not mean offering new courses in convergence.
- For journalism students to emphasize the right areas of study and take the right courses so they will be able to defend themselves against the evils of convergence, prosper in that new world, and contribute to the effort to sustain informed self-government.

Haiman said," If we decide to teach anything about convergence at Poynter, that is the lesson I hope we'll teach." To students, Haiman said that the journalists who will be the most successful in the converged world are the same ones who are the most successful today, and they are the ones who are best trained in six areas: reporting, writing, editing, ethics, and media law, research techniques and specialized knowledge such as business, finance, law, science, health, aging, and the environment. Since the top reporter in education Haiman mentioned can hardly survive the converged media world, our question is whether gaining knowledge in these six areas is sufficient and what else, if any, students need to learn. Do students need to learn any new skills? What new skills do news practitioners need?

Also, we would like to see how the attitudes of the respondents from these three groups toward media merger affect their views of how to train future journalists. As South and Nicholson commented," If the industry doesn't agree on what new skills journalists need, it will be hard for journalism schools to know what to teach."

LARGER CONTEXT OF THE STUDY

The questions concerning teaching skills vs. critical thinking and training specialists vs. generalists are not new. They have been contextualized in ongoing conversations across disciplines over decades on many campuses in the United States. But such conversations take on new meanings in journalism schools when many reporting jobs today are becoming high-tech-oriented and many news companies are demanding high-tech skills from new hires upon their graduation.

The impact of such industrial demands on universities brings us back to the core issue-the role of the university in the shaping of the young souls in its charge. In other words, how should a university achieve the desired product-a truly educated human being for newsrooms.

The question of teaching skills vs. critical thinking winds down to a perennial competition between acquiescing pervasive vocationalism with its emphasis on skills training in an attempt to enable college students to survive outside academic institutions and establishing the relevance of the broad spectrum of knowledge to the career goals and lives of individuals. E. D. Hirsch argues: "Narrow vocational education, adjusted to the needs of the moment, is made ever more obsolete by changing technology... What is required is education for change, not for static job competencies".

Probably no one has better expressed than Joanne G. Kurfiss the importance of imparting critical thinking as skills of analyzing and constructing arguments, as construction of meaning, and as the manifestation of a contextual theory of knowledge. "Critical thinking can result in a new way of approaching significant issues in one's life or a deeper understanding of the basis for one's actions. Or it might result in political activity".

Along the similar line as Kurfiss's critical thinking theory and unlike Allan Bloom, who condemns the introduction of non-Western materials into the university curricula so as to protect the curriculum from the contamination of ideological conflict, Jerry Herron also highly promotes the teaching of critical thinking by calling on faculty to bring their conflicting ideologies into open engagement so that students can discover what is at stake in different ideas and can see their representational meaning.

The questions are whether universities should totally give up the teaching of skills today and how the needs of the job market and the goal of college education can be in harmony. In other words, can the teaching of common traditional content and the teaching of higher order skills join forces? Patracia Graham, ex-dean of the Harvard Graduate School of Education, argues that we need both commonality and flexibility in American education and there is no reason we cannot have both at once.

The question of training specialists vs. generalists is an extension of a larger conversation about reforming the fragmented curricula in higher education. Often classified as "cultural right," Ernest Boyer, Allan Bloom, and E. D. Hirsch share similar views about the problems in higher education. They point out that the university now is anarchistic. There is no vision of what an educated human being is. The curriculum is disjointed and disciplines are fragmented into smaller pieces.

Undergraduates find it hard to see patterns in their courses and relate what they learn to life. Careerism conflicts with the liberal arts. And finally, schools have failed to thoroughly carry out the educational goal of promoting mature literacy for all our citizens. They all agree that an educational reform is needed to teach more common traditional content apart from the higher-order skills that are commonly emphasized.

Boyer calls for a balance between individual interests and shared concerns while the actual priority is given to the latter. To promote a liberal education, Boyer advocates the "integrated core" or "enriched major"-a programme of general education that introduces students not only to essential knowledge, but also to connections across the disciplines, and, in the end, to the application of knowledge to life beyond the campus.

Boyer points out, knowledge becomes important only when we use it and apply it to humane ends; therefore, the undergraduate experience should not only generate new knowledge, but channel that knowledge to the service of the society. It is a matter of invigorating "the claims of community while protecting with full vigour the dignity and origins of each individual," to use Boyer and Kaplan's words.

In a similar vein, Bloom calls on teachers to look toward the goal of human completeness and to provide students a liberal education, in which learning is both synoptic and precise. To Bloom, liberal education feeds the student's love of truth and passion to live a good life. It also requires that a student's whole life be radically changed by it.

Bloom offers an ivory tower vision of the university-"the good old Great Book approach"-undergraduate students spend four years reading certain generally recognized classic texts for answers to philosophical questions of personal and human identity and aspirations. Bloom thinks that man may live more truly and fully in reading Plato and Shakespeare than at any other time because then they are participating in essential being and are forgetting their accidental lives.

In accordance with Boyer's and Bloom's points of view, Hirsch argues that "the greatest human individuality is developed in response to a tradition, not in response to disorderly, uncertain, and fragmented education" and "only by accumulating shared symbols, and the shared information the symbols represent can we learn to communicate effectively with one another in our national community".

However, Hirsch places emphasis more on the content of education, ensuring that students acquire all the "right" elements of knowledge that will enable them to get along in the Real World. He believes that neither the content-neutral curriculum of Rousseau and Dewey nor the narrowly specified curriculum of Plato is adequate to the needs of a modern nation. Hirsch calls for a curriculum, including extensive curriculum and intensive curriculum with an emphasis on the former, which is traditional in content and provides students with a common core of cultural information. "The conception of a two-part curriculum avoids the idea that all children should study identical materials" Hirsch says.

Based on our literature review, media convergence in our study is defined as the assimilation of media content for multiple media platforms. Media convergence may involve any combination of the convergences of media contents, media forms, media companies, and roles of news practitioners. Our general research question is how college professors should prepare students to cope with media convergence. To be specific, should college professors prepare generalists who can competently work in multiple media platforms or prepare specialists who know inside out how to work for one particular medium platform? And how should journalism schools balance the teaching of critical thinking and technical skills?

Corresponding to these two questions, we also would like to find out if college journalism educators themselves are both theoretically equipped and technologically prepared to teach their students about media convergence. The study serves both as an attitude finder and a fact finder. We believe that professors, editors, and news professionals are the best candidates to answer these questions. Editors represent the media companies to hire news staffers with news reporting abilities desired by the company. News professionals work in the forefront of news reporting and know best about what news reporting abilities they need.

The attitudes of the editors and the current generation of news professionals toward media convergence will have a great implication on future journalism education. Professors run journalism schools, and they have the final say about where their schools are going. Their attitudes toward journalism education in terms of media convergence will have the most direct influence on the kind of education journalism students will receive and how the students will perform in tomorrow's media.

Editors include daily newspaper editors in charge of newsroom operations or online news operations and news directors in charge of newsroom operations in a commercial TV station with news content, both in the United States.

News professionals refer to non-management news staff, such as reporters, anchors, photographers, designers, producers, Web staff, etc., working in American media companies. Journalism professors are defined as full-time instructors with any academic rankings who teach journalism courses in a U.S. journalism school, department, programme, or division, which could be administratively affiliated with an institution with a name like College of Communications or Department of Communications Studies.

To obtain opinions about media convergence, we could have targeted our survey only at those editors and news professionals in a converged media environment. The opinions obtained from those editors and news professionals, however, could be biased. Those media companies that have not gone through convergence must have a reason for not doing so. We also wanted to find out what they are doing about convergence. Balanced views both from the converged and un-converged media companies will better assist colleges in their strategic planning.

We conducted a national survey among editors, news professionals, and journalism professors with three different versions of online survey questionnaires posted on a school Web site. Respondents were asked to fill out the questionnaire online and submit answers online as well. The answers went through a commercial form handler and reached the primary investigator's email address. By doing so, the primary investigator had no way to detect who answered the questionnaire unless the respondent voluntarily revealed his/her email address to request the findings from the study.

There were twenty-two questions in each of these three questionnaires. Almost all questions were close-ended. About half of the questions used a 5-point Likert Scale from "Strongly Agree" to "Strongly Disagree." Some questions across the three questionnaires shared similarity, so that comparisons could be made when analyzing data. A text field was created for respondents to provide feedback to the survey freely.

The textual answers in the text field will be reported along with the statistics to illustrate and explain the quantitative findings. All questionnaires went through pilot tests. The unit of analysis was each participant.

In order to conduct a systematic random sampling of editors and news professionals, we needed a list of newspaper editors and TV news directors in the United States and a list of newspaper and TV news staffers. We found that such lists did not exist, though lists of newspapers and lists of TV stations did exist in multiple places online like Editor & Publisher Yearbook and Broadcasting Sr Cable Yearbook. Therefore, we decided to construct our own. To do so, we went through two steps. First, we constructed a combined list of daily newspapers and TV stations so that we could sample these news institutions. Second, we visited the Web sites of all sampled news institutions to find the email of the editor/news director and the email of one news professional randomly chosen.

After further research, we decided that newslink.org's daily newspaper list was the most comprehensive and workable list for sampling daily newspapers. In total, 1,190 U.S. daily newspapers with a valid URL were listed alphabetically by state. We sampled one out of every four dailies. Then, we visited each of those Web sites to find the email address of the managing editor, chief editor, online editor, or equivalent in each of those dailies and sent out a survey invitation email to him/her. If an individual email address was not available, we replaced it with a generic email address listed on their Web site and specified that the email was for the editor.

In total, there were 1,093 companies ordered alphabetically by state. From the list, we removed PBS network companies, which mostly did not provide staff information, companies that did not generate news content such as WB network companies and UPN network companies, religious TV stations, and foreign language stations. In total, we extracted 674 TV stations with a valid URL. Since this population is smaller than that of the newspapers, we over-sampled it. Instead of sampling every other four, we sampled every other station. Then, we visited each of those Web sites to find the email address of the news director or equivalent in each of those TV stations and sent out a survey invitation email to him/her. If an individual email address was not available, we replaced it with a generic email address and specified that the email was for the news director. In total, we successfully sent out invitation emails to 523 newspaper editors and TV news directors as our sample.

We also sampled one news professional out of each of the sampled U.S. dailies and TV stations for the survey. Since there was always more than one professional in a company, we simply randomly clicked on one name and picked him/her and made sure that s/he was on the news staff. Then, we sent him/her a survey invitation email. If an individual email address was not available, we replaced it with a generic email address and specified whom the email was for. S/he was asked to fill out a questionnaire that was worded in a slightly different manner. In total, we successfully sent out invitation emails to 398 news professionals.

We also needed to conduct a systematic random sampling of college journalism professors, but we were disappointed that all lists we found had many J-schools, even major ones, missing. Therefore, a new list was built upon the existing lists and upon the findings from a more careful search in the Yahoo U.S. Colleges and Universities site. In total, the new list contains 205 alphabetically ordered U.S. J-schools that contain 2,194 journalism professors.

We sampled one out of every four professors from the virtually running list of all journalism professors across the schools. For instance, if a school had six journalism professors, we picked the fourth one; then, the second journalism professor from next school was picked. We sent an invitation email to every professor in the sample. In total, we successfully sent out 500 emails.

The three samples of editors, news professionals, and professors included 1,421 cases. We understood that nonresponse had been a serious problem with online surveys in recent years. In order to counter possible low response rates in our survey, we created three samples for editors, news professionals, and professors containing roughly 500 people for each group, which were much larger than the sample sizes for populations recommended by Mildred Patten in her book Understanding Research Methods: An Overview of the Essentials so that, if low response rates occurred, we could base our confidence limits on the actual number of responses themselves. We also sent out one reminder email to the samples, which drastically boosted the response rates, especially for professors and news professionals.

After two weeks of online data collecting in November 2002, we received 223 responses from professors (a 44% response rate), 151 responses from editors (a 29% response rate), and 142 responses from news professionals (a 35% response rate). The overall response rate is 36%. As Singletary notes, returns of 30% to 40% are common in mail surveys. The response rates of this online survey seem typical. However, the response rates are still comparatively low. A response bias is potentially present. Many respondents (41%) left textual answers to explain and illustrate their answers to the close-ended questions and/or made comments on the topic.

- What is the status quo of media convergence in the industry?

By the end of 2002, 19% of the newspapers and comme-rcial television stations with news content in the United States had gone through media mergers. Being merged or not has to do with the size of a company. Larger companies tend to have been merged while smaller ones have not. Roughly half of the news professionals surveyed (48%) reported that they produced news content for multiple media platforms on a routine basis; that was true both in merged media (50%) and non-merged media (48%). In other words, media merger is not the precondition for practicing news for multiple media platforms. The pressure on news professionals to learn to produce multimedia content is also felt in many non-merged media companies. This finding confirms that media convergence is not necessarily related to media merger.

A typical editor or news director was a man (71%) between 36-45 years old (42%) with a bachelor's degree (76%) who had worked for at least two media (57%) for more than 20 years (53%). A typical news professional was either a man (52%) or woman (48%) between 26-35 years old (43%) with a bachelor's degree (84%) who had worked for at least two media (60%) less than ten years (62%).

Editors had generally worked for more years than news professionals, but they did not have more multiplatform experience than news professionals. As more news companies are practicing cross-media reporting with or without their companies being merged, it is important that editors with multiplatforrn experiences are chosen to direct newsroom businesses. Many editors need cross-media training more urgently than news professionals do if the news company they work for produces news contents for multiple media platforms on a daily basis.

- Should J-schools train specialists or generalists?

Gil Thelen said that writers should learn how to write for multimedia and still photographers should learn how to shoot videos, but he was not interested in hiring people with multiple sets of skills. We designed four questions to test how popular Thelen's opinion was.

The majority of the respondents (84%) agreed or strongly agreed with Thelen that journalism students should learn how to write for multiple media platforms. One-way ANOVA shows significant difference among the means for professors (4.35), professionals (4.05), and editors. Tukey HSD post hoc tests show that professors were more positive on this statement than editors and professionals, while no significant difference existed between editors and professionals.

A similar number of respondents (85%) agreed or strongly agreed with Thelen that journalism students with a visual emphasis should learn how to produce and edit photos, videos, and online interactive images. One-way ANOVA shows significant difference among the means for professors (4.55), professionals (4.22), and editors. Tukey HSD post hoc tests show that professors were more positive on this statement than professionals, while professionals were more positive than editors.

Most respondents (78%) agreed or strongly agreed that all journalism majors should learn multiple sets of skills, such as writing, editing, TV production, digital photography, newspaper design, and Web publishing.

Oneway ANOVA shows significant differences among the means for professionals (4.28), editors (3.99), and professors (3.86). Tukey HSD post hoc tests show that news professionals who worked in the forefront of news production felt this need more deeply than other respondents. Editors also had such an expectation for them. There is no significant difference between editors and professors. These findings support the growing evidence that news professionals are being asked to wear multiple hats. The findings also indicate that Thelen's view has its market at this moment when news professionals with multiple sets of skills are highly desirable but not easy to find. Such a view may change as more journalism graduates equipped with multiple sets of skills enter the job market.

The professors' textual answers show that some of the difficulties J-schools have come across include the lack of a friendly curriculum, lack of credit hours to include the components of convergence content, lack of willing cooperation among faculty from different sequences, and lack of expertise, interest, or even time for some professors to develop new courses on convergence. When asked whether journalism students should still have a specialization, such as writing, photojournalism, broadcasting, and new media, over half (63%) of the respondents agreed or strongly agreed. Over a quarter of the respondents (28%) were negative and 9% were not sure. One-way ANOVA mean comparisons show no significant difference of attitude among professionals (3.42), editors (3.51), and professors (3.72).

Comparing the support rate for this question to those for the first three questions, it is fair to argue that editors, news professionals, and professors emphasized the importance of cross-media training more than that of specialization, though they believed that specialization should not be neglected either. Currently, students in many J-schools specialize in one area by subscribing to a sequence such as news-editorial, magazine, photojournalism, and broadcast. When asked whether sequences should be reorganized considering the trend of media-platforms merging in the industry, 56% of the professors agreed or strongly agreed, 22% were not sure, and another 22% disagreed or strongly disagreed.

The concept of sequences is being shaken among professors though it is still being accepted as a legitimate means of training students in various specialization areas in some J-schools. Speaking on behalf of herself and her colleagues, Professor offered some special insight on this issue: We can't teach for the" now." We have to prepare students for when they graduate...which in most instances is now five years out. And, we feel a commitment to expose them to all types of writing in all platforms so they can be flexible about their career choice at the front end of their academics. Then, they can apply the skills to a specialty area where they are totally proficient.

"Flexible" is a key term repeatedly seen in editors' and news professionals' textual answers as a suggestion for future journalists. Editor's statement is typical:

Our job descriptions are open ended and new hires understand that they are being hired for their skills. They may be hired today to cover the city beat. In six months or in two weeks, if necessary, a person with Quark skills may be asked to fill in or shift duties to include pagination of a particular section. It is important that hires stay flexible. The new hires, wrote Editor, "need to understand that the information they gather and process can have many different uses, audiences and shelf lives. They need to understand the complexities of the audience mix and be able to respond." "Those unwilling to be flexible may find themselves in a difficult scenario later in their careers".

From a different perspective, Professional concurred: "Students must be flexible, have a vigorous skill set and be prepared to get laid off and move around in the changing media arena." In short, "young journalists must be prepared to fill a variety of roles if they hope to succeed". "The most successful journalists are those that take on assignments willingly, can learn and want to learn". Specialization in journalistic jobs is still honored, but is losing its favour to cross-media capability in converged media. Today, professionals with different specializations team together to work on multiple media projects. Tomorrow, it is likely that one-man bands will be more and more desired in newsrooms.

- How should J-schools balance the teaching of critical thinking and that of technical skills?

Most respondents (93%), especially professors, agreed or strongly agreed that journalism students should both learn technical skills, such as online information search and Web design, while learning critical thinking skills in media law, ethics, etc.

One-way ANOVA shows significant difference among the means for professionals (4.35), editors (4.38), and professors (4.76). Tukey HSD post hoc tests show that professors were more positive on this point than editors and professionals, while no significant difference existed between editors and professionals. But, should journalism students spend more time on learning critical thinking skills than on technical skills? Opinions were divided.

More than half of the respondents (62%) believed that should be the case, but 19% of the respondents were not sure and another 19% of them did not agree. Oneway ANOVA shows significant difference among the means for professors (3.21), professionals (3.87), and editors (4.3). Tukey HSD post hoc tests show that editors were more positive on this point than professionals, and professionals were more positive than professors. Throughout all the answers from the three groups of respondents, critical thinking was highly regarded as being more important than technical skills.

Editors, news professionals, and professors all liked to see good stories, and good stories come from good thinking ability. An editor said: "Journalism graduates need to have a broad, well-rounded education; be critical thinkers; have the ability to write clearly; have a serious work ethic; and know computer basics - in that order". "You can teach a monkey to type," echoes a writer. Therefore, he strongly suggested that J-schools "get more critical thinking skills pounded into the skulls of the students". While highly emphasizing the importance of critical thinking ability, editors did not mean to neglect the importance of teaching technical skills in schools.

We will develop this point when we discuss the next question. Comparing the professors' highest mean for the first question and their lowest mean for the second question, it is clear that professors saw critical thinking as highly important, but preferred a comparatively balanced approach for the teaching of the two sets of knowledge. One professor's comment illustrated this observation:

Knowing technical skill alone will not make you a "good" journalist. Critical thinking is vital not just to a career but to life itself. Without developing your ability to discern and evaluate, you will become "the prey" of society. Next, a technical skill is critical to a career in journalism today. Even print Journalism is very high tech these days and all electronic media require extensive computer knowledge as well as other technical skills. I would place critical thinking skills first on your list of things to do because a developed mind will make it that much easier to develop a creative and technically sound understanding of the technical side of the business. From a holistic view, there was no substantial disagreement between classrooms and newsrooms when we examine the issue of teaching critical thinking vs. teaching technical skills.

Compared to Terry's 2000 poll, this study shows that professors gave a higher status to technical skills in journalism curricula in 2002 than they did in 2000.

This is a period during which media convergence garnered its momentum. In short, all respondents generally agreed that J-schools should place emphasis on teaching critical thinking, but at the same time, should not neglect teaching technical skills.

- Should technical skills be learned at work or in school?

News professionals were asked, "If you wish to possess the technical skills you don't have now, do you prefer to learn them at work or wish you had learned in school?" Editors were given the same question with a slightly different wording.Chi-Square test shows that the difference between editors and news professionals is significant. This finding well supplements the findings from the preceding questions. It suggests that editors not only looked at future journalists' critical thinking ability, but also hoped that future journalists would already possess the skills needed in a converged newsroom when they are hired.

On the other hand, most professionals preferred that they spend most of their school time on gaining critical thinking ability and learn skills largely at work. The professionals' general preference, to some extent, also reflected their need for technological update at their current positions, so that they can better qualify for multimedia productions.

Many editors and reporters said that school is the best place for journalism students to explore every facet of the media and acquire basic technical skills, though some advanced skills can only be learned on the job. Learning skills while in school, they said, can build confidence and an expansive and broad understanding of the entire field and help with damage control and communication in newsrooms. "If editing and the technical skills were more prevalent in college courses," wrote a multi-tasking editor, "I think I could stave off a lot of headaches when the students become professionals."

An internship was the news professionals' and editors' most recommended venue for enhancing and learning more technical skills and gaining other practical experience. Reporter said: "While I value my college education, my internship and first job provided me with the most valuable skills today." Another reporter said: "While education is great, students who work in media while in school fare much better in the real world." Some editors had complaints about graduates with a 3.5 GPA but no practical experience and no published news work. An anchor/reporter said that it is important even "for a freshman or sophomore in college to visit a newsroom and shadow someone. So many students wait until they are juniors and seniors to do this and then they realise they made a mistake in selecting their major. You will learn more by watching and doing". One reporter said, "To remain competitive, education must continue throughout a career".

The implication of the discrepancy from this finding suggests that Jschools should place emphasis on teaching critical thinking, expose students to new technology, and design a comprehensive internship programme for students to gain real-world knowledge and further develop their crossmedia technical skills.

- What skills do news professionals need to learn most at their current positions?

Both editors and news professionals were given this unstructured question with slightly different wordings. We read through all the answers, and categorized them into the following nine facets in random order:

Multimedia production: producing and editing news stories on video, for the Web, and for print; re-purposing the same story for different media. New technology: knowledge of software for producing video, Web sites, graphics, newspapers, and magazines; knowledge of how to operate a computer and use the Internet.

Good writing: knowing how to write to make people remember and/or take action, write about the beats with an expert's view.

Good editing is also expected:

- *Critical thinking:* Having good news judgment, understanding what is legal and ethical, knowing how to report with insight, knowing how to crunch statistics.
- *Computer-assisted reporting*: Expert's knowledge of conducting online information search, database knowledge.
- *On-camera exposure*: How to report like a TV news anchor before a camera for a newspaper reporter.
- *Visual production*: A newspaper writer must know how to take photos, or a TV reporter must know how to shoot video.
- *Second language*: Knowing how to fluently speak and read a foreign language.
- *Time management*: Well organizing time to work for multiple media platforms; the ability and willingness to work as a team to produce multimedia news stories.

Then we ranked these facets according to the percentage scores each facet got separately from the editors and the news professionals: This ranking shows more agreement than disagreement between editors and news professionals. No matter how technology changes and whether media are converged, editors and news professionals believed that learning how to write good stories is still the top priority and writing is the very basic skill all news professionals should learn. One editor pushed the importance of good writing to the extreme:" I've worked in markets 170 to 20, and having training in multiple media will not help you get a job, but being a good writer will". Most editors and news professionals, however, did believe that learning multimedia production, new technology, and computer-assisted reporting are also among the top priorities." I would strongly urge students to prepare themselves to the best of their ability to be able to report/edit the news in a variety of platforms and to learn how to truly engage readers/listeners/viewers in what they are writing about," said Editor.

Editors and news professionals both believed that it is not very important for a newspaper reporter to learn how to talk like an anchor in front of a video camera. This skill was even regarded as being less important than knowing how to speak a second language. Some editors and news professionals also mentioned learning how to manage time for producing multimedia news stories. Editor hoped that journalists in a converged environment would learn to avoid" extra" work by working" smarter" and with greater awareness of the requirements of the different publishing media. This finding, again, shows that editors valued critical thinking ability more than news professionals did. Editors wanted news professionals to be good thinkers first, and the latter wanted most to learn how to express their thinking in different media.

- If news professionals have to re-purpose their work for multiple media platforms, will the quality of their work suffer?

Since some authors such as Haiman expressed the concern about the possible decline of work quality if news professionals have to "re-purpose" stories for multiple media platforms, we tried to find out to what extent this concern was shared by editors and news professionals. Opinions split.

Thirty-eight per cent of the editors and professionals agreed or strongly agreed that the quality would deteriorate, 40% disagreed or strongly disagreed, and the other 22% were not sure. Editors and professionals showed no significant difference on this attitude T-test. Such a concern was not prevalent in the news industry.

In response to such concerns, the news director from a converged media company wrote: "When reporters do cross platforms we give them the time to finish the project for all three platforms. Quality does not suffer. If we were to try to force reporters to cross platforms while operating under daily deadlines then quality could suffer depending on the nature of the story and the extra time consumed". Another editor summed up this issue: "Some employees can capably handle multiple media and tell stories effectively. Others cannot. Certainly strong technical skills and training can help, but it's not just dependent on that; it depends more on the attitude and aptitude of the journalist". Quality multimedia work also involves a solid understanding of different cultures in different media. Editors both for and against media convergence noted the difficulty of merging different media with different cultures, and editors in those merged media called for flexibility in aptitude and willingness to cooperate across platforms.

For instance, Editor wrote: Clarity of what convergence means to the news organization is vital and often lacking. This causes unneeded anxiety. Managers have to realise that each medium has its own culture, language, skill set and timetable and is naturally skeptical of anything unfamiliar. It is also true that these same journalists' stock in trade is learning a new culture, language, skill set and timetable-on a daily basis. Therein lies the hope for an efficient news operation running on all cylinders and an effective -maybe even happy-staff.

If most editors and news professionals are not concerned about the quality of the work prepared for multiple media platforms and if news professionals are given enough time to complete their cross-media work, there is little reason to worry that future journalists, if well trained both theoretically and technologically for multiple media platforms, will produce work of poorer quality. Training students to practice news in multiple media platforms will help bridge newsroom cultures from different media and eventually erase such differences. We have noticed that no significant statistical differences existed between the editors and news professionals from the converged media companies and their counterparts from the not-yet-converged media companies when they answered the questions reported above.

- How are J-schools coping with media convergence?

From 1998 to 2002, about 60% of the J-schools in the United States redesigned their curricula or developed new courses to prepare students for practicing news in multiple media platforms. A typical journalism professor was a man (71%) between 46-55 years old (42%) with a doctoral degree (63%) who worked in news media for one to ten years (48%), may still be practicing news (45%) in one way or another, and conducted academic research (66%).

More professors claimed that they were theoretically equipped (81%) than technologically prepared (53%) to teach students how to report news in multiple media platforms. More than half of the professors (57%) had not taught any journalism courses in the last five years where skill sets were beyond their own expertise; 25% of the professors taught one such course and 11% taught two.

Nevertheless, the majority of the professors (84%) added content about media convergence either to their existing courses or to new courses or participated in cross-media team-teaching in the last five years.

Worries, concerns, and, sometimes, misconceptions about media convergence appeared in professors' textual answers. For instance, a professor from Montana said: "convergence is not happening". A professor who no longer practiced news said, "In my judgment, the writing portion of preparing news for print and for the Web is exactly the same". Another professor maintained that it was not necessary to teach cross-media news practicing because "few 'want ads' for newspaper reporter and editor positions specifically listed multimedia platform skills as required or preferred experience for new hires". Many professors worried that media mergers would restrict the number of voices in a community. They regarded media mergers as a grand experiment in the profession and waited for the FCC's ruling on the cross-ownership of different media in the same market.

Wait-and-see-that was the strategy some universities took for teaching media convergence. One professor said that he needed to see the substantive contribution media convergence could make before he would be more serious about this phenomenon. He said that J-schools should be cautious about embracing convergence. Some other universities didn't have the time and resources to teach convergence courses or make major curriculum changes.

Most professors, however, did believe that media convergence was a reality; and "anybody serious about practicing media needs at minimal an acquaintance with various media and at best multiple competencies," as Professor said. Many professors (and editors and news professionals as well) had a clear opinion as to which comes first, teaching critical thinking or teaching technical skills.

While acknowledging the need for incorporating media convergence content in curricula, especially the technological components, professors cautioned against sacrificing conceptual and theoretical courses such as law, ethics, history, cultural studies, critical perspectives, etc. Professor analogized critical thinking as meat and potatoes and technical skills as dessert and side dishes and argued that "the meat and potatoes need to come before one begins to worry about the dessert and side dishes (or side shows)." This viewpoint was popular. Professor wrote:

It's the message, not the medium, that is of paramount importance. If students cannot understand and appreciate the underlying concepts, principles and ethics of journalism, then they cannot produce the type of content that will be of value to a free society. A thorough grounding in journalism must come before any training in tools. The tools are means to an end, not the end in and of themselves.

Incidentally, a reporter had similar thoughts: The medium isn't the message, the message is the message. In short, the fundamental analytic and synthetic skills of the news writer are paramount to the message.

The medium does not alter the reporter's craft of interpreting news events in the context of the society in a way that will make sense for the receiver of the information.... Additional skills may be desirable, but for the most part they can be learned on the job.

Obviously, the more skills one can offer, the better the employment opportunity. Those ancillary skills should not come at the expense of thorough proficiency as a news writer.

We fully understand why these respondents emphasize the teaching of critical thinking and the fundamentals of good reporting over the teaching of technical skills, and we strongly agree with their opinions. But, we also see the danger of over-stretching the point by treating the two sets of knowledge as two opposing poles.

Those arguments are based on the presumptions that message and medium can be easily separated, content and form can be detached, and readers for different media are from the same population. But, is that right? It is true that content is the king. It is true that "the medium does not alter the reporter's craft of interpreting news events."

News practice, however, is not only about news-gathering and writing. It also includes production, editing, and delivery. Without a solid grasp of grammar and style, how can a writer effectively express his/her good analytical thinking? Without knowing the available features and limitations of online news delivery, how can messages be constructed to their fullest potential?

Without understanding the technical difference between video news and print news, how can messages be constructed appropriately? In the digital era when almost all steps of news transmission involves technology, if professors don't teach students technical skills, will the computer majors, who know little about news practices, be expected to produce newspapers, TV news, and online news?

Writers, for instance, do not necessarily have to be conversant in constructing news reporting with Flash for online presentation or know how to operate a video camera to shoot video stories.

But knowing the principles and rules of news video-taping and what Flash or other software can offer will surely help writers more effectively convey their messages and better cooperate with visual reporters. Creativity distinguishes artists and artisans. Critical thinking ability distinguishes master journalists and technical writers. But artists must first know what artisans know and a master journalist must possess all that a technical writer knows for a living. Skills are intrinsic instead of extrinsic to ideas.

Teaching critical thinking and teaching technical skills are not mutually exclusive. Teaching journalism students how to express their critical thinking with conversant technical skills in different media seems to be a big challenge for J-school professors in the years to come.

From the professors' textual answers, we have observed different philosophical approaches to teaching convergence. Unlike some professors who took the wait-and-see approach, a professor from the University of Texas at Austin claimed that "convergence is already happening, and journalism schools should be leading the parade and not following it".

A popular viewpoint was that "skills across platforms must be taught, but more importantly storytelling, ethics, and critical thinking skills should be even more important in the journalism school curriculum".

One professor from Texas Christian University said that it maintained the existing sequences but required broadcast students to take print courses and vice versa.

Team-teaching was an often-used approach in some J-schools such as Indiana University for courses involving multiple sets of skills while professors learned from each other. Another professor, from the University of Colorado at Boulder, said convergence meant that "students work together to produce multimedia content for the Web-not that each individual should attempt to become proficient in all media". To overcome the hurdle of the ratio limited by the ACEJMC accreditation standards between journalism courses and liberal arts courses, a professor from Bowling Green State University suggested that journalism undergraduate students stay for five years and devote the fifth year entirely to practice. Some professors said that journalism students only need to know a little about the practices in media other than their own while some other professors firmly maintained that students should "be the master of many arts and the explorer of all".

- Who benefits from media convergence?

All respondents were asked, "Do you think that merging media companies such as television station, newspaper, radio station, and online news from a local area will benefit any of the parties listed on the left? Check all entries that apply." The entries included "The general public," "News professionals," "Media companies," "Nobody," and "Not sure." We designed this question about the legitimacy of media merger as a barometer for testing the respondents' political view on media convergence. We presumed that a respondent's answer to this question could be related to his/her way of answering other questions regarding teaching media convergence or requirement for new hires. Most respondents (66%) from all three groups pointed to media companies as the beneficiary of media mergers. In comparison, only 37% of the respondents said that media mergers also benefit the general public, and even fewer (27%) said that media mergers benefit the news professionals.

By reading the percentage numbers horizontally, we can find that consistently fewer respondents believed that media mergers benefit the general public or news professionals; also consistently more respondents believed that media mergers benefit media companies. It is also noticeable that 47% of editors believed that media mergers benefit the general public while the other 53% didn't. Editors' opinions on this point were roughly equally split. This finding indicates that media merger is a grand experiment in the media industry. Its benefits to the general public, which can better legitimize media mergers, are to be explored in the years to come.

By reading the percentage numbers both vertically and horizontally, we also find that editors were the most positive about the benefits media mergers could bring to all three parties while professors were least sure of such benefits. It is logical to reason that management personnel, such as editors and news directors and the companies they represent, are the primary forces behind today's media merger movement. The question is that, since most professors, editors, and even news professionals believed that media mergers do not benefit news professionals and hardly benefit the general public, why do most news professionals still want to be trained to be cross-media practitioners and why are so many Jschool professors enthusiastic about training such graduates? Considering the editors' most positive attitude toward media convergence, we wonder if news professionals are under the pressure to do so, and J-school professors are under the pressure to follow the industrial trend. Our surmise is partially corroborated by some textual answers. A news anchor from a merged media company agreed that new hires should have received cross-media training in writing and visuals and should possess multiple sets of skills. She showed her understanding for media mergers:

The merging of media companies is almost a daily occurrence. The pool of entities providing news services is shrinking. I think there is a danger that the public will lose in this race for media giants to accumulate wealth. At the same time, with the amount of competition in the industry from cable networks, the Internet, DVD's etc., I see the financial need for companies to merge to survive. A newspaper reporter also from a merged media company expressed a similar feeling: "I am not all for the media convergence... At the same time I find it quite beneficial to be savvy in all branches of the industry. It helps the journalist become more knowledgeable about her or his job". News professionals were not alone in having such feelings. Here are two excerpts from two professors who have expressed similar feelings:

It's a harsh reality that I checked the box saying that news companies are the ones that are sure to benefit from media convergence. It may not be great for the public or even for news professionals who are going to be asked to bring more and more skills to the table and to have more and more responsibility on the job. Even so, convergence in one way or another is gonna happen and we need to prepare our students. Finally, my answer on merging media companies... reflects my disdain for the corporatization and concentration of control in the media. I think we ought to train mass communicators for a converged world, but as professors we ought to fight like hell against media mergers.

Very few respondents (19%) believed that media mergers benefit all three parties, the general public, news professionals, and media companies, but about one third of the respondents (35%) believed that media companies are the only beneficiaries to such a practice. These 35% respondents, who were almost equally proportionally found in editors, news professionals, and professors groups, could be regarded as the most critical toward media mergers. We compared these 35% respondents with the rest of the sample and found no significant difference in their answers concerning the necessity of teaching journalism students cross-media writing and visuals and teaching multiple sets of skills. Always, more respondents believed that professors should teach all those things. In short, the respondents' political view was not directly tied to their views of teaching students cross-media practices.

12

Social Responsibility of Media

An important consideration in doing ethnographic research in the study of new electronic media is the social presence attributes of the technology itself. Short, Williams, and Christie were apparently the first researchers to conceptualize the construct they called social presence, which they defined as being a quality of the communications medium itself. As they elaborated, social presence "varies between different media... affects the nature of the interaction... and interacts with the purpose of the interaction to influence the medium chosen by the individual who wishes to communicate".

Media perceived as high in social presence are generally judged (on Semantic Differential Scales) by users as warm, personal, sensitive, and, sociable; those low in social presence as cold, impersonal, insensitive, and unsociable. Chief among the reasons for differentiating media in their degree of social presence is the medium's ability to restrict stimulus-conveying information. More specifically, media that are less able to convey nonverbal elements are more likely to be judged as being low in social presence.

In another sense, social presence is the degree to which a medium is perceived as conveying the "presence" of the communicating participants; it is dependent not only on the words involved in the communication but on the full range of verbal and nonverbal cues, and the communication context. Thus CMC technologies typically would be judged lower in social presence than face-to-face communication (FTF) because of the lower bandwidth of information conveyed by the former (vis-a-vis verbal and nonverbal messages).

This notion of the bandwidth of the medium is closely related to media richness, a construct developed by Daft and Lengel. Rice describes the term as the: Extent to which media are able to bridge different frames of reference, make issues less ambiguous, or provide opportunities for learning in a given time interval, based on the medium's capacity for immediate feedback, the number of cues and senses involved, personalization, and language variety. The essential underlying element in both of these notions is that a good match between the medium's characteristics (high in social presence or media richness) and the intent of the communication activity (getting to know someone, strategic decision making) should lead to higher performance and satisfaction. The importance of all of this to ethnographic research is, how can one adequately do participatory research with media that are judged low in social presence or media richness?

Stated another way, how will the ethnographic researcher be able to make adequate sense out of communication that restricts important cues such as nonverbal behaviours? in their study of e-mail in organizations, Garton and Wellman have discussed the consequences of e-mail's exclusion of nonverbal cues: E-mail does not supply nonverbal interactional cues to group members, such as eye contact, gestures, nodding approval, frowning, or hesitating before replying.

There are no contextual cues, either: Participants cannot use seating arrangements to identify coalitions and cleavages, or choose meeting sites to identify the importance of sponsorship of meetings. Because e-mail users typically are identified by name only, people are not constantly reminded of the social roles cues others have beyond the narrow confines of the task group.

Users may not be aware of another group member's gender, race, expertise, or organizational position. One approach to this dilemma is to take account of the ways participants do compensate at times for the restricted bandwidth of the medium by providing clarifying cues in their messages.

Social role cues can be transmitted in e-mail (either implicitly or explicitly) by adding status information to their "signatures," by their writing style, or by forwarding communications to (or from) important persons. Baym also found the standard components of Usenet posts for a soap opera news group—e.g., "from" line, "subject" line, "organization" line (site of message's origin), and the quotation system, in addition to signatures—to provide subtle contextualizing cues about the sender's interests and status.

Other examples of clarifying cues are:

- Emotions used to pictorialize emotional states (e.g., the computer "smiley face"),
- Meta-messages included to communicate physical states (e.g., using " " to designate jocularity),
- Acronyms used to designate degree of emotion (e.g., "FOTFL" to represent "failing on the floor laughing," or a greater degree of merriment beyond a mere smile or grin).'

As Walther, Anderson, and Park noted in their meta-analysis of computer mediated interaction, the interpersonal effects expected to accrue rapidly in face-to-face interactions can (and do) occur in CIVIC, but these interpersonal cues require extended time interactions. That is, interactional, contextual, and social cues that provide immediate feedback in FTF communication have to be stated explicitly in CIVIC and require more time to develop. Deep knowledge of an organizational culture may also enhance the participants' hermeneutic ability to embellish an e-mail with meaning.

Of course, social cues do more than merely clarify or boost informational richness in FTF or CMC encounters; they also mark a person's identity (e.g., gender, age, ethnic, class, sexual, cultural, occupational, etc.) as being of a certain moral or political character. Gender norms, for example, are a powerful means of designating the inappropriate or disvalued behaviours of men and women in specific contexts and vary widely from ideologically dominant expressions to the communication contexts and media of subaltern groups.

Thus, women ethnographers learn very quickly how their bodies—not only skin colour and body shape, but also aspects of clothing, adornment, hair style, and facial, gestural, and speech styles—affect the way they are perceived in the field, and the roles and motives attributed to them.

Embodiment in all of its forms is not a condition that can be controlled independently or somehow neutralized. Rather, it is through the ethnographic body performing with other cultural members that one learns the schemes of cultural valuation. Practical problems of "fitting in" are of a piece with issues of acculturation which are enormously important to understanding the scene being studied. In CMC environments, where perceptions of identity derive almost totally from what and how one writes, the notion of representational reality collapses and the ambiguity of action becomes foregrounded. Multiple identities are tried on, and specific traits or behaviours may be expressed more boldly in the widespread use of aliases, aptonyms, and role-playing domains in which players build characters for themselves. By detaching self-expression from the politics of the body, CMC liberates its users from certain kinds of discriminatory practice and promotes a low-risk, often playful, exploration of skill sets.

Certainly, the texts one writes may unwittingly leak signs of personal identity which could be attributed by readers to the author's embodied self.

As long as there are other users supervising the actors and the threads of their discourse, standards of plausibility, coherence, and trustworthiness will still apply to the textual contributions. Ultimately, the CMC ethnographer should be prepared to confront the ambiguity of identity performance as a central fact of virtual life, worthy of study on its own terms.

Concerns about testing the informational richness, or the authenticity, of virtual action against criteria of embodied action may be much less important to the project of ethnography than issues of how computing worlds are socially constructed, what recognizably human purposes they serve, and how they relate to a range of other "possibility spaces." Reduced social presence also affects the way in which researchers enter virtual scenes. Interaction management seems to function similarly in FTF and CMC in the opening and closing phases of encounters, but in CMC the choice of names and the use of attention-getting strategies are critical decisions. The risks of field entry may be lessened by learning the norms of such strategies in advance. Thus the "outsider" designation one usually expects in the first stages of an FTF project may be less of a problem in entering a virtual space once the right level of competence has been gained via observation. On the other hand, veteran members often do not suffer novices gladly, and the ethnographer may need to ask for the cooperation of the group (or its influential members) in order to be heard, or to engage them in directed queries or tasks. Researchers face subtle differences in the social makeup and interactional preferences of virtual scenes, which may require them to devise different strategies for entry and field positioning than in FTF situations.

SOCIAL STRATEGIES

Matters of self-presentation and scope of action are critical to the relations built among researchers, the virtual "places" populating the Internet, and the cultural membership. Correll, for example, was able to convey the location, look, and meanings of the "furniture" of the Lesbian Cafe mostly from her observations of electronic postings, but also from interviews. Compared to Leal's analysis of the relation of TV sets to the domestic material culture in working-class Brazilian homes, the mise-en-scene of the Cafe is not nearly as dense, tactile, and sensuous.

Despite this possibly unfair comparison, "the sense of a common reality [in the Lesbian Cafe] was used by patrons much like physical settings are used by co-present conversationalists—as a source of mutually relevant topics". Like the dialogue one hears in a radio play, conversationalists in the Lesbian Cafe must include many more references in their ordinary talk to objects, the current status of the objects, and the presence or absence of people in and around those objects in order to maintain orientation and sustain a convincing sense of as-if reality. The lean exposition Correll offers would likely be unacceptable in other forms of ethnographic work, but it turns out to be the one that matters to the women who "drink" and socialize there.

Media ethnographers begin their on-line presence in a variety of ways. One mode used by some is that of the unknown, unobtrusive observer. Over a three-year period, Harrington and Bielby collected and printed messages posted on two soap opera BBS's by subscribers to two commercial on-line computer services. They do not report interactions of any kind between themselves and the posters.

Presumably, the computer services were not notified of the initiation of the research activity, nor were the BBS system operators. Interestingly, while the authors appear unconcerned about their own lurker posture, they note the suspicion held by many of the BBS users that their conversations were being overheard by "industry insiders". Scodari also relies on transcripts of fan BBS discourse in interpreting critical reactions to changes in the soap, Another World, although she aligns her own interests much more closely with the fans she quotes than Harrington and Bielby. Open participation characterizes the approach of several other studies and more closely resembles normative field practice. Baym started as an unabashed soap fan and news group contributor and found it easy to continue openly as an analyst of the group:

My position in the [rec.arts.arts.soaps, or r.a.t.s., newsgroup] is that of a participant at least as much as a researcher. As a long-time fan of soap operas, I was thrilled to discover this group. It was only after I had been reading daily and participating regularly for a year that I began to write about it. As the work has evolved, I have shared its progress with the group members and found them exceedingly supportive and helpful. They have acted as research participants as well as subjects and have treated me more as an ambassador than a researcher. The confidence each party had in the other paved the way for Baym to obtain other forms of data besides the news group's messages, especially electronic mail correspondence with several participants and responses to open-ended questions she posted to r.a.t.s. Similarly, Correll's membership in the Lesbian Cafe, and the approval she got from the bar's founder, assisted her in posting queries and interviewing several of the patrons both by e-mail and in person.

Some researchers actually run the facilities that enable computer users to "find" the research project. In an early study, Myers operated a university BBS for two months and set up a number of networked research tools in order to investigate the perceived social context of CMC: on-line surveys, a focus group, and a role-playing game.

More recently, Lindlof et al. launched a Web home page for X-Men fans that offered graphic content (thus participating in the X-Men array of more than 60 Internet locations), links to other X-Men sites, a survey to capture data, and a solicitation for dialogues with on-line X-Men users and page producers. Like the Baym and Correll studies, the research purpose was stated openly in order to invite cooperation; however, its sudden appearance and the research team's initial contacts with users were sometimes met with suspicion, critique (of their knowledge of X-Men), and humorous skepticism.

It became clear that the World Wide Web page of hypertext URLS's (Uniform Resource Locator) that linked to other pages related to the X-Men topic constituted the study's "gatekeeper" in the traditional sense of enabling an initial contact. The study also hints at the possibilities of participatory design in which ethnographers may act as the interpreters of diverse voices, usage interests, and aesthetic tastes in the design of networked systems. A final strategy for consideration moves the researcher physically alongside the user in order to "read" his or her real-time decision making and styles of engagement. The user's dyadic interplay with a computer forms a focal interest, but included in this arena would be the material context of computing (e.g., its location in a room, the CD-ROM's on hand), the institutional culture (e.g., considering open viewing of sex sites as sexual harassment), interpersonal resources or constraints (e.g., informal rules for sharing URL's), and the specific reality of what it means to "do computing" that these signify for users.

Models for this approach exist in the literature on social television viewing and family computer usage. However, since Internet usage is typically a solitary venture, the more promising route would seem to lie in some version of the "shopping with consumers" protocol from the field of consumer behaviour. Accompanying users on their way through the kinetic pathways of virtual space and eliciting talk on a wide range of subjects, either retrospectively or on-the-spot, enables the researcher to understand the more embodied dimensions of CMC. In effect, the researcher shadows the user's on-site computing. The advantages of the approach are its close proximity to the user and setting, and the ability to comprehend computing performance as an activity that has a rich, localized back stage—that is, as more than lines of type scrolling down a screen.

In ethnographies of embodied social scenes, the researcher must continually negotiate with the culture membership and convince them of the value of the study and the reasonableness of the person doing the research. It is not unusual for ethnographers to have to adjust their persona somewhat differently as they pass through a scene, or disclose different versions of the project, since the members of a group often relate asymmetrically or even conflictively to each other.

CMC ethnographies, as we have shown, also involve some degree of negotiation when anonymous observation is not the method of access. Virtual spaces offer a limited window in which to explain one's purpose, and electronic text is not the most suitable medium for engaging in a sensitive interaction. Trust tends to be a heightened concern where entry and exit and unbridled information disclosure are easily accomplished. Mistakes, once made, can have disastrous results, and be very hard to rectify. Institutional principles for informed consent are now being formulated for research on the World Wide Web, but it will take longer for ethnographers themselves to develop a consensus around protocols for responsible virtual space entry and ways to insure the fair treatment of those they study without compromising very seriously the conduct of inquiry.

TECHNICAL UTILITIES

In this section, we discuss the use of technical utilities for accomplishing research tasks. Some computer systems allow asynchronous communication interactions to be studied either by saving the individual messages, or archiving all postings for later perusal. Most of these have been around for some time. The ones we discuss here are electronic mail, news groups over Usenet, and list servers. Electronic mail is asynchronous (users generally are not communicating in realtime), quick (in terms of transmission and reply), text-based, and configured for dyadic or multiple connections (can be sent one-to-one, one-to-many, or many-to-many). Moreover, e-mail can be stored and manipulated. As Garton and Wellman noted in a recent review:

E-mail can be stored in external memory for future retrieval, searching, editing, and forwarding to others. People can edit their own or other's messages to change their meaning. The historical record of interaction may be used for surveillance of individual and group interactions, to review past decisions (as Oliver North belatedly learned), and to bring new members up to date. What makes this modality particularly suitable for ethnographic research are its personal-contact and archival functions.

For example, in his 9-month participant-observation study of "Zytech," a computer systems firm, Workman utilized e-mail in the following ways:

- Being placed on the company's various distribution lists, which on a daily basis delivered internal documents, minutes of meetings, meeting agendas, and announcements;
- Scheduling interviews;
- Accessing hundreds of BBS's, including Zytech correspondence going back several years;
- Communicating with informants, including follow-ups to FTF interviews.

Though the staggered progress of e-mail interviewing does not promote the same qualities of rapport or spontaneity as personal interviews, it does permit a more elastic time frame for both interviewer and participant to think carefully about the meanings of questions and replies. In another organizational study, special software was used to automatically save the headers (but not the message content) of all departmental e-mail to a designated file whenever a user read or transmitted a message, yielding a nonreactive means of learning who communicates with whom, when, and about what. For ethnographic purposes, the value of this procedure lies in its capacity to augment such methods as interviews or on-site observation.

However, the ability to retrieve and store this information without the users' permission (or below their conscious awareness, even when permission is granted) carries the potential for ethical abuse at worst, and suspicion on the part of participants at best. Usenet is a protocol that describes how groups of messages can be stored on and sent between computers, many of which lay outside of the Internet. In actuality, Usenet forms a "virtual forum" for the electronic community that is divided into a plethora of news groups dedicated to varied areas of interest. News group articles are read and written through programs called newsreaders that keep track of articles that have been read, allow users to edit what has been read, and enable readers to reply to previously posted messages in the aforementioned study, Baym reported her participant-observation of a news group made up of soap opera aficionados.

Even though some Usenet sites can archive messages off-line, Baym herself saved the messages posted on the r.a.t.s group while she was an active member. Even working with a medium often described as low in social presence or media richness, she was able to develop a "thick" description of the personalities of this community based on features of their postings:

- Signature files (files automatically attached to postings containing identifying information about the sender),
- Humour in the messages,
- Self-disclosure,
- Comments made about personal lives.

By capitalizing on the features of Usenet news groups, variations of focus group interviewing become possible. During a two-month period of operating a public BBS, Myers set up a computer-mediated focus group "to determine what motivated frequent and active BBS use". As an alternative to a simple discussion, a focus group consisting of a theoretically interesting set of users could work on a virtual task. MacGregor and Morrison describe an editing-group protocol in which groups of people were given the opportunity to re-edit existing news reports (including video footage) in order to produce a more "ideal" version, thereby enabling them to understand viewers' journalistic values more concretely.

It is not difficult to see how this task could be adapted to computer news groups and the multimedia capabilities of high-end work stations, although techniques for training and monitoring the users in their editing-group activities would need to be developed. Listserv groups (managed by listserver software) are similar to news groups in that they are discussion groups, but they operate in a completely different way by using the Internet e-mail system to exchange messages. Once a person subscribes to a Listserv group (or Listproc group, as they are called on networks other than the early Bitnet), their name is added to a mailing list that receives postings from everyone else subscribed to the list. Many listservers offer features that allow users to search and retrieve files that are archived, and search the archives using keyword searches. Thus, anyone from a remote site can access archived messages for study from the host computer.

This capability raises interesting ethical issues: How does one receive consent to study the stored communications of users of a particular listserver? Is open access to a person's communications implied in the use of this service? Are the archived files considered the property of the individual subscribers, or are they "owned" in some form of fiduciary relationship by the listserv operator? Because the Internet has developed so rapidly, many such legal and ethical questions have yet to be resolved. The CMC technologies mentioned above have been in place for a while and are generally well known to most researchers. Most of the communication from these sources is asynchronous, i.e., it is archived for later review and becomes an excellent database. However some of the newer systems allow for the actual observation of synchronous, or real-time, communication behaviour. It is to these we now turn.

Some of the more recent real-time technologies are:

- Internet Relay Chat (IRC) systems, or" chat lines";
- The entire gamut of multiple-user technologies, e.g., MUDs (Multiple User Domains, formerly known as Multiple User Dungeons), MOOs (MUD Object-Oriented), and MUSHes (Multi-User Shared Hallucination);
- Groupware,
- Desktop videoconferencing over the Internet. All of these systems operate synchronously and as such more approximate face-to-face communication.

Internet Relay Chat (IRC) is a multi-user synchronous communication capability available worldwide to users with Internet accessibility.

These real time" chat lines" provide for mutithreaded conversations from more than two users in something very similar to an" electronic cocktail party". In these" chat rooms" users are able to don bogus" personas" (false identities) and communicate with interactants from all over the globe. These chat lines are very popular on commercial services like America Online and are now available through various web browsers (e.g., students can" chat" with the president of a university via its Web site).

One step up from IRC is a whole family of computer programs that allow more than just written conversation in real time. These are multi-user programs that, in addition to providing text, allow the additional depiction of a physical environment. Multiple User programs are designed to offer a pseudo-physical dimension via its object orientation. In MOOs, for examples, individuals" virtually" move through" rooms," interact with virtual" objects" such as chairs, doors, and the like, and have virtual conversations with others. As Reid has remarked, in MUDs," text replaces gesture and has even become gesture itself".

A third, more recent technology is found in a generation of software called" groupware." Unlike MUDs, MOOs, MUSHes, MUCKs, and the like that are used more for entertainment and amusement, groupware is being developed mainly for business and professional uses.

Most of the newer groupware programs use Web-based technology and allow not only for sharing e-mail but for conducting synchronous multiuser conferencing. The promise for ethnographers in this technology lies in the" common thread" that runs through all these programs--i.e.," the construction of shared memory" and recording of group discussions. In essence, groupware allows for observing the" virtual office," i.e., electronic mail, conferencing, scheduling, shared documents, electronic" whiteboards," and so on, and recording these interactions. All of this can function in real time or be archived for later study. Appearing now on the horizon is the capability to use the desktop computer for real time videoconferencing. Using fairly inexpensive video cameras attached to desktop computers, and software such as CU-SeeMe technology, mediated FTF interactions are now available for study. As soon as compression capabilities for full-motion video are perfected, these dispersed FTF interactions, mediated by the computer, can be recorded and used in data analysis.

When considering all these new technologies, the type of research done may have to be dictated by the characteristics of the medium. That is, for asynchronous media, the type of research conducted would be more akin to that for studying other forms of written communication, while synchronous media enable types of research more equivalent to naturalistic observation--i.e., observing the unfolding of communicative events in real time.

It was inevitable that interpretive analysts would turn their attention to the profusion of common culture now moving through the Internet. Forms of ethnographic inquiry are being applied to many of the events that occur in virtual space, although questions remain about how well these approaches engage CMC phenomena. One such question is the appropriateness of" community" as a conceptual device. The conventional idea of community as a stable locus for the practice of ritual, custom, and moral obligation applies to cyberspace groups, albeit in the context of a shifting sense of commitment.

When members can easily come and go, when many" members" do not even post, and when identities cannot be verified beyond the current situation, the power of a community ethos may be weakened considerably. The structural properties of the Internet also raise questions about how far a user community extends. For example, can any array of Web sites found by a search term be considered a" community," and if not, what criteria do we use for including a site in the community set?

Finally, what is the relationship of computer-mediated action to local social networks? It has been suggested, for example, that the growing reliance on computer technology for communicating with distant others may undermine the vitality of public life in so-called real communities or play a role in their economic and social fragmentation. Answers to these and other important issues about virtual community await further and more inventive empirical studies.

If there is one theme that runs through the differences between FTF (embodied) and CIVIC (virtual) ethnography, it is the problem of participation. CIVIC ethnography moves us into questions of what it means to engage in and explain" experience" without being co-present with others. Screen-life is a social sphere of its own with vocabularies, motives, and expectations that increasingly re-interpret the meanings of off-screen-life (e.g., mail becoming known as" snail mail").

Objectifications of life in the screen world are also a part of that world. Computer users do act as textual performers and analysts, and knowingly comment on the skills of other text-makers. The use of symbolic codes like" FOTFL" and the real-time deployment of a character in a MUD are operations that create the affect of participation for users, and it would be unusual for ethnographers; not to consider their situated usage.

However, the sites of semiotic action in CMC are not the texts, but the persons who produce them. The text-threads from a Usenet news group or a stack of e-mail messages exnominate the moments in which they were created and read, and the influences of local institutions on their users' action are seldom seen in the messages themselves. In the years ahead, ethnographers will be struggling with basic questions of what it means to" participate" in simulated worlds as well as with developing tactical ways to participate as researchers.

Closely related to the problem of participation are issues of trust and ethical conduct to which we have alluded at various points in this chapter. These issues assume even more importance than usual in research practice due to the greater potential for engaging in covert surveillance of CIVIC social life and the still-unsettled distinctions between" public" and" private" behaviour across the range of cyberspace contexts.

The problem of the stable identifiability of persons who post in Usenet news groups, respond by e-mail, or visit a Web site may also confound the principle of informed consent as a precondition for engaging a human subject's participation. Generally, there is little debate about the need to provide as much disclosure as possible about research procedures to those who are asked to participate, and to shelter them from the possible harmful consequences of participation and subsequent publication.

However, as King notes, extremely wide ranges of" group accessibility" and" perceived privacy" exist on the Internet. The highest accessibility characterizes those public BBS groups that are unmoderated and unregulated, while the least accessible community is" a private, closed e-mail group where the subscription address is not published and there are enforced requirements to join".

Perceived privacy varies in terms of both the sensitivity of the information (in which, for example, a substance abuse support group would seek a very high level of privacy) and the need to disseminate information to the widest possible client group (the National Communication Association's CRTNET would seek a low measure of privacy). Yet a great many Internet conversations can in fact be monitored with relative ease, which complicates the understanding of what is permissible to study and whether observation is truly" covert" if no barriers are erected to keep one from observing.

Of course, it probably does matter to many virtual groups whether it is a naive visitor who is stopping briefly at their fora, or a person whose goal is to cast a long-term, analytic eye on their activities and publish the result. The conventional view holds that any research of on-line participants should" strive to obtain some degree of informed consent whenever possible.... Most importantly, researchers should negotiate their entry into electronic communities, beginning with the `owner' of the discussion, if one exists".

Preserving the dignity and empowerment of the persons being studied, even if their" real" identities and locations are unknown, demands that the researcher take steps to explain all of the elements of the study that may bear on their decision to participate voluntarily. Taking a different view, Jones argues that the highly elusive, evanescent presence and essentially unknowable identity of most of the subjects in cylberspace obviates the need in most cases for pursuing consent formally:" If the research does not involve identifiable subjects, there is no risk to subjects, and therefore the protection of these rights and interests no longer applies".

Jones goes on to argue that the strict application of conventional human subject protections would be especially detrimental to the study of cyberspace, which exists as an arena in which individuals can enjoy the freedom of withholding, revealing, and even fabricating information about themselves.

Somewhere between these positions is King, who states that" the perceived level of privacy with which most members of cyberspace forums post notes is the level that researchers are obligated to protect".

At the stage of publication, she advocates the removal from messages of all headers, signatures, references to the name and type of the group (e-mail, Usenet news group, etc.), and references to any person's name or pseudo-name. It may be that the evolving use of networked systems will alter the customs and arguments for what constitutes" privacy" and" autonomy," in turn informing the ethical practice of ethnography.

Finally, the implications of computer networks for the construction of the research text are of great importance. One can adapt the same hypermedia programming tools used in other scholarly efforts to the production of ethnographies that would in turn be fully compatible with the World Wide Web's system architecture. An example of such an effort is the Survivors of the Shoah Visual History Foundation, which has set out to videotape oral histories of all living Holocaust survivors and digitize them in hypermedia format along with maps, documents, photos, and written texts of the interviews.

The files, perhaps numbering 150,000 by the end of the decade, will be fully cross-referenced and accessible for on-line searches by key words. Similarly, ethnographies of CMC culture can be envisioned which would provide the discursive threads that underpin an analysis, along with field notes, full-text interviews, generations of Web page design, graphic material, and URL's to the ethnographic sites themselves and related research projects. Presumably the author would also be" available" in a rather immediate sense to readers via the research text's Web site or e-mail.

What distinguishes an archive a reader can navigate at will from a research text is that the latter usually embodies arguments, claims, and evidence in a style conventionalized within the discipline. While readers have always had non-linear access to a text, it is the linear narrative designed by the author that academic communities recognize as the only one subject to critique.

The capabilities of hypermedia threaten this formulation of the research product and the concept of authorial control that stands behind it. If readings of an ethnography are neither the ones an author intended nor the ones deemed important or legitimate by a discipline, then its use-value becomes as widely distributed among communities of practical interest as the Internet itself. The move to modular, multi-threaded (but not necessarily plotless) research texts not only reduces the researcher's story to the stature of one among a potentially limitless number, it also accelerates the epistemological decentering of inquiry that began with the challenge to objectivist ethnography nearly twenty years ago.

Index